Routledge Revivals

Index to the London Magazine

Index to the London Magazine

Frank P. Riga
Claude A. Prance

First published in 1978 by Garland Publishing, Inc.

This edition first published in 2018 by Routledge
2 Park Square, Milton Park, Abingdon, Oxon, OX14 4RN
and by Routledge
52 Vanderbilt Avenue, New York, NY 10017, USA

Routledge is an imprint of the Taylor & Francis Group, an informa business

© 1978 by Frank P. Riga and Claude A. Prance

All rights reserved. No part of this book may be reprinted or reproduced or utilised in any form or by any electronic, mechanical, or other means, now known or hereafter invented, including photocopying and recording, or in any information storage or retrieval system, without permission in writing from the publishers.

Publisher's Note
The publisher has gone to great lengths to ensure the quality of this reprint but points out that some imperfections in the original copies may be apparent.

Disclaimer
The publisher has made every effort to trace copyright holders and welcomes correspondence from those they have been unable to contact.
A Library of Congress record exists under ISBN:

ISBN 13: 978-0-367-13787-8 (hbk)
ISBN 13: 978-0-367-13792-2 (pbk)
ISBN 13: 978-0-429-02858-8 (ebk)

INDEX TO
THE LONDON MAGAZINE

GARLAND REFERENCE LIBRARY
OF THE HUMANITIES
(VOL. 103)

INDEX TO THE LONDON MAGAZINE

Frank P. Riga
Claude A. Prance

GARLAND PUBLISHING, INC. • NEW YORK & LONDON
1978

© 1978 by Frank P. Riga and Claude A. Prance
All rights reserved

Library of Congress Cataloging in Publication Data
Riga, Frank P
  Index to The London magazine.
  (Garland reference library of the humanities; 103)
  Bibliography: p.
  Includes index.
  1. The London magazine (London, 1820–29)—
Indexes. I. Prance, Claude Annett, joint author.
II. The London magazine (London, 1820–29).
III. Title.
AP4.R53   052   77-83391
ISBN 0-8240-9846-3

Printed on acid-free, 250-year-life paper
Manufactured in the United States of America

Contents

ACKNOWLEDGEMENTS	vii
THE LONDON MAGAZINE, 1820–29: A BRIEF HISTORY	xi
PLAN AND USE OF THE INDEX	xxxi
Monthly Contents with Identification of Contributors	xxxiii
Index of Authors and Contributors	xl
Index of Signatures	xlii
Book Review Index	xliii
Bibliography	xlv
Abbreviations	xlvi
Summary Directions	xlvi
PART ONE: MONTHLY CONTENTS WITH IDENTIFICATION OF CONTRIBUTORS	1
Volumes I–X	3
New Series, Volumes I–X	112
Third Series, Volumes I–III	157
PART TWO: INDEX OF AUTHORS AND CONTRIBUTORS	173
PART THREE: INDEX OF SIGNATURES	235

PART FOUR: BOOK REVIEW INDEX 249
    Author List 251
    Title List 277

BIBLIOGRAPHY 303

APPENDIX: LIST OF ILLUSTRATIONS IN THE LONDON 321

Acknowledgements

We are sensible of our heavy borrowings from the work of others, but hope "that a grateful mind By owing owes not, but still pays, at once Indebted and discharged." Throughout this volume we have tried to document our research with precision, so here we wish to acknowledge the more direct and personal of our debts. Walter Houghton, editor of *The Wellesley Index to Victorian Periodicals,* directed us to an important group of manuscript letters from W.H. Leeds to Dawson Turner. Busy as he necessarily was, he answered all of our enquiries and offered encouragement. The influence of *The Wellesley Index* on our efforts needs no comment. For permission to use manuscript materials in their possession, we wish to thank Mr. R.W.P. Cockerton and Mr. Michael Brooke-Taylor, both of Bakewell, Derbyshire. One of the authors is deeply indebted to Mr. Cockerton for his hospitality and personal generosity.

Canisius College and several of its members made many contributions toward the completion of this volume. Dr. Joseph F. Bieron, Dean of the College of Arts and Sciences, provided a grant to help defray the costs of preparing the final typescript. The College's Faculty Research and Publication Committee awarded one of the authors two summer research grants and a publication grant. Melvin W. Schroeder, Chairman of the English Department, allowed the departmental budget to absorb a good number of clerical and mailing expenses. He also permitted Gretchen Bouliane, the department secretary, to type more of the early stages of the manuscript than even she desired, and we are grateful for her endurance. Peter J. Laux, the College's chief librarian, read and criticized part of the manuscript, and his staff was relentless in tracking down copies of rare books. The Rev. John J. Jennings, S.J., of the Classics Department, provided the Greek characters for the typewriter, and Dr. Rose

Ann Martin found that the most expeditious way of teaching us to use them was to do the job herself. The College's Secretarial Pool typed parts of an early version of the Book Review Index. Susan McCrillis, Secretary to the Dean of Students, agreed to do the final typescript and then learned later why Gretchen refused. For her perceptive criticisms of the manuscript and her help with proofreading, we affirm the Pyrrhic claim that M. Patricia Frederick has read every word of this volume. And for Dr. Paul Dowling of the English Department, we hope his students profit as much from his reading of their work as we did from his reading of ours.

We are indebted to a number of libraries for making certain manuscripts available to us. The Houghton Library, Harvard University, permitted us to use the typescript copies of eight letters from John Scott to Robert Baldwin and the thirty-one manuscript letters from B.W. Procter to John Taylor. For the use of John Taylor's autograph Commonplace Book, No. I, we are indebted to the Berg Collection, The New York Public Library. The British Museum Library allowed us places in the Reading Room and the Manuscript Room and the use of a number of manuscript letters in the Egerton collection. The Keats Museum, Hampstead, allowed us to examine the volumes of the *London* owned and marked by John Hamilton Reynolds, and the library of the Charles Lamb Society permitted us to examine its various holdings. We wish to thank Trinity College, Cambridge, for allowing our reader, Ms. Brendel Lang, to take notes from the letters of W.H. Leeds to Dawson Turner, deposited in the University Library; and Mr. T. Kaye of the Trinity College Library, who sent us a photocopy of a letter from Henry Southern to William Whewell. We are indebted to Dr. Williams's Library, 14 Gordon Square, London, where we read H. Crabb Robinson's manuscript diary and found several of Henry Southern's letters. The National Library of Scotland, Edinburgh, made available to us several manuscript sources that aided our work considerably.

In our attempt to trace manuscript materials we incurred debts with the keepers of records in England and Brazil, and the English community in Brazil. For answering our letters, we wish

Acknowledgements • ix

to thank N.G. Cox of the Search Department, Public Record Office, London, and J.G. Parker and S.G. Roberts, Research Assistants of The Royal Commission on Historical Manuscripts, London. P.E. Penner da Cunha, Chief da Divisas de Documentacao Diplomatica, Ministero das Relacoes Exteriores, Brasilia, answered our letter of enquiry. Other letters to Brasilia were answered by T.T. Macan, First Secretary of the British Embassy, who wrote for the Ambassador, and D.J. Spiller, Books Advisor of The British Council. We are indebted to P.J. Truman, Central Administrator of the British Burial Fund, Rio de Janeiro, who not only answered our letter, but also placed an enquiry in the local English newspaper.

We also wish to acknowledge other correspondents and other libraries that aided us in our work. For answering our letters and sending others of their own, we wish to thank Mr. Tim Chilcott of the United States International University, Sussex; Canon Kenneth Harper of Brampton, Cumbria, for his comments on Solomon Atkinson; Dr. Charles E. Robinson of the University of Delaware for his many letters; and Dr. William S. Ward of the University of Kentucky, who sent several bibliographic items. For letting us use their facilities and for easing our work in many ways, we wish to thank the following libraries: The Buffalo and Erie County Public Library; The Firestone Library, Princeton University; Gozo Public Library, librarian Paul Cassar; Guildhall Library, London; The Lockwood Memorial Library, State University of New York, Buffalo; Malta University Library, librarian Dr. Paul Xuereb; St. Bride Printing Library, London; and the University Library, University of London.

Can this weight of indebtedness support any more debits? We wish to thank our families for patience and understanding. John T. Riga went through the alphabet countless times for us. And to our wives we owe a profound debt of gratitude for their "little, nameless, unremembered acts of kindness and of love."

The London Magazine, 1820–29:
A Brief History

The history of *The London Magazine* is briefly told in the accomplishments and failures of its four editors. During the fourteen months of his editorship, 1820–21, John Scott succeeded in establishing the *London* as one of the finest literary periodicals of the nineteenth century. John Taylor, the second editor, maintained the high quality of the magazine by securing many excellent writers. But by the end of 1825, the first year of Henry Southern's editorship, the magazine had lost most of its distinguished writers. When Charles Knight began editing the *London* in 1828, its great period was already a memory.

In his response to Robert Baldwin's offer to edit a new literary periodical, John Scott could little anticipate the role *Blackwood's Edinburgh Magazine* was to play in his personal destiny, but he was fully aware that the Scottish periodical was the model to imitate and, if possible, to surpass. Scott was making a careful study of the plan and content of current periodicals, and *Blackwood's* seems to have arrested his attention.[1] Earlier magazines were "storehouses of miscellaneous information, repositories of all sorts of facts and fancies."[2] *Blackwood's* established the format and content of the modern magazine, one primarily made up of original literary material and independent critical opinion.

Scott understood this new conception of the literary periodical and embodied it in the first number of the *London*. Appearing in January 1820, with 120 pages in double column, the *London* was crammed with all kinds of features, including "magazine" items of the old-fashioned sort—meteorological reports, colonial intelligence, summaries of foreign and domestic news, births, marriages, deaths, stock prices, and so on. But more importantly, as Walter Graham has noted, "the *London* began its career . . . with considerably more of its contents devoted to writers and books than is to be found in any preceding periodical of the kind."[3] Among the items in the first number was the opening article of Scott's "Living Authors," a series which demonstrates that the editor was among the most discriminating critics of his time. Scott's notice of a French criticism of Goethe's *Werther,* his critical acumen aside, revealed his interest in foreign literature and criticism, an interest he wished to make into a principal feature of the *London.* The first number also included prose contributions from William Hazlitt, T.G. Wainewright, B.W. Procter, and Charles Eastlake, and verses from Bernard Barton and Horace Smith. In short, almost three-quarters of the first number was devoted to original literary material and critical opinion. That copies of volume one exist with the words "second edition" on the title page suggests that the *London* had attracted some attention.[4]

Scott knew that a magazine of this kind depended on the quality of its contributors. He believed that the writers for *Blackwood's* had considerable talent, "but a magazine in London on the same plan would have several advantages over it. . . ."[5] One of the advantages available in London was a wide range of distinguished writers, many of whom were acquaintances or friends of Scott. To secure these writers he knew he would have to pay good rates. When Baldwin suggested ten guineas a sheet for contributions, the same rate he was paying for review articles in the *British Review,* Scott argued against it. Since "original communications" required twice as much writing as review articles, the proposed rate was barely half enough. He then made his principal point: "Now, for this sum I do not think you can expect any writer of distinguished Talent."[6]

Scott himself was a "writer of distinguished Talent," but he demonstrated his editorial genius by securing many excellent contributors and by stimulating them to do some of their best work. During the first year Scott could point proudly to such items as Hazlitt's *Table Talk* and Charles Lamb's Elia essays. The *London* had some share at this time in bringing the work of John Clare, the peasant poet, to general notice through an article contributed by Octavius Gilchrist. To provide lighter fare Scott secured the services of "Janus Weathercock," T.G. Wainewright. This dilettante, who ended his life as a transported felon, sent Scott amusing articles on art and kindred subjects. Another excellent contributor secured by Scott was J.H. Reynolds, the friend of Keats. Scott's encouragement of his authors' individual talents and his combining them all under one governing spirit were to assure the *London* the high place it holds in English periodical literature.

Scott meant the *London* to represent its namesake and to rival the Scottish periodicals that had dominated the field until then. This intention is manifest in Scott's negotiations with Baldwin during 1819 and in the Prospectus to the *London* that grew out of these negotiations. Responding to Baldwin's request that the magazine have a "distinguishing feature," Scott argued:

> The Readers of your work ought to acquire confidence, from experience, in opening the pages of each No. that something will be found within, on every subject of interest, foreign or domestic, properly belonging to the month. It ought to be looked to as affording the best panoramic view of all that is going forward in Literature, Art, Science, & Politics, throughout Europe. This comprehensiveness of information would soon become of itself a *distinguishing feature*, and, unless I am much mistaken, it would be one that would excite a considerable degree of expectation.[7]

As Scott then announced in the Prospectus, such comprehensiveness and cosmopolitanism would convey "the very image, form and pressure" of London. He also noted in the Prospectus:

> We have been induced to revive the Title of a once well-known but discontinued Magazine, and to appropriate it to our new undertaking, in consequence of its occurring to us as singular, that while secondary towns of the Kingdom give name and distinction to

popular journals, the METROPOLIS should remain *unrepresented* in the now strenuous competition of Periodical literature.

The *London* under Scott rectified this situation, giving the "secondary towns of the Kingdom," mainly Edinburgh, "strenuous competition."[8]

Finally, Scott understood that if *Blackwood's* was in many ways the model for the modern magazine, its errors in policy suggested that "some improvement might be made as to the plan."[9] These errors were mainly in style and tone. The *London* would have its political articles and literary criticism but, unlike *Blackwood's,* would avoid anything that smacked of personalities. All criticism would be vigorous and forthright, but aimed at policies and issues, not persons. Scott sought to raise his periodical above the kind of practices ridiculed by the *New Monthly* in 1820:

> Few literary changes within the late changeful years have been more remarkable than the alteration in the style and spirit of the Magazines. . . . Now they are full of wit, satire and pungent remark—touching familiarly on the profoundest questions of philosophy as on the highest varieties of manners—sometimes overthrowing a system with a joke, and destroying a reputation in the best humour in the world.[10]

Blackwood's chequered career was perhaps the most obvious example of this "style and spirit." The *London* under Scott eschewed such reprehensible ways of attracting readers.

As 1820 progressed Scott became more and more critical of *Blackwood's Magazine,* an attitude fiercely reciprocated by the Scottish periodical. The object of Scott's criticism was *Blackwood's* practice of abusing an author in one issue and praising him in another. The contributions were anonymous, but often the contradictory articles were written by the same hand. Eventually the dispute degenerated to personalities, mainly between Scott and

John Gibson Lockhart, the man Scott thought was the editor of *Blackwood's*. A challenge was issued that culminated in a duel between Scott and Jonathan Christie, a young barrister who was acting as Lockhart's second in the negotiations. Scott was critically wounded in the duel that took place 16 February 1821 and died a few days afterwards. For the *London*, Scott's death was a great loss, for it was never to have as good an editor again.

After Scott's death, the publishers continued issuing the *London*, apparently intending to find a new editor. Robert Baldwin probably carried out part of the immediate editorial duties, assisted by Hazlitt[11] and perhaps Wainewright. According to H. Crabb Robinson, Thomas Noon Talfourd thought of applying for the editorship, but he did not do so.[12] But by April of 1821, the publishers had not found a suitable editor and decided to sell the magazine.

Taylor and Hessey, Keats's publishers, were looking for just such a publication, and after some negotiations on the purchase price, they paid Baldwin, Cradock and Joy £ 500 for the goodwill of the *London*.[13] Though many of the old contributors were willing to continue with the magazine, the number of subscribers was small. When Taylor and Hessey bought the *London*, Taylor believed the circulation was 1,800 copies. After publishing the first number in July 1821, Taylor revised his estimation of sales. Claiming the circulation for July was 1,700, he added, "I suspect the Sale had actually sunk to 1600 when we entered on the Work."[14] This was an ominous figure, for when Taylor and Hessey sold the magazine to Henry Southern in 1825, the circulation again stood at 1,600 copies.[15] The significance of this number can better be appreciated when it is recalled that of the Scottish periodicals, both the *Edinburgh Review* and *Blackwood's* sold some 14,000 copies each issue.[16]

The new owners seriously considered both Hazlitt and Henry Francis Cary, the translator of Dante, for the editorship, but eventually John Taylor himself assumed the position. Though not Scott's equal as an editor, Taylor was a man of intelligence and learning. The list of authors published by his firm, including Keats, Clare, Lamb, De Quincey, and Coleridge, indicates he recognized good writing when he saw it. Taylor knew many of Baldwin's best contributors and was able to retain most of them for the *London*, while adding others of distinguished talent. He was also a convivial man, and during 1821, he began giving his famous "Magazine dinners." These functions, delightful in themselves, helped establish a sense of comradeship and mutual interest among his contributors.

Taylor was also able to secure a number of able coadjutors. He hired Thomas Hood as "a sort of sub-editor." Hood took over "The Lion's Head," which contained the editorial notes of the *London*, and contributed poems and articles regularly. J.H. Reynolds became a more frequent contributor and no doubt helped with the editorial duties.[17] Taylor's partner, James Augustus Hessey, took a share in the business management and acted for Taylor when the latter was absent. Unfortunately, this very abundance of editorial help, which augured well at the commencement, was later to prove harmful.

During the latter half of 1821 and all of 1822, Taylor was able to publish contributions of a very high caliber. Charles Lamb continued to send some of his best essays and Thomas De Quincey contributed many notable papers. The poems of John Clare began to appear regularly. The number for September 1821 had the distinction of carrying the first part of De Quincey's "Confessions" and Lamb's famous "The Old Benchers of the Inner Temple," as well as excellent items from Clare, Cary, Allan Cunningham, C.W. Dilke, and Reynolds. These contributors, with Hazlitt and Hood, made 1822 the peak year during Taylor's editorship.

In view of the magazine's excellence, Taylor could not understand why the circulation was not larger. He speculated, "the Flam of Blackwood and the namby pamby of Colburn are more suited it seems to the Taste of the Age."[18] Perhaps the standard was too high. In "The Lion's Head" for April 1822, Hood quoted one correspondent who complained that "the *London* is too full of Literature." Hood humorously remarked that with his correspondent's assistance this could soon be put right. Whatever the precise cause of the failure of the *London* to achieve a large circulation, the lack of subscribers was an obvious danger to the continuance of the magazine. Writing to Taylor in November 1822, Hessey complained that a circulation of 1,600 did not pay for expenses.[19]

Though Taylor managed to obtain many good contributions in 1823, this was perhaps the last consistently excellent year for the *London*. In July, Walter Savage Landor's "Imaginary Conversation between Southey and Porson" appeared, but he did not follow it up with other items. This year George Darley became a frequent contributor. Some excellent essays appeared from Richard Ayton, which, although collected and reprinted by Taylor and Hessey in 1825, are now forgotten. Lamb's famous letter to Southey appeared this year, but the disagreement between them was settled by private letters. De Quincey's "On the Knocking at the Gate in Macbeth" appeared in October, and Thomas Carlyle contributed the first part of "Schiller's Life and Writings" in the same month. The year closed with Lamb's outstanding "Amicus Redivivus," the account of George Dyer's immersion in the New River.

The year 1823 was also notable because Hazlitt almost embroiled the *London* in a lawsuit. In February, Hazlitt included a severe criticism of Sir Walter Scott in his review of *Peveril of the Peak*. According to Taylor, the firm "had a narrow Escape from Libel. In Hazlitt's Review of Peveril he spoke in such terms of Walter Scott as seemed without doubt actionable. . . ."[20] The terms were indeed strong ones, and read in part:

> ... the reputed author is accused of being a thorough-paced partisan in his own person,— intolerant, mercenary, mean; a professed toadeater, a sturdy hack, a pitiful retailer or suborner of infamous slanders, a literary Jack Ketch, who would greedily sacrifice anyone of another way of thinking as a victim to prejudice and power, and yet would do it by other hands, rather than appear in it himself.[21]

Somehow Taylor allowed the printing of this passage. Procter and Wainewright drew Taylor's attention to the possibly libellous nature of Hazlitt's remarks, and the passage was hurriedly suppressed by altering and reprinting the relevant page. A few unaltered copies of the *London* had already been distributed, but Scott took no action. The passage seems to have escaped notice until August 1824, when *Blackwood's* made it the principal example in an article on the profligacy of the periodical literature of London. Quoting the offensive passage, the writer attempted to demonstrate the villainies of which Whig partisans were capable. Taylor answered the charges in the number for October, but nothing like the Scott-Lockhart controversy was initiated.

In January 1824 the magazine claimed that it had lost none of its old contributors and gained several new ones, but this was not strictly accurate. De Quincey and Darley were the most constant, but Hazlitt and Wainewright had dropped out, while some others contributed less frequently. Lamb, one of the most famous names associated with the magazine, sent nothing for the first eight months of the year, but made up in September with his "Blakesmoor in H——shire." More than this was needed, however, and the items submitted by the new contributors were not of the same standard as the old. They included work by Mary Shelley, Stendhal, and Henry Taylor. Competition from the *New Monthly Magazine* was keen, and many of the *London's* old contributors were now sending items to the rival monthly.[22]

Taylor's shortcomings as an editor now began to affect the quality of the magazine. His methods of refusing and cutting articles were resented by such contributors as Cary and Procter, and especially Hazlitt, who terminated his connection with the *London* by the end of 1823. This failure in tact manifested itself in other ways. For example, De Quincey reviewed adversely Carlyle's translation of *Wilhelm Meister,* but the review was included in the same issue that contained Carlyle's "Life of Schiller," a fact that Carlyle did not forget. Taylor also alienated his authors by his financial arrangements. His rate of payment for contributions was good, but he was not quick to pay for work completed.[23] By contrast, *Blackwood's* was noted for the promptness of its payments, a policy much appreciated by the writers. Taylor also attempted to control the copyright on materials that appeared in the *London,* demanding as much as two-thirds of the profits of later reprintings.[24]

Editorial direction itself seemed confused. This may well have been caused by too many sub-editors. Hood was hired to serve in this capacity and Reynolds was no doubt assisting. Hessey was always doing some form of editorial work, and in December 1822, Procter was put on to conduct a new feature, "The Miscellany." In a contribution of January 1823, Wainewright put his finger on this weakness when he expressed his doubts as to who was the editor: "he is without form—I can't make up my mind to believe in such a *nominis umbra*." This babel of sub-editors accentuated what was becoming the editor's principal weakness. Taylor had increasing difficulty in combining the various efforts of his writers under a single governing spirit. As Hazlitt remarked of the *London* of this time, "all is in a confused, unconcocted state, like the materials of a rich plumpudding before it has been well boiled."[25]

Towards the end of 1824 Taylor began to take a less active role in editing the magazine. As he reported to his family in Bakewell on 4 December 1824, "A proposal was made to us by Southern, who wrote the Article on the 'Personal Character of Lord Byron,' to take a share of the Magazine, and to become its future editor."[26] This was Henry Southern, founder of *The Retrospective Review* and co-editor of the *Westminster Review*. He assisted Taylor in the editorial department and acted as his business manager. He became editor at the beginning of the new year, though not yet the proprietor.

Probably at Southern's instigation, the December number announced a new title for the magazine, *The London Magazine and Review*. There were also grandiose editorial promises of "vast additional strength being called into use." The journal increased its size and the double columns were replaced by a single column that was easier to read, but this was poor compensation for inferior literary articles. That Southern was finding greater difficulty in attracting original literary contributions of a high standard seems borne out by his announcement that in the future the magazine would contain more reviews.

The January 1825 issue started what was described as a new series. Almost the only survivors from the great days were Lamb and Darley. During 1825 Lamb had contributions in every issue from January to August, including such delightful pieces as "Barbara S—," "The Superannuated Man," and "The Wedding." But they were almost his last, for Lamb knew the *London* was a sinking concern. Writing to Bernard Barton on 10 February 1825, Lamb complained:

> Our 2nd No [under Southern] is all trash. What are T. and H. about? It is whip syllabub, "thin sown with aught of profit or delight." Thin sown! not a germ of fruit or corn. Why did poor Scott die! There was comfort in writing with such associates as were his little band of Scribblers, some gone away, some affronted away, and I am left as the solitary widow looking for water cresses.[27]

Within six months, Elia, the pride of the *London*, could no longer be counted among the Londoners.

About this time, June 1825, Taylor and Hessey decided to dissolve their partnership, and realizing that the magazine was the principal source of their losses, they sought a purchaser. Writing to his brother James on 31 May, Taylor mentions the balance sheet for the *London*:

> Hessey has completed the statement of Incomings & Outgoings on the Mag. account, of which it appears that the chief of our loss is after all this work. He makes the Deficiency if we sell it for 1000£ — as much as 1500£. It is high Time that we had done with it.[28]

As this statement reveals, Taylor, like John Scott before him, failed to make a financial success of the *London*.

Southern, the new editor, had been negotiating with Taylor and Hessey for the purchase of the magazine since May, and both Reynolds and John Stuart Mill contemplated joining him in the venture.[29] By July or August Southern had bought the magazine on his own for a sum of £1000.[30] Letters between

Southern and Taylor and Hessey reveal that for editorial and other work during 1825, Southern was to receive one-third interest of the magazine's copyright. When Taylor and Hessey decided to sell the *London,* they wanted a minimum of £1500 for it. If they did sell it for more, Southern was to receive only one-third of the sale price above the minimum. He apparently was not to receive the one-third interest of the copyright. If he were to buy the magazine himself, he was to have it for one-third less than the minimum price. He was angered over Taylor and Hessey's dealing and said so:

> You are certainly not entitled to sell my interest in the Magazine without my concurrence. You engaged to give me a third of the copyright on the condition that I performed a certain task. When I have half done that task you tell me that you do not want the work to be finished—and that I must lose my labour. The manifest injury which such a course must do me gives me a right to be considered and a claim to have every opportunity of remedying it afforded to me.[31]

Eventually they came to terms, Taylor and Hessey no doubt accepting Southern's proposal that they receive £500 immediately and the remainder within a year.[32]

Under Southern's ownership, the names of Hunt and Clarke of Tavistock Street, Covent Garden, appeared on the title page as publishers. Henry Hunt was Leigh Hunt's nephew and his firm's business acumen was in doubt. Clarke was Charles Cowden Clarke, a friend of Keats and more successful as an author and lecturer than as a publisher. This was not a happy combination. As H. Crabb Robinson noted in his Diary, "That Magazine cannot possibly succeed, and I fear Southern will involve himself deeply in a losing concern. It is enough to ruin the work that Hunt is the publisher."[33] In June 1825, furthermore, the circulation of the magazine was 1,600 copies.[34] Prospects for the magazine's resuscitation were not good and did not improve.

In November 1824, while Taylor was still editor, Southern

began attacking the publication practices of Henry Colburn. These attacks were continued throughout 1825 and much of 1826, with such articles as "Colburniana; or, Puffs of the Month" and with adverse reviews of books published by Colburn. Southern's recurring point was that Colburn advertised his books in a number of periodicals and newspapers under the guise of independent reviews. As he noted in the *London* for June 1826, "no, the Times has nothing to do with Colburn's books, because it has the ugly habit of putting ADVERTISEMENT over paragraphs for which it has received money." For whatever reason, he discontinued his campaign before the end of 1826, and what began as a minor attempt to free reviewing from publisher control came to nothing. A few years later *The Athenaeum* would take up the same struggle more extensively and would again identify Henry Colburn as a principal offender.

Southern continued to fill the magazine with a great deal of material during his first year or so, including contributions from Stendhal, Ugo Foscolo, Sarah Austin, John Neal, and Thomas Jefferson Hogg. But the life and sparkle had gone out of it, in part as a result of Southern's decided bent toward Utilitarianism. As co-editor with John Bowring of the *Westminster Review*, his connections with the Utilitarians were obvious and continuous. Commenting on the decline of the *London,* Thomas Hood was to mourn, "worst of all, a new editor tried to put the Belles Lettres in Utilitarian envelopes. . . ."[35] Such "envelopes" no doubt discouraged many of the older contributors, who continued to defect to the other periodicals. By the time Southern sold the *London,* not one of the Londoners he had directed early in 1825 was writing for him.

Southern's inability to retain the older contributors and his failure to attract new ones was aggravated by his failure to pay for work done. In the manuscript diary for 14 December 1826, H. Crabb Robinson noted that Southern "does not pay anyone . . . who writes for either of the works" (i.e., the *London* or the *Westminster*). Sarah Austin put his financial practices in the strongest terms when, in a letter to Francis Place of 31 December 1828, she commented on Southern's dealings with Fortunato

Prandi, who assisted him on the *Westminster*: "*He* of course cheated him as he did me & every body."[36] As a consequence of this and other editorial shortcomings, during the final two years of his directorship Southern was writing more and more of the magazine himself, mostly slight reviews fattened out with excessive quotation from the books reviewed.

By the end of 1827, Southern had attracted neither new contributors nor new subscribers, and by the early part of 1828 he was looking for someone to purchase the magazine. The number for March 1828 had an announcement of a new Third Series and a statement that the magazine had changed hands. It had, in fact, been bought by Charles Knight, who became part proprietor and co-editor with Barry St. Leger. Hunt and Clarke ceased to act as publishers and shortly afterwards became bankrupt; their place was taken by Henry Hooper of 13 Pall Mall East. Writing some years later Knight said:

> Our undertaking promised no great pecuniary advantage; for several years of bad management had reduced the Miscellany to a much lower level than that of the brilliant days of Charles Lamb and Hazlitt and Hood and De Quincey. But it furnished us agreeable employment from the spring of 1828 till the summer of 1829.[37]

What he apparently did not know was that the *London* had given "no great pecuniary advantage" to any of its former proprietors.[38]

Perhaps the most notable contributor at this time was W.M. Praed. Some very able articles on foreign authors and statesmen were contributed by the French political exile Frederick Degeorge. But the co-editors wrote most of the magazine themselves, as Southern had done before them, and their writing engaged some of the principal social issues of the day. Charles Knight dealt with the religious world and popular education, while Barry St. Leger wrote on reforms in the law and Catholic emancipation. Articles on Irish subjects and Irish books appeared regularly. Knight's concern with the Society for the Diffusion of Useful Knowledge and his plan for the Library of Entertaining Knowledge were revealed in the pages of the magazine. The treatment of such subjects indicates that Knight and St. Leger were perhaps planning to establish a new purpose for the *London,* one which, like the famous Victorian periodicals, would involve it in the shaping of public opinion on important, current issues. If so, the plan was stillborn.

In June 1829, the editors gave up the attempt to keep the *London* going. St. Leger had been ill during the year and died on 20 November. Since 1828, Knight had become increasingly involved with the work of the Society for the Diffusion of Useful Knowledge, at first only supervising its publications, but by March 1829 serving as publisher. The *London* was obviously of little consequence to him, and perhaps, for him, his editorship was nothing but "a short period of promiscuous literary work."[39] Ironically, the *London* was absorbed by what had become its chief rival, the *New Monthly Magazine.* As Allan Cunningham observed, "The old London Maga is departed this life—or rather had tied its dead body to Campbell's Mag. . . ."[40]

The fortunes of *The London Magazine* under its various editors, then, account for both its rise to eminence and its decline and downfall. Under Scott's directorship, the magazine developed into one of the great English periodicals. Scott was both an excellent writer and a discriminating critic, but of more importance for the *London* were his abilities as an editor. He quickly discovered the direction in which the modern literary periodical was developing and applied this knowledge to his conduct of the *London.* To maintain the literary and critical excellence demanded by his conception, he enlisted an exceptional corps of writers and was able to foster the best in them. He then unified their varied efforts under a single governing spirit. The *London* maintained its high quality for most of Taylor's editorship. Taylor retained many of Scott's writers and added some new ones of talent. But by 1824 the *London* was on the decline. As an editor Taylor kept too tight a hand on his authors and had a tendency to curtail their work. Besides, he was slow in paying for contributions. During his last year or so, moreover, much competition sprang up from rival publications, notably from the *New Monthly Magazine.*

Southern's editorship was marked by a continued decline in the magazine's literary quality. A measure of this decline is Southern's use of the title "Table Talk" for one of his features. Under that title during the early years of the *London*, Hazlitt produced many exceptional, perceptive essays; under the same title, Southern merely excerpted passages from other publications without observation or comment. Moreover, he could attract neither contributors nor subscribers. And like Taylor, he was slow in paying the contributors he did have. When Knight took over in 1828, he was apparently aware that the previous three years of mismanagement had seriously damaged the magazine's literary quality. He and St. Leger evidently wanted to reestablish the magazine on a new plan centered more on social rather than literary issues. But their attempt was short-lived.

The fact remains, however, that during its best period, from 1820 to 1823, *The London Magazine* included the work of some of the foremost prose writers of the day and, for a time, gave vigorous competition to its rivals. The accomplishments of this brief period place the *London* high among the best literary periodicals of the nineteenth century.

Notes

1. A good deal about the plans and policies of the early *London* is revealed in John Scott's letters to Robert Baldwin, hereafter referred to as the Scott/Baldwin Letters. See Bibliography for details on these unpublished manuscript sources.

Robert Baldwin was the senior partner of the long established and prosperous firm of Baldwin, Cradock and Joy, the founders and first publishers of the *London*. A man of ability and a member of the Court of Stationers, Baldwin showed his good sense by appointing Scott as editor of the new magazine and by leaving him a free hand to deal with it. At the time, Scott was best known as a former editor of *The Champion*, as contributor to Baldwin's *British Review*, and as the author of some excellent travel books.

2. Walter Graham, *English Literary Periodicals* (New York, 1930), p. 271.

3. *Ibid.*, p. 281.

4. At the exact same time another publisher, Gold and Northhouse, issued a *London Magazine and Monthly Critical and Dramatic Review*. There was some dispute between Gold and Baldwin as to priority of title, but it came to nothing. When Taylor and Hessey bought Baldwin's *London* in 1821, they also purchased Gold's *London,* paying £50 for the goodwill. See Edmund Blunden, *Keats's Publisher* (London, 1940), p. 123.

5. Scott/Baldwin Letters; 24 January 1819, from Milan.

6. Scott/Baldwin Letters; 25 April 1819, from Rome. Scott may not have won this argument. In a letter of 1821, H.F. Cary quotes Baldwin's rates as ten guineas a sheet for prose and fifteen for verse. Quoted in R.W. King, *The Translator of Dante* (London, 1925), p. 130.

7. Scott/Baldwin Letters; 14 August 1819.

8. For Scott, *Blackwood's* was always the chief competitor. In a letter to Baldwin of 9 November 1819, Scott discussed the

Prospectus and contributors. Of the latter he states, "I am sorry to find you telling me that Coleridge gave nothing like a *promise to us. I would again impress upon you the necessity of securing him, if it were only to keep him out of Blackwood's Tent"* (Scott/ Baldwin Letters).

9. Scott/Baldwin Letters; 24 January 1819.

10. "Modern Periodical Literature," *New Monthly Magazine,* XIV (September 1820), 309.

11. P.P. Howe, *The Life of William Hazlitt* (London, 1947), pp. 285–86.

12. H.C. Robinson, MS Diary, 3 March 1821. See Bibliography for details on the manuscript diary.
Talfourd did become a contributor about this time.

13. Blunden, p. 123. Taylor and Hessey's office was in Fleet Street, but they soon acquired additional premises at 13 Waterloo Place, mainly to facilitate dealing with the magazine and to keep the operation separate from their other publications.

14. Quoted in Olive M. Taylor, "John Taylor, Author and Publisher," *London Mercury,* XII (July 1925), 262.

15. Brooke-Taylor MSS; letter from H. Southern to J.A. Hessey, 22 June 1825. See Bibliography for details on these unpublished manuscript sources.

16. Graham, p. 236, gives the figure for the *Edinburgh* in 1818; and Tim Chilcott, *A Publisher and His Circle* (London, 1972), p. 133, gives the figure for *Blackwood's.*

17. Blunden, p. 246n.

18. Quoted in Taylor, p. 264. Henry Colburn was the publisher of the *New Monthly Magazine,* soon to be the *London*'s principal rival.

19. Blunden, p. 140.

20. Quoted in Taylor, p. 264.

21. Quoted in "Profligacy of the London Periodical Press," *Blackwood's Edinburgh Magazine* (August 1824), p. 180. Italics and capitals removed.

22. Comparing the *London* and the *New Monthly*, Hazlitt noted, "we believe many of the writers are the same in each" (*Works*, XVI [London, 1930–34], 231). Hazlitt made this comment in May 1823, and it was obvious to him that the *New Monthly* was the chief rival of the *London*.

23. Taylor was at least paying Baldwin's old rate: ten guineas a sheet for prose and fifteen for verse. Some variations were made, for H.F. Cary received sixteen guineas a sheet for his "Continuation of Johnson's Lives of the Poets." Charles Lamb was the highest paid contributor at twenty guineas a sheet. See King, pp. 130–32.

24. King, p. 176.

25. Hazlitt, XVI, 232. This analysis of the end of Taylor's editorship should not undermine his value to the *London*, nor his considerable service to literature generally by his promotion of the work of many talented authors.

26. Quoted in Taylor, p. 265. Hood seems to have ceased to act as sub-editor about this time, although he sent a few contributions in 1825. Charles Wentworth Dilke many years later claimed to have acted editorially for the *London*, and if this is correct, it may have been at this time.

27. *Letters*, ed. E.V. Lucas, II (London, 1935), 460. Lamb's dissatisfaction with the *London* had been growing for many months. The previous July, for example, he was asked by a colleague at the India House to recommend periodicals suitable for a club. He suggested *Blackwood's* for scandal and the *New Monthly* for light articles and humor without offence, but he does not mention the *London* (*Letters*, II, 432).

28. Bakewell MSS. See Bibliography for details on these unpublished manuscript sources.

29. Blunden, p. 133.

30. Bakewell MSS; the price is mentioned by Taylor in a letter to his brother James, 31 May 1825.

31. Brooke-Taylor MSS; H. Southern to John Taylor, 6 June 1825.

32. Brooke-Taylor MSS; H. Southern to J.A. Hessey, no date but certainly around June or July 1825.

33. H. Crabb Robinson, MS Diary for 8 November 1825. Also in *Henry Crabb Robinson on Books and Their Writers,* ed. E.J. Morley, I (London, 1938), 324.

34. Brooke-Taylor MSS; letter from H. Southern to J.A. Hessey, 22 June 1825.

35. "Literary Reminiscences. No. IV," *Hood's Own* (London, 1839), p. 550.

36. Margaret C.W. Wicks, *The Italian Exiles in London, 1816–1848* (Manchester, 1937), p. 220.

37. Charles Knight, *Passages of a Working Life,* II (London, 1864–65), 27.

38. At the time of purchase, financial matters must have been weighing on Knight's mind. The years 1824–25 had been ones of considerable difficulty in the economic life of England, and many banks and some publishers failed. Taylor and Hessey had felt the insecurity of the times, carrying on their business at a loss, and though they did not fail, the dissolution of their partnership was prompted by these hard times (Taylor, p. 266). Knight was also directly affected by the financial panic, and in 1827 he was forced to place his affairs in the hands of trustees (*DNB*).

39. *DNB*, XI, 246.

40. Quoted in C.C. Abbott, *The Life and Letters of George Darley* (London, 1928), p. 48.

Plan and Use
of the Index

Fifty years ago, in *The Life and Letters of George Darley,* C.C. Abbott noted that "a marked file of the *London Magazine* would fill a great gap."[1] Such a file would indeed have been invaluable for the compilers of the present index. Yet since Abbott published his book, the research of many careful and thorough scholars has uncovered nothing like complete publishers' lists or marked files. As a result, the writers of the items that appeared in the *London* had to be identified by more difficult, time-consuming methods of research. T. Rowland Hughes, in 1931, made the first, excellent attempt to fill the lacuna. Others such as E.L. Brooks have added many new items. In recent years, the discovery of the autograph Commonplace Book of John Taylor, in which he noted contributors and their contributions between August 1821 and October 1824, has allowed for the reaffirmation of earlier identifications and the addition of new ones. At the time we began our research a number of years ago, the writers of many articles, stories, and poems that appeared in the *London* had been identified. Our own work, based largely on newly discovered or hitherto unused manuscript material, has allowed us to identify hundreds of new items and to correct others wrongly attributed. In part, then, the Index that follows is our compilation of this collective effort to identify the writers of *The London Magazine.*

In the early stages of our work, we decided that the Index would include every piece of writing that appeared in the *London.* Articles, poems, stories, and even front and end matter would be listed, and as far as it was within our power, we would

1. (London, 1928), p. 47.

identify the writers of each item. The Index lists the contents for the entire run of the *London*, but our attempt to identify all of the items is uneven. For the first six years of the *London*, our percentage of identifications is high, reflecting the success of our own research and that of our predecessors. This period covers the editorships of John Scott (1820–21) and John Taylor (1821–24) and the first year of Henry Southern's (1825). The period also includes by far the most important time in the life of the *London*.

Beginning with the editorship of Henry Southern, the quality and importance of the *London* declined rapidly. When Charles Knight took over the magazine in 1828, it was perhaps not dead but certainly lingering. Our identifications of authorship also decline for this period. There are several reasons for this. Since the magazine's content was not as distinguished as in its earlier days and its circulation was not large, few contemporaries bothered to comment on it. Moreover, there is no reason to believe that any of the better writers of the day contributed to the *London*, at least during the last two years of Southern's editorship. By the end of his editorship, Southern was no doubt writing most of the magazine himself. The *Athenaeum* for 7 March 1828 tells us as much:

> A review of "New Books" is a thing that may be swallowed with avidity and digested to boot, but a whole Magazine of Reviews, *"thirteen* to the dozen," is insupportable. Neither is the matter mended in consequence of their being "done by the same hand." Five-sixths of the *London Magazine* for the present month is taken up with notices of and extracts from "Irving's Columbus," "Sayings and Doings" and "Memoirs d'une contemporaire."[2]

Charles Knight, with the assistance of Barry St. Leger, also wrote most of the magazine himself.

Our efforts to discover manuscript sources for the years

---

2. No. 13, p. 204.

Plan and Use of Index • xxxiii

between 1826 and 1829 have met with no success. An extended search for Southern's papers, reaching down to South America, where Southern spent his later years, resulted only in the location of some official letters written while he was in the diplomatic service and a few letters written earlier. Southern's papers seem to have perished. Knight's papers for this period are also lacking. For these years, then, external evidence is scarce, and we have been forced to make a greater use of internal evidence than we wished.

When we realized that the number of identifications after 1825 could not be increased substantially, we seriously considered listing the complete contents for the first six years of the *London* and giving only the items we could identify thereafter. However, the independent value of listing contents was made apparent in a number of reviews of the first volume of *The Wellesley Index to Victorian Periodicals*. For scholars who do not have the *London* conveniently at hand, the titles of the articles, poems, and stories will provide some assistance. Even when a library has a full run of the magazine, the Monthly Contents will enable the user to locate items more easily and quickly than would an examination of each issue of each volume. This observation is especially true when microfilm must be used. Readers having to work with a number of titles listed over several issues, as for serials, will find that the Monthly Contents facilitates their task. The inclusion of the Book Review Index in this volume, moreover, requires a complete listing of contents. In fact, the inclusion of the Book Review Index itself gives greater significance to the years where our identifications fall off, for during 1826 and 1827 Southern filled issue after issue with long book reviews.

Part One:
Monthly Contents
with Identification of Contributors

The listing of the Monthly Contents includes all articles, poems, stories, and end matter that appeared in the *London*. Except for

Plan and Use of Index • xxxiv

the specific items discussed here, each title has been given a separate index number. All end matter has been gathered under one title with one index number. This material consists of tables of various sorts; reports of births, marriages, bankruptcies, and deaths; stock and currency exchange prices; and other such matters, none of which warranted separate entry. Under the first general entry of this type, the various headings that appear in the magazine are given, and every entry thereafter contains a cross-reference to the first. We have departed from our general rule of assigning one index number to each item in other places. Contributors sometimes sent items that were printed among the editorial notes in "The Lion's Head." We have listed all of the significant items that appeared there, but under the one index number assigned to that month's "Lion's Head." At various times during the history of the *London*, moreover, the editor gave a general title to a group of book reviews. Under Scott such a feature was entitled "Critical Notices of New Books," and under Knight a similar feature was entitled "The Editor's Room." These appeared monthly. We have assigned one index number to each monthly appearance of such features, regardless of the number of books reviewed. Finally, for five numbers, beginning in December 1822, B.W. Procter conducted a feature entitled "The Miscellany," which included brief items from many contributors. Each appearance of this feature has been assigned one index number.

Standard entries in the Monthly Contents contain as few as three and as many as six distinct units. Following is an example of a six-unit entry:

> 721   Beauties of the Living Dramatists, No. V.
>   Processions. Signed: P*.   37–48.   JOHN POOLE.
>   Repr. <u>Christmas Festivities</u>.

All entries have an index number, title, and inclusive pagination. When an item is signed with a pseudonym, letters, or symbol, it is placed between the title and pagination. When the writer of an item is known, the name is placed after the pagination. The final unit in an entry is the evidence for the identification.

The index number allows for convenient cross-reference within the Monthly Contents. For example, when the evidence for a later attribution is the same as an earlier one, especially when the statement of evidence is lengthy or complex, a simple "See No. so-and-so" saves a good deal of repetition. Index numbers are also collected together and placed, with brief titles, under the writer's name in the Index of Authors and Contributors. This arrangement allows for an easy cross-reference to the more complete information in the Monthly Contents. Index numbers are also included in the Book Review Index and in the Index of Signatures to direct the reader to the information he may need.

Although no thorough attempt has been made to duplicate the typography of titles as they appear in the *London,* titles are substantially accurate and almost always complete. Titles have been reproduced as they appear over the item within the magazine, and not as they appear on the contents pages of the magazine. At times this has resulted in a longer or more descriptive title. At other times, when the title on the contents page provided information not included in the interior title, that information has been added silently. Our guiding principle in constructing titles has always been to give as much descriptive information as feasible. In a few instances, however, where the title within the magazine tended to be as long as an eighteenth-century title page, a short version has been established. The word *verse* in square brackets follows the title of every poem where nothing in the title, such as the words *stanza, verse,* or *song,* indicates that it is a poem. Since this volume includes a Book Review Index, no effort has been made to fill out the titles and authors of reviewed books by such means as editorial brackets.

The third item in a six-unit entry is always the word *signed,* followed by a colon and then by pseudonym, letters, or symbol. The author's real name is never placed in this unit. The reason for this is to keep clear the distinction made in the evidence unit between the words *signed* and *signature.* When an item is signed with the writer's real name, either in full or substantially, pagination follows the title unit immediately. In the evidence unit, then, the word *signed* is given as proof for the attribution. When the

Plan and Use of Index • xxxvi

word *signature* appears as the evidence for attribution, it means that in the *London*, the identified writer used the pseudonym, letters, or symbol given earlier in the entry. The following example should clarify this distinction:

    36   Sentimentalities on the Fine Arts, No. I.
           Signed: Janus Weathercock. 136–40. T.G.
           WAINEWRIGHT. Signature; repr. <u>Essays and Criticisms.</u>

The word *signature* in the evidence unit above refers to the pseudonym, Janus Weathercock, which follows the word *signed* given earlier in the entry. The next example uses the word *signed* as evidence:

    1125   Song.   604.   JOSIAH CONDER.   Signed; repr. <u>Star in the East.</u>

The word *signed* which follows CONDER means that the writer's real name appeared in the *London* over that item.

    The fourth item in a six-unit entry is the inclusive pagination where the piece of writing will be found in that particular issue of the *London*. Generally this is straightforward and requires no special explanation. However, mispaginations that appear in the magazine are so noted in this unit. Moreover, certain front matter that appears in the magazine without pagination is indicated by [n. p.], an abbreviation for "no page numbers."

    The fifth item provides the name of the person who wrote or contributed that piece. Because of the varying degrees of certainty of the evidence, the names of the writers appear in three different forms. When the evidence for an attribution is fully convincing, the writer's name stands alone in capital letters. When the evidence is less than fully convincing, the writer's name is entered in capital letters followed by "prob.," an abbreviation for *probably*. If an attribution is made on the basis of informed speculation, we have made use of the formula "Untraced, perhaps so-and-so."

The evidence for an attribution occupies the last place in a six-unit entry. Whenever possible, attributions are based on external evidence. To obtain it, we have gone through a great number of published letters and journals, reprintings of anonymous and pseudonymous items, published reminiscences and biographies, John Taylor's autograph Commonplace Book, manuscript letters, marked issues of the *London*, and scholarly books, articles, and dissertations. Internal evidence of various kinds has also been used. This includes direct and indirect statements of authorship within the *London* itself, autobiographical circumstances, likely subjects, and stylistic considerations. We have accepted the attributions of modern scholars where the evidence or argument seemed to warrant it, or where we could not find better evidence of our own. When authorities have indicated some reservation about an attribution, it is concisely stated. Where they merely give the attribution without a statement of evidence, the abbreviation "attr.," for "attributed by," ordinarily precedes the name of the person making the attribution. When we had doubts about an attribution or when we felt our own speculations could support an attribution, we have added our thoughts. At times the evidence or argument for an attribution conflicts. If we have not been able to decide one way or the other, we have presented the conflict as fully as concision would allow and have cited the places where the point can be pursued more fully.

The abbreviation "repr.," for "reprinted in," means that the item in the entry was reprinted, either exactly or substantially, in the book cited. For a reprinted item we have cited only the title of the volume in which it appears and, where necessary, the volume number. The title of the item in the *London* will guide the reader to the appropriate place in the volume where it was reprinted. In some instances, the items that appear in the *London* itself are reprintings of older material, translations, or items from other periodicals. When necessary we have cited the original authors, the translators, or the contributors of the items, usually giving whatever information we have. Whenever practicable we have given the title of a volume in which the item is reprinted. Sometimes the reprinting is the evidence of authorship. At other times the reprinting is mentioned for the convenience of the person using the Index. The article, story, or poem can thus be read in libraries that may not own the *London,* but have copies of the books in which the items are reprinted.

Two other points relative to the evidence unit should be mentioned. When the evidence is "See No. so-and-so," this means the evidence for the entry referred to applies precisely to the present entry. If we felt some confusion might arise from a cross-reference, an explanation was added. Secondly, short forms of citation have been devised for the evidence unit. This was done to abbreviate citations and thus to reduce the bulk of each entry. All of these brief citations are fully elaborated in the Bibliography at the end of the volume. One other form of brief citation needs a word of explanation. Some entries contain an index number, followed by a specific page number. This means that the proof for the identification is located on that specific page in that item of the *London* itself. An example should make this clear:

    2155   Scotch Note Bill.   54–63.   CHARLES KNIGHT.
             Editorial admission of authorship in No.
             2212, p. 607; style.

The phrase "Editorial admission of authorship in No. 2212, p. 607" refers to the article entitled "The Money Market," which appeared in the *London* for December 1828 and in which, on p. 607, the editor, Charles Knight, admitted that he wrote "Scotch Note Bill." Thus, the phrase "editorial admission" defines the nature of the proof, the index number locates the time and place of the item's publication by reference to this Index, and the page number reveals precisely where this evidence is found in the *London*.

The user of this Index who wishes fuller bibliographical information should be aware of a number of conventions used in the short forms of citation. Whenever a book is cited in evidence without author, this means that the volume will be found in the

Bibliography under the name of the writer of that particular index entry. Whenever a citation appears with two names, the Leeds/Turner Letters, for example, the item will be listed in the alphabet under the first name. If we have used only one title by a particular authority, the evidence unit will contain only his surname or last name, followed by a volume number where applicable and a page number. Volume numbers are indicated by Roman numerals, page numbers by Arabic numbers. If we have used more than one title by a particular authority, the evidence unit will contain his last name, a brief title for the appropriate volume, and the volume and page numbers. The last name of the authority will direct the reader to the proper place in the Bibliography, and the brief title will allow for the discrimination between the several titles. When the name of an authority appears in the evidence unit without volume or page numbers, this indicates that, in the work itself, the information we used was listed either alphabetically under the author concerned or tabularly according to the volume and page numbers of the *London*.

For the most part, the evidence in support of an attribution is given in the Monthly Contents following the writer's name. Often several pieces of evidence in our possession led to the same conclusion. The evidence unit reflects this availability of coincidental proof with several citations. When this occurs, each piece of evidence is separated by a semicolon. In some instances, the Index of Authors and Contributors will contain information—such as the writer's list of works in the *London*, his vocation, or a stated argument—that will help corroborate an attribution. For each of the identifications, the user of the Index should be able to trace the grounds of the attribution from the sources or argument given.

The work of attribution is fraught with uncertainties, and so a word of caution seems appropriate. Such caution applies most obviously to items ascribed on the basis of subject and style, with little or no external evidence. Attributions of this kind are uncertain, and we have alerted the reader to this by the way we have qualified the writer's name in the entry. Yet even when an attribution of authorship is given without qualification, there is

Plan and Use of Index • xl

still a possibility that the attribution may be mistaken. Too often during our research we have discovered external evidence that was later shown to be inaccurate. Some of the most flagrant examples of this are the attributions made by Alaric A. Watts, in his letters found among the Blackwood Papers in the National Library of Scotland. Unless there was corroborative evidence, attributions made by Watts were not to be trusted. In every instance, then, the evidence had to be scrutinized and weighed. Even after such painstaking and time-consuming evaluations, the validity of all our attributions cannot be guaranteed, though we feel certain of most. In all instances, however, we believe the evidence leads clearly to the conclusions we have made.

Part Two:
Index of Authors and Contributors

The Index of Authors and Contributors is a complete listing of all the writers whose articles, poems, or stories we have traced in *The London Magazine.* Here individual contributions are arranged under the author's name by brief title and index number, and taken together, they provide a complete list of the writer's work in the magazine as far as we know it. In many cases, we have discovered, or brought together conveniently, what amounts to new items by well-known writers and others not so well known. The inclusion of an author index, as Walter Houghton has pointed out in *The Wellesley Index,* makes a volume of this sort a bibliography in a double sense since the user may need either of two pieces of information. He may need to know who wrote a specific item in the *London,* thus the Monthly Contents, or he may need to know that a particular writer contributed to the *London,* thus the Index of Authors and Contributors.

Several specific features of the Index of Authors and Contributors need a word or two of explanation. The brief titles provided here should facilitate the use of this volume. Had only index numbers been provided, the user would have had to check every number under a contributor's name against the

Monthly Contents to locate any one title needed. The present form is particularly convenient when the writer being researched wrote a great deal for the *London*. The index numbers of serials are gathered under one title, letting the user know how many parts are involved and where each of the parts can be located. Full information for the item or items can then be located by turning to the appropriate index number or numbers in the Monthly Contents. Many regular features appeared every month, or almost every month, and were provided by the same contributor. Several of these features are listed under a formula that gives the first and last index numbers involved and the inclusive dates. Thomas Hood, for example, was responsible for "The Lion's Head" for over two and a half years. This item appears under his name as follows:

> The Lion's Head, from No. 445 (July 1821) monthly to No. 1185 (March 1824), except for October 1823.

This formula is used only for monthly features.

A writer's contributions are listed chronologically since this follows the order in which they appeared in the magazine and shows his development in the *London*. The only exception to the order by date is the listing of all numbers of a series under the first reference. The opening entries for Sir John Bowring illustrate this arrangement.

> BOWRING, SIR JOHN, 1792–1872, linguist and translator.   DNB.
>
> A Promenade on the Prado at Madrid, 258.
>
> Spanish Romances, 935, 957, 981, 1022, 1042, 1101, 1122, 1157.
>
> Ode on the Death of Marco Bozzari, 1118.

The third title in the list returns to the chronology that was interrupted by the serial listing of the "Spanish Romances."

No distinction is made in the Index of Authors and Contributors between firm and probable attributions. For such information the Monthly Contents must be consulted. However, attributions that appear in the Monthly Contents under the formula "Untraced, perhaps so-and-so" are listed at the end of the entry for that particular writer under the phrase "See also Nos...." and without brief titles. The Index of Authors and Contributors is also a concise biographical checklist of the Londoners, giving, so far as we could, full name, life dates, vocation, and at least one source of our biographical information. In a few instances, the Index of Authors and Contributors contains the names of writers who have been identified as Londoners, but for whom we have been unable to locate contributions. We have done this with the hope that other investigators, once alerted to the name, will have better success. In these entries, we have given the writer's full name, life dates, vocation, the source that identifies him as a contributor, and a brief statement of the claim.

Part Three:
Index of Signatures

The Index of Signatures lists the pseudonyms, letters, and symbols used by writers in the *London*. Prompted by the excellent example of *The Wellesley Index,* we have included all of the signatures given in the *London,* whether or not we have broken them. Where we have discovered the writer's identity, the signature is given, followed by the writer's name. We have then added in parentheses the index number of the item where the author first used this signature. Often the first use of a signature is the only use. Anyone seeking further information must then consult either the Monthly Contents or the Index of Authors and Contributors. Where we have been unable to discover the writer's identity, the signature is given, followed by all of the index numbers of the items where it was used. In the instances where several items are involved, a user who can identify one of the items will then be able to locate conveniently the others written under that signature. All too often, however, several writers used the same initials for a signature. P.G. Patmore used "A" as a signature for No. 167, while Richard Ayton used it for No. 973. An unidentified contributor then used it for No. 1505. In the Index of Signatures the entry for "A" appears as follows:

> A.--Richard Ayton (973), Peter G. Patmore (167), 1505.

Several other points should be mentioned. Letters and words in the Greek alphabet are listed after the letter "Z," followed by asterisks and symbols used as signatures. Other Greek words, transliterated by Roman letters, appear alphabetically in the English list. Where initials are used they are listed under the first initial, for example, W.H., not H.,W. A doubtful attribution of a signature is indicated by placing a question mark before the name.

Part Four:
Book Review Index

The Book Review Index is a feature of this volume that we believe will be useful to scholars interested in the reception of books published between 1820 and 1829. Some four hundred books were reviewed in the *London,* and their listing here will facilitate the location of specific authors and titles. Where possible we have included the author's name, and since many of the volumes were published anonymously or pseudonymously, the compilation of the list necessitated some bibliographic research. Each ordinary entry in the Book Review Index contains three units: the author's name, the title of the book, and the index number or numbers of the review in the *London*. When necessary and available, pseudonyms or the names of editors or translators have been added. No reference has been made here to the writers of the reviews since their names, when traced, appear in the Monthly Contents.

The Book Review Index contains two lists, an Author List

and a Title List. This was done because we had no way of knowing which piece of information a user might need. At times a book review is referred to more than once in the Author List. It may appear once under the name of the writer, where the main entry is given, and then under a pseudonym, the names of other writers in instances of multiple authorship, the name of a translator, or the name of an editor. In a few instances, when we do not know the author's name, the principal entry is given under the name of the translator or editor. Where we have been unable to discover a relevant name, the review is entered only in the Title List. Users who do not find the book review in the Author List, then, should also check the Title List. Book titles used in both lists are brief. Thus H.I. Todd's *Some Account of the Life and Writings of John Milton, Derived Principally from Documents in His Majesty's State Paper Office, Now First Published* is entered as *Some Account of the Life and Writings of John Milton*. This practice was adopted to reduce the length of the Index.

The lists include all reviews that appeared in the *London*, whether a review was extensive or cursory. Brief notices and announcements of publication have been excluded. Moreover, a distinction has been made between reviews and extracts from books. Though it can be argued that the reprinting of parts of a book without comment or criticism is a kind of review, such extractions have not been included in the Book Review Index. Such excerpts will ordinarily be noted in the Index of Authors and Contributors under the name of the writer. Part of Walter Scott's *Chronicles of the Canongate*, for example, was reprinted in the November 1827 issue of the *London*. This entry will be found under "Scott, Walter" in the Index of Authors and Contributors. The review of the *Chronicles*, curiously enough in the same issue of the *London*, will be found in the Book Review Index under Scott's name and the book's title. At times this distinction between extraction and review was more difficult to maintain, particularly in the case of translations preceded or followed by a note. The first group of extracts from Cuvier's *Animal Kingdom*, for example, was preceded by an editorial note, but in the second only extracts were given. How was this to be listed? Was the first to be given as a review and the other as excerpts listed under the author's name? In this specific case each of the index numbers is listed in the Book Review Index. Though we have tried to maintain this distinction, then, some fairly arbitrary decision had to be made.

Bibliography

The Bibliography covers works listed in all sections of this volume. It does not include, however, all of the works and papers we have examined, nor does it list every significant item in which the *London* is mentioned or discussed. In compiling this Bibliography, the selection of items was determined by the specific needs of this volume. All works are listed under one alphabet, which includes books, articles, manuscripts, dissertations, and marked copies of the *London*.

Abbreviations

attr.	attributed by
K-SJ	*Keats-Shelley Journal*
MLN	*Modern Language Notes*
[n.p.]	no page numbers
prob.	probably
PQ	*Philological Quarterly*
repr.	reprinted in
TLS	*Times Literary Supplement*

Summary Directions

The summary schema that follows is incomplete and epitomizes only the most obvious features of the Monthly Contents with Identification of Contributors. It is not meant to be a substitute for the full information provided in the Plan and Use of the Index. For readers pressed for time, however, it does include enough information to allow for a quick, though minimal, use of the Index.

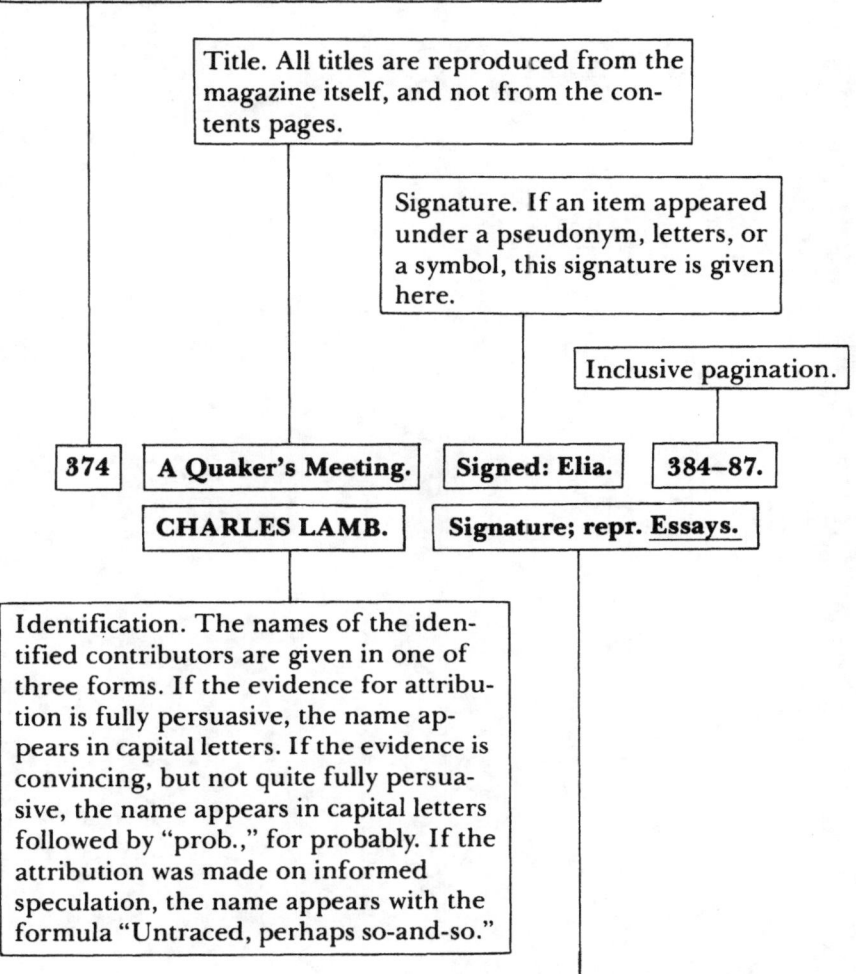

PART ONE:

MONTHLY CONTENTS

WITH IDENTIFICATION OF CONTRIBUTORS

VOLUME I. NUMBER I
JANUARY 1820

1 Preface and Prospectus of The London Magazine. iii-vii. JOHN SCOTT. Robert Baldwin, the publisher, made some alterations of Scott's draft. Scott/Baldwin Letters.

2 Editorial Notes. 2. JOHN SCOTT. The context and other evidence make it clear that these notes are by the editor. Occasional contributions from others were printed here.

3 General Reflections suggested by Italy, seen in the Years 1818 and 1819. 3-7. JOHN SCOTT. Scott's footnote on p. 3 of the second edition of volume I refers to his forthcoming Sketches of Manners.

4 Some Account of John Clare, an Agricultural Labourer and Poet. 7-11. OCTAVIUS GILCHRIST. Signed; B. M. Egerton MS 2245/19.

5 Living Authors (Being a Series of Critical Sketches) No. I. The Author of the Scotch Novels. 11-22. JOHN SCOTT. See No. 303.

6 Modest Offer of Service from Mr. Bonmot to the Editor and Ancestral Enormities (Taken, with liberties, from the French). 22-24. T. G. WAINEWRIGHT. Repr. Essays and Criticisms.

7 The Memoirs of Mr. Hardy Vaux (A Family Man) now residing at New South Wales for the Public Good. 25-31. JOHN SCOTT, prob. Scott refers to this review of Barron Field's book in No. 253, p. 511; style.

8 Tomb-Stone Warehouse; or magasin des Modes Monumentals, at Paris, 1819. Signed: W. 31-34. B. W. PROCTER. Signature used by Procter elsewhere in London as in No. 90; style.

9 The Influence of Religious and Patriotic Feeling on Literature. 34-41. JOHN SCOTT. Scott's footnote on pp. 36-37 refers to his article in the British Review, X (Nov. 1817), 434-84.

10 The Traveller, No. I /verse/. 41. JOHN SCOTT.
    Attr. Brooks, Dissertation.

11 The Advantages and Disadvantages of Rome, as a
    School of Art; With Descriptive Criticism on the
    French, Italian, and German Artists in Rome, in-
    cluding particulars of the various Institutions
    established in that Capital for the Encouragement
    of Art. 42-48. CHARLES L. EASTLAKE. Eastlake,
    95.

12 French Criticism on a Celebrated German Work. 49-
    52. JOHN SCOTT. See No. 34. Introduction is
    editorial, the rest a translation from a French
    periodical criticism of Werther. Scott believed
    the use of foreign periodicals necessary to the
    London; and in a letter to Baldwin of 18 Oct. 1819,
    he mentions that he intends to write an article on
    French criticism for the first number: Scott/
    Baldwin Letters.

13 The Searching of the River Tyber for Remains of
    Antiquity. 52-56. CHARLES L. EASTLAKE.
    Eastlake, 95.

14 Letters from Venice. By an Italian. Signed: C.
    56-58.

15 Farewell in England, Written off the Land's End,
    December 1819 /verse/. Signed: H. 58-60. HORACE
    SMITH. N.L. of S. MS 1706/178.

16 Midnight Hours, No. I. 60-61. Untraced, perhaps
    John Scott. One of the poems, "The Wanderer," is
    reminiscent of Scott's House of Mourning, and other
    poems in the series show a knowledge of French
    poetry which Scott possessed.

17 The Collector, No. I. 61-62. JOHN SCOTT, prob.
    Each month Scott was to provide three sheets of
    original and selected matter and notices for the
    London. He undoubtedly conducted this feature,
    though others contributed items to it. See Scott/
    Baldwin Letters.

18 The Ivy, Addressed to ---- /verse/. 62-63.
    BERNARD BARTON. Signed; repr. Poems.

19 Sonnet. From the French of Scarron. Signed: R. H.
    63. REGINALD HEBER. Attr. Brooks, Dissertation.

20 Winter. Bath /verse/. 63. J. H. REYNOLDS, prob.
    Attr. Hughes as conjecture.

21 The Drama. No. I. Signed: L. M. 64-70. WILLIAM
    HAZLITT. Repr. Works, XVIII.

22 Notices of the Fine Arts. No. I. 70-71. JOHN
    SCOTT. An introductory article which quotes the
    Prospectus and refers to Wilkie, Scott's favorite;
    style.

23 Gleanings from the Foreign Journals. 72-76. JOHN
    SCOTT or W. H. LEEDS. After Scott's death in
    February 1821, W. H. Leeds was definitely provid-
    ing the material for this item, but in his letter
    to Baldwin of 14 Aug. 1819, Scott states his re-
    sponsibility for it. However, they may both have
    provided material. Scott/Baldwin Letters and
    Leeds/Turner Letters.

24 Critical Notices of New Books: I. Anastasius, or
    Memoirs of a Greek, 76-79; II. Ivanhoe, a Romance.
    By the Author of Waverley, 79-84; III. A Sicilian
    Story, by Barry Cornwall, 84-86. JOHN SCOTT.
    The Editorial Notes for April 1820 (No. 85) and the
    Scott/Baldwin Letters assign this column to Scott,
    but others contributed items. The evidence of
    Scott's style would often weigh heavier here than
    elsewhere in the London. Scott's note in Apr. 1820
    (I, 437) specifically acknowledges the review of
    Ivanhoe.

25 Literary and Scientific Intelligence. 86-88. JOHN
    SCOTT. Scott/Baldwin Letters. As with all of the
    regular features for which Scott was responsible,
    others may have contributed here. For Hazlitt's
    possible assistance here, see Brooks, Notes and
    Queries.

26 Report of Music. No. I. 89-92. Untraced, perhaps
    R. M. Bacon. See No. 211.

27 Rural Economics. 92-95. A Mr. VANCOUVER. Scott/
    Baldwin Letters. This is probably Charles
    Vancouver. See DNB.

28 Medical Article. No. I. 95-96. Untraced, perhaps
    Dr. George Darling who later attended the dinners
    given by Taylor and Hessey for contributors.

29 Commercial Report. 97-98. JOHN SCOTT. In his
    letter to Baldwin of 14 Aug. 1819, Scott states
    his responsibility for providing this kind of item
    and specifically mentions "markets." Scott/
    Baldwin Letters.

30   Historical and Critical Summary of Public Events.
     99-106. JOHN SCOTT. Scott supplied "the News of
     the Month," for which see No. 85.

31   Monthly Register. 106-20. JOHN SCOTT. Scott/
     Baldwin Letters. The heading for this mis-
     cellaneous group of items appears regularly in the
     London. Under it are included such items as colon-
     ial intelligence, public documents, new patents,
     ecclesiastical preferments, bankruptcies, births,
     marriages, deaths, foreign news, domestic news,
     works preparing for publication, books newly im-
     ported, markets, and so on. Most of these items
     appeared monthly and are mainly notices, short
     summaries, and tables. As Scott's letter to Baldwin
     of 14 Aug. 1819 makes clear, he was to provide
     these items, though others might contribute (Scott/
     Baldwin Letters). Some of the notices and articles
     were signed by other contributors. This number in-
     cluded signed contributions by J. M. RICHARDSON,
     WOLFE and EDMONDS.

                  VOLUME I. NUMBER II
                    FEBRUARY 1820

32   Editorial Notes. /n.p./ JOHN SCOTT. See No. 2.

33   Poetry and Prose, by a Member of Parliament and a
     Free Mason. 121-26. JOHN SCOTT, prob. Sentiments
     expressed here are the germ for his article on
     Byron (No. 303); style.

34   The Spirit of French Criticism, and Voltaire's
     Notices of Shakespeare. 126-32. JOHN SCOTT.
     Sentiments are similar to No. 12. Scott acknow-
     ledges his authorship of present article in No. 60.
     He also refers the reader to his review of Morgann's
     Falstaff, No. 51, as a continuation of this subject.

35   Observations on the Nature and Importance of Medical
     Jurisprudence. Signed: W. M. I. 132-36. Untraced,
     perhaps J. Gordon Smith. As reported in the London
     for April 1820, Smith "expressed his intention of
     devoting himself particularly to this hitherto much
     neglected, though important subject" (I, 468).
     This may have been a trial article.

36   Sentimentalities on the Fine Arts, No. I. Signed:
     Janus Weathercock. 136-40. T. G. WAINEWRIGHT.
     Signature; repr. Essays and Criticisms.

37 Gymnastic Exercises in Germany: their Influence on Personal Character and Public Spirit. 140-46. Untraced, perhaps John Scott. The article was collected and arranged from the Annals of Literature, a periodical published in Vienna, and Scott was interested in using material from foreign periodicals in the London.

38 On the Dramatic Art, as Influenced by the present Practice of the Theatre. Signed: From a Foreign Contributor. 146-49. Perhaps John Scott, attr. Hughes; or C.L. Eastlake, attr. Brooks, Dissertation.

39 Lines written on New Year's Day, 1820. Signed: N. T. H. B. 149.

40 On the Oracles of the Ancients. 150-56. GEORGE CROLY, prob. Attr. Hughes; subject and style.

41 Hereafter. A Poem. Signed: B. C. 156-58. B. W. PROCTER. Advertisement in Morning Chronicle, 1 Feb. 1820; repr. Poetical Works, III.

42 The Collector, No. II. 158-60. JOHN SCOTT, prob. See No. 17. Contains a hitherto unpublished letter of Napoleon.

43 The Traveller, No. II /verse/. 161. JOHN SCOTT. Attr. Brooks, Dissertation.

44 The Drama, No. II. 162-68. WILLIAM HAZLITT. Repr. Works, XVIII.

45 Report of Music, No. II. 169-72. Untraced, perhaps R. M. Bacon. See No. 211.

46 Notices of the Fine Arts, No. II. The Descent from the Cross. Signed: Janus Weathercock. 172-73. T. G. WAINEWRIGHT. Signature. Exhibition at the Great Room, 173-74. Signed: T. WILLIAM HAZLITT. Signature.

47 Gleanings from the Foreign Journals. 174-78. JOHN SCOTT or W. H. LEEDS. See No. 23.

48 Medical Article, No. II. 179-80. Untraced, perhaps George Darling. See No. 28.

49 Rural Economics. 180-82. A Mr. VANCOUVER. See No. 27.

50 Commercial Report. 182-85. JOHN SCOTT. Scott/Baldwin Letters.

51 Critical Notices of New Books: I. Lectures on the Literature of the Age of Elizabeth, by W. Hazlitt, 185-91. JOHN SCOTT. Attr. Butterworth, 17. II. Anecdotes, Observations and Characters of Books and Men &c, By the Rev. Joseph Spence, 191-94. OCTAVIUS GILCHRIST. Taylor, London; and N.L. of S. MS 1706/45. III. An Essay on the Dramatic Character of Sir John Falstaff. By Maurice Morgann, 194-98. JOHN SCOTT. Scott claims this in No. 34 above. IV. Memoirs of the Private Life, Return, and Reign of Napoleon in 1815, 198-200. JOHN SCOTT, prob. Context; style, for which see No. 24.

52 Literary and Scientific Intelligence. 200-03. JOHN SCOTT. Scott/Baldwin Letters. See No. 25.

53 Historical and Critical Summary of Public Events. 204-13. JOHN SCOTT. See No. 85.

54 Monthly Register. 213-38. JOHN SCOTT. See No. 31. Signed contributions by J. M. RICHARDSON, WOLFE and EDMONDS.

VOLUME I. NUMBER III

MARCH 1820

55 Editorial Notes, Mr. Bonmot's Visit to the Editor. 240. JOHN SCOTT and T. G. WAINEWRIGHT. See No. 2 and Curling, 379.

56 Notices of some of the Early French Poets. 241-44. JOHN SCOTT. Page 242 repr. from British Review (Aug. 1818), 54-55.

57 News from Rome. 245-50. CHARLES L. EASTLAKE. Eastlake, 95.

58 The Phenomena of Diseased Imagination. 250-54. Untraced, perhaps George Croly on subject and style.

59 A Literary Gem. Original Dramas, By James Plumtre. 254-63. J. H. REYNOLDS. Attr. Brooks, Dissertation.

60 On the Comparative Refinement of the Age that preceded and that which followed the Commonwealth; With Further Observations in Reply to the French Critics. 263-67. JOHN SCOTT. Passage on Montaigne and Amiot substantially repr. Sketches of Manners. On p. 263 he acknowledges authorship of No. 34.

61   The Priestess of Vesta [verse]. Signed: *******.
     267-68. Untraced, perhaps B. W. Procter on style.

62   On Human Perfectibility and the Progress of Society.
     269-71. JOHN SCOTT, prob. Context; style.

63   The Last Song. Signed: L. 272. B. W. PROCTER.
     Repr. Poetical Works, III.

64   The Traveller, No. III [verse]. 272-73. JOHN
     SCOTT. Attr. Brooks, Dissertation.

65   Charles the Fifth, and a Monk. Signed: W. 273-75.
     B. W. PROCTER. Signature; style.

66   Living Authors, No. II: Wordsworth. 275-85. JOHN
     SCOTT. London Magazine, II (Nov. 1820), 515.

67   Sentimentalities of the Fine Arts, No. II. Signed:
     Janus Weathercock. 285-89. T. G. WAINEWRIGHT.
     Signature.

68   Midnight Hours, No. II [verse]. 289. Untraced,
     perhaps John Scott. See No. 16.

69   Postscript to the News From Rome. 290-91. JOHN
     SCOTT and CHARLES L. EASTLAKE. Editorial note and
     an addition to No. 57.

70   The Collector, No. III. 291-95. JOHN SCOTT, prob.
     See No. 17.

71   Extract from Lord Byron's Journal. 295-96. JOHN
     SCOTT and LORD BYRON. Editorial note and excerpt
     from Byron's unpublished journal.

72   The Contrast [verse]. Signed: H. 296-97. HORACE
     SMITH. Repr. Poetical Works, I.

73   The Drama, No. III. 297-304. WILLIAM HAZLITT.
     Repr. Works, XVIII.

74   Report of Music, No. III. 305-08. Untraced,
     perhaps R. M. Bacon. See No. 211.

75   Notices of the Fine Arts, No. III: Exhibition of
     Revelli's Picture of the Spanish Inquisition, 309.
     Untraced, perhaps John Scott on style. The British
     Institution. Signed: T. 309-10. WILLIAM HAZLITT.
     Signature. Balneum Bathshebae and Provincial
     Antiquities. Signed: Janus Weathercock. 310-13.
     T. G. WAINEWRIGHT. Signature; repr. Works, XVIII.

76   Gleanings from Foreign Journals. 313-14. JOHN
     SCOTT or W. H. LEEDS. See No. 23.

77   Medical Article, No. III. 313-17. Untraced,
     perhaps George Darling. See No. 28.

78   Rural Economics. 317-18. A Mr. VANCOUVER. See No.
     27.

79   Commercial Report. 319-21. JOHN SCOTT. Scott/
     Baldwin Letters.

80   Critical Notices of New Books: I. Song to David,
     by the late Christopher Smart. 321-23. JOHN
     SCOTT. Taylor, London. II. Poems descriptive of
     Rural Life and Scenery. By John Clare. 323-27.
     JOHN SCOTT. Taylor, London.

81   Address to a Copy of Clare's Poems Sent to
     Octavius Gilchrist. 328. JOHN CLARE. Attr.
     Hughes, who saw the presentation copy.

82   Literary and Scientific Intelligence. 328-29. JOHN
     SCOTT. Scott/Baldwin Letters. See No. 25.

83   Historical and Critical Summary of Public Events.
     329-39. JOHN SCOTT. See No. 85.

84   Monthly Register. 340-66. JOHN SCOTT. See No. 31.
     Signed contributions by MARK BEAUFOY, J. M. RICHARD-
     SON, WOLFE and EDMONDS.

VOLUME I. NUMBER IV
APRIL 1820

85   Editorial Notes. 368. As Scott was ill this
     month, Robert Baldwin or William Hazlitt may have
     written this. Since this note is often cited for
     Scott's contributions, we quote the following
     sentence: "There is a deficiency in this Number in
     our Notices of New Books; also an omission of the
     usual Political Article, and of the News of the
     Month: these have been occasioned by the severe
     illness of the Conductor of the Magazine."

86   Memoirs of the Life and Writings of Sir John
     Suckling. 369-79. OCTAVIUS GILCHRIST. Taylor,
     London; B. M. Egerton MS 2245/82.

87   Endymion, A poetic Romance, By John Keats. 380-89.
     P. G. PATMORE. Taylor, London; Champneys, II, 226.

88 The Bag-Piper in Tottenham Court Road. Signed: Vitruvius. 389-90.

89 Song. Signed: M. 390. B. W. PROCTER. Repr. Galignani.

90 Melancholy /verse_/. Signed: W. 391. B. W. PROCTER. Taylor, London; repr. Poetical Works, III.

91 On the State of the Cultivation of the Ancient Literature of the North at the Present Period. 391-401. Untraced, perhaps George Croly on subject and style.

92 Sentimentalities on the Fine Arts, No. III. Signed: Janus Weathercock. 401-08. T. G. WAINEWRIGHT. Signature.

93 Observations on some Distinctions between the English and Scottish Systems of Law. 408-14.

94 Sonnets, No. I, To the Author of Childe Harold. Signed: P. 415. P. G. PATMORE. Taylor, London.

95 The Grave /verse_/. Signed: P. 415. P. G. PATMORE. Taylor, London.

96 Extracts from the Journal of an English Traveller in Palestine. 416-19. Untraced, perhaps George Croly, as he published Views of the Holy Land in 1842.

97 The Leper of the City of Aosta: A Tale. 419-22. JOHN SCOTT and HELEN M. WILLIAMS. Scott comments after quoting the Williams translation of a tale by XAVIER DE MAISTRE.

98 Sonnets, Amatory, Descriptive, and Incidental. Signed: W. Cornelius, Chelsea. 423. CORNELIUS WEBB. Signature; repr. Sonnets.

99 Biographical Notices of the late Duke of Kent and Strathearn. 423-31. "This brief Memoir was drawn up by one of his Royal Highness's Household, who, in its illustrious subject, had the high honour and happiness of a patron and protector."

100 To My Mother in Heaven. /verse_/. Signed:Cistus, 431.

101 The Drama, No. IV. 432-40. WILLIAM HAZLITT. Repr. Works, XVIII.

102 Report of Music, No. IV. 440-47. Untraced, perhaps R. M. Bacon. See No. 211.

103 Notices of the Fine Arts, No. IV: Mr. West. 447-48. B. R. HAYDON. Attr. Brooks, Dissertation. British Institution (continued from March). 448-49. WILLIAM HAZLITT. See No. 75. Criticisms. Signed: Janus Weathercock. 449-50. T. G. WAINEWRIGHT. Signature.

104 Gleanings from Foreign Journals. 451. JOHN SCOTT or W. H. LEEDS. See No. 23.

105 Medical Article, No. IV. 451-54. Untraced, perhaps George Darling. See No. 28.

106 Rural Economics. 454-56. A Mr. VANCOUVER. See No. 27.

107 Commercial Report. 456-60. JOHN SCOTT. Scott/Baldwin Letters.

108 Critical Notices of New Books: I. Observations from a Memorandum Book, by Edward Meissner. 460-67; II. London in 1819. 467. JOHN SCOTT, prob. for both. Attr. Brooks, Dissertation.

109 Literary and Scientific Intelligence. 468-69. JOHN SCOTT. Scott/Baldwin Letters.

110 Monthly Register. 469-86. JOHN SCOTT. See No. 31. Signed contributions by MARK BEAUFOY, J. M. RICHARDSON, WOLFE and EDMONDS.

VOLUME I. NUMBER V
MAY 1820

111 Editorial Notes. 488. JOHN SCOTT. See No. 2.

112 On May Day. 489-92. B.W. PROCTER. Taylor, London.

113 Lord Byron: his French Critics: the Newspapers; and the Magazines. 492-97. JOHN SCOTT. Taylor, London.

114 The Chronicle of Don Pierre Nino, Count of Buelna; by Guttiere Diez de Gamez, his Standard Bearer. 497-501. JOHN SCOTT. Editorial footnote on p. 501; style.

115 Euphrosyne and Melidore, A Tale /verse7. Signed: Drue Digby. 501-03. LEIGH HUNT, prob. Signature; Louis Landre, Leigh Hunt; see No. 141.

116 Ancient State of the Jews in England. 503-10. GEORGE CROLY. Attr. Hughes.

117 Extracts from Dr. S. H. Spiker's Tour through England, Wales and Scotland. 510-13. JOHN SCOTT, prob. This is largely a selection of excerpts with two paragraphs of introduction.

118 Spanish Literature and Language. 514-19. Untraced, perhaps John Bowring. Bowring was a specialist in this subject and later contributed articles on it to the London.

119 On Fighting. Signed: A Young Gentleman of the Fancy. 519-22. B. W. PROCTER. Taylor, London; N. L. of S. MS 1706/131.

120 Goethe on Art and Antiquity. 523-25. JOHN SCOTT. Editorial comments precede and follow translated excerpts from J. W. VON GOETHE, Ueber Kunst und Alterthum. Two excerpts: On Mr. Haydon's Account of Two Ancient Heads of Horses and Manfred by Lord Byron.

121 On the Character and Writings of James Shirley. Signed: K. Q. X. 525-30. JOHN PAYNE COLLIER. Taylor, London; N. L. of S. MS 1706/158.

122 Sonnets. Signed: W. Cornelius. 531-32. CORNELIUS WEBB. Signature; repr. Sonnets.

123 Vindication of Eustace, from the Charges brought against him in Mr. Hobhouse's Notes and Illustrations to Childe Harold. 532-37. CHARLES L. EASTLAKE. Attr. Brooks, Dissertation.

124 Curious History of a Soldier's Daughter. Signed: Veteranus. 538-41.

125 On the Nile and the Niger. 541-42. JAMES GREY JACKSON. Signed.

126 Midnight Hours, No. III [verse]. 542. Untraced, perhaps John Scott. See No. 16.

127 The New Schools [verse]. 543. Untraced, perhaps J. H. Reynolds, attr. Hughes; or P. G. Patmore, attr. Brooks, Dissertation.

128 Sonnets. Signed: P. 544. P. G. PATMORE. Signature.

129 The Collector, No. IV. Signed: T. R. 544-45. John Scott probably conducted this feature, but the present item is a letter from T. R. See No. 17.

130 Critical Notices of New Books: I. The Cenci, by
     Shelley. 546-55. JOHN SCOTT. N. L. of S. MS
     1706/182. II. Memoirs of the Late R. L. Edge-
     worth. 555-65. JOHN SCOTT. Taylor, London. III.
     The Monastery, by the Author of Waverley. 565-68.
     JOHN SCOTT. Attr. Zeitlin, p. 241.

131 The Drama, No. V. Signed: L. 569-78. WILLIAM
     HAZLITT. Repr. Works, XVIII.

132 Report of Music, No. V. 578-81. Untraced, per-
     haps R. M. Bacon. See No. 211.

133 Notices of the Fine Arts, No. V: Mr. Haydon's
     Picture of Christ's Triumphal Entry into Jeru-
     salem. 581-87. JOHN SCOTT. Editorial admission
     in No. 157, p. 3; Haydon, II, 70.

134 Gleanings from Foreign Journals. 587. JOHN
     SCOTT or W. H. LEEDS. See No. 23.

135 Literary and Scientific Intelligence. 587-89.
     JOHN SCOTT. Scott/Baldwin Letters.

136 Historical and Critical Summary of Public Events.
     590-91. JOHN SCOTT. See No. 85.

137 Monthly Register. 591-606. JOHN SCOTT. See No.
     31. Signed contributions by MARK BEAUFOY, J. M.
     RICHARDSON, WOLFE and EDMONDS.

                    VOLUME I.   NUMBER VI
                        JUNE 1820

138 Editorial Notes. 608. JOHN SCOTT. See No. 2.

139 Nero:--Elliston &c. or, The Emperor Actor and The
     Actor Emperor. 609-16. JOHN SCOTT. Taylor,
     London.

140 On Musical Style; principally with reference to the
     English and Italian Schools of Music. 616-21.
     CHARLES L. EASTLAKE. Eastlake, 95.

141 Fiametta and Boccacio, A Tale [verse]. Signed:
     Drue Digby. 622-25. LEIGH HUNT, prob. In Auto-
     biographical Recollections, John Bowring quotes
     Hunt as saying, "I contributed largely to the
     London Magazine" (p. 61). That this and No. 115
     are two of his contributions is indicated by P. G.
     Patmore's prose parody of Hunt, entitled "Boccacio
     and Fiametta," which he included in Rejected

Articles (1826). Patmore mentions that the reading of a "tale in verse" suggested the parody. See No. 115.

142   Janus's Jumble: Enterlaced with hys iourney to Town and his visite to the Exhibition and Covent Garden theatre. 625-34. T. G. WAINEWRIGHT. Signature; editorial note on p. 628 states this is by Janus Weathercock.

143   Das Niebelungenlied. 635-40. Untraced, perhaps George Croly on subject and style.

144   On Fighting /concludes No. 119/. Signed: A Young Gentleman of the Fancy. 640-45. B. W. PROCTER. N. L. of S. MS 1706/131.

145   Table Talk, No. I: On the Qualifications Necessary to Success in Life. Signed: T. 646-54. WILLIAM HAZLITT. Repr. Works, XII.

146   Memory (Old Parr loquitur) /verse/. Signed: g. 654. OCTAVIUS GILCHRIST. Attr. Brooks, Dissertation.

147   On the Panorama of Venice /verse/. Signed: L. 655. B. W. PROCTER. Attr. Butterworth, 15.

148   A Recollection /verse/. Signed: g. 655-56. OCTAVIUS GILCHRIST. Attr. Brooks, Dissertation.

149   Much Ado About Nothing. Signed: E. B. 657-61. T. G. WAINEWRIGHT. Signature; Curling, 380.

150   The Collector, No. V. 661-65. JOHN SCOTT, prob. See No. 17. Includes a letter of John Locke sent to Scott by a MR. WATKINS. Scott/Baldwin Letters.

151   Critical Notices of New Books: I. Winter Evening Tales, collected by James Hogg. 666-71. JOHN SCOTT, prob. Context. II. Travels in various countries, by E. D. Clarke and Travels through Sweden, Norway and Lapland, by Vargas Bedemar. 671-79. Untraced, perhaps John Scott as he was the heaviest contributor of these reviews. III. The Fall of Jerusalem, by H. H. Milman. 679-86. JOHN SCOTT. Taylor, London.

152   The Drama, No. VI: Mr. Kean's Lear. Signed: T. 686-92. WILLIAM HAZLITT. Attr. Works, XVIII. The Lady and the Devil. Signed: X. 692. B. W. PROCTER. Signature. Virginius. 692-95. Untraced, perhaps John Scott on style.

153   Notices of the Fine Arts, No. VI: The Exhibition
        at the Royal Academy. 695-700. JOHN SCOTT, prob.
        Context. Janus Weathercock's Dialogue on the Ex-
        hibition at Somerset House. 700-04. T. G. WAINE-
        WRIGHT. Signature.

154   Gleanings from Foreign Journals. 704-06. JOHN
        SCOTT or W. H. LEEDS. See No. 23.

155   Literary and Scientific Intelligence. 706-09.
        JOHN SCOTT. Scott/Baldwin Letters.

156   Monthly Register. 709-26. JOHN SCOTT. See No.
        31. Signed contributions by MARK BEAUFOY, J. M.
        RICHARDSON, WOLFE and EDMONDS.

                    VOLUME II. NUMBER VII
                         JULY 1820

157   The Lion's Head. 3-8. JOHN SCOTT. Until Dec.
        1824, the formerly untitled editorial notes appear
        under this heading. See No. 2. Here he reprints
        WORDSWORTH's poem "Dion," and some verse frag-
        ments on the queen.

158   The History of Madame Krudener, a Religious
        Enthusiast. 9-22. JOHN SCOTT, prob. Style and
        sentiment similar to his Sketches of Manners.

159   Table Talk, No. II: On the Difference Between
        Writing and Speaking. Signed: T. 22-33. WILLIAM
        HAZLITT. Repr. Works, XII.

160   Mr. Bowles--As Editor of Pope. Signed: L. S. C.
        33-34. L. S. COSTELLO. Brooks, K-SJ, 107.

161   Lines, Written by a Spaniard. 34. Untraced, per-
        haps John Bowring. This is similar to his Spanish
        romances. See No. 118.

162   To--On a Dispute Concerning the Comparative Beauty
        of Black Eyes and Blue Eyes /verse/. Signed: X,
        Lincoln's Inn. 35. B. W. PROCTER. Signature as
        in No. 330; style.

163   On the Character and Writings of James Shirley, No.
        II. Signed: K. Q. X. 36-41. JOHN PAYNE COLLIER.
        N. L. of S. MS 1706/158.

164   A New Bibliographical Work. 41-43. OCTAVIUS
        GILCHRIST. Attr. Brooks, Dissertation.

165 To--/vers_e/. 43. JOHN SCOTT. Attr. Brooks, Dissertation.

166 La Danse /vers_e/. 44.

167 Mr. Hunt's Hero and Leander and Bacchus and Ariadne. Signed: A. 45-55. P. G. PATMORE. Taylor, London.

168 Sonnets: Amatory, Descriptive and Incidental. 56. CORNELIUS WEBB. Signed; repr. Summer.

169 The Collector, No. VI. 56-59. JOHN SCOTT, prob. See No. 17. Here he includes Dr. Johnson's account of the coronation of George III.

170 Critical Notices of New Books: I. The Diary of an Invalid. 59-65. JOHN SCOTT. Scott/Baldwin Letters. II. Sintram and his Companions. 65-71. JOHN SCOTT, prob. Subject; style, for which see No. 24. III. The Fancy, by J. H. Reynolds. 71-75. B. W. PROCTER. Rollins, Keats Circle, I, 117. IV. Marcian Colonna. 75-81. V. The Glory of Regality. 81-88. JOHN SCOTT. Scott/Baldwin Letters.

171 The Drama, No. VIII. Signed: L. 88-93. WILLIAM HAZLITT. Repr. Works, XVIII.

172 Report of Music, No. VI. 94-98. Untraced, perhaps R. M. Bacon. See No. 211.

173 Literary and Scientific Intelligence. 98-99. JOHN SCOTT. Scott/Baldwin Letters.

174 Historical and Critical Summary of Intelligence. 100-05. JOHN SCOTT. See No. 85.

175 Monthly Register. 105-20. JOHN SCOTT. See No. 31. Signed contributions by MARK BEAUFOY, J. M. RICHARDSON, WOLFE and EDMONDS.

VOLUME II. NUMBER VIII
AUGUST 1820

176 The Lion's Head. 122-24. JOHN SCOTT. See No. 157.

177 Goethe and his Faustus. 124-42. GEORGE CROLY. Attr. Bauer, 288; Hughes.

178 Recollections of the South Sea House. Signed: Elia. 142-46. CHARLES LAMB. Signature; repr. Essays.

179 The Traveller, No. IV. Lines. 146-49. JOHN SCOTT. Attr. Brooks, Dissertation.

180 Description of certain frescos. 149-54. Untraced, perhaps Charles Macfarlane. This was from a correspondent in Rome who was not a professional artist. Macfarlane had been in Italy and was interested in the subject of art.

181 Midnight Hours, No. VI [verse]. 154-55. Untraced, perhaps John Scott. See No. 16.

182 The Jewels of the Book. 155-61. J. H. REYNOLDS. Taylor, London; Gold's London Magazine, Oct. 1820.

183 Mr. Ebert, and Mr. Dibdin. Signed: One of the Fancy. 161-63. OCTAVIUS GILCHRIST. Attr. Brooks, Dissertation.

184 Living Authors, No. III: Godwin, chiefly as a writer of Novels. 163-69. JOHN SCOTT. Editor admits he wrote this in No. 253, p. 515.

185 Bibliographia Curiosa, No. I. Signed: A. B. 170-75. OCTAVIUS GILCHRIST. Attr. Brooks, Dissertation.

186 Christian VII of Denmark and his Queen. 176-79. GEORGE CROLY. Attr. Brooks, Dissertation.

187 Supposed to be spoken by a Dying Son to his Mother [verse]. 179. JOHN SCOTT. Attr. Brooks, Dissertation.

188 A Portrait [verse]. 179.

189 The Character of Pope; Mr. Bowles. 180-81. OCTAVIUS GILCHRIST. Signed.

190 Stanzas written in a Forest. Signed: B. 182. B. W. PROCTER. Signature; style.

191 Excursion to the Top of Skiddaw. 183-85. B. W. PROCTER. Attr. Hughes.

192 Critical Notices of New Books: I. A Letter to Earl Bathurst. 185-90. JOHN SCOTT, prob. Material possibly supplied by Barron Field as this book is about New South Wales. II. The Life of Wesley, by R. Southey. 190-94. R. HEBER. Attr. Brooks,

Dissertation. Heber did a review of Southey's book for the Quarterly. III. Poems, by Bernard Barton. 194-97. JOHN SCOTT, prob. Zeitlin, p. 241; style.

193   The Drama, No. VIII. Signed: T. 197-202. WILLIAM HAZLITT. Repr. Works, XVIII.

194   Report of Music, No. VII. 202-206. Untraced, perhaps R. M. Bacon. See No. 211.

195   Notices of the Fine Arts: Mr. Haydon's Address to the Public. 206-09. B. R. HAYDON. Signed. Haydon's statement is headed by editorial note of JOHN SCOTT.

196   Gleanings from Foreing Journals. 209-12. JOHN SCOTT or W. H. LEEDS. See No. 23.

197   Literary and Scientific Intelligence. 212-16. JOHN SCOTT. Scott/Baldwin Letters.

198   Historical and Critical Summary of Intelligence. 216-22. JOHN SCOTT. See No. 85.

199   Monthly Register. 222-40. JOHN SCOTT. See No. 31. Signed contributions by MARK BEAUFOY, J. M. RICHARDSON, WOLFE and EDMONDS.

VOLUME II.   NUMBER IX
SEPTEMBER 1820

200   The Lion's Head. 242-44. JOHN SCOTT. See No. 157.

201   Old Stories, No. I: The Lying Servant; The Castle-Goblin. 245-49.

202   The Character of Pope. 249. W. L. BOWLES. Contents page.

203   Table Talk, No. III: On the Conversation of Authors. Signed: T. 250-62. WILLIAM HAZLITT. Repr. Works, XII.

204   Sbogar, the Dalmatian Brigand. 262-68. JOHN SCOTT. Attr. Zeitlin, p. 241; context and style support attribution.

205   The Jewels of the Book, No. II. 268-76. J. H. REYNOLDS. Taylor, London; Gold's London Magazine, Oct. 1820.

206   Italy, Sonnet imitated freely from the Italian of
        Filicaia. 276. Untraced, perhaps Charles Strong.
        Strong was later to contribute a series of sonnets
        translated from the Italian.

207   Stanzas. Signed: B. B. 277. BERNARD BARTON.
        Signature.

208   German Descriptions of Hogarth's Works: Harlot's
        Progress. 277-84. W. H. LEEDS and JOHN SCOTT.
        Leeds/Turner Letters and context. Translation of
        G. C. LICHTENBERG's description by Leeds and
        editorial introduction by Scott.

209   On Italian Tragedy: Introductory to remarks on Il
        Conto di Carmagnola. 284-91. GIOVANNI BERCHET.
        Attr. Hughes.

210   Drab Bonnets /verse7. 292. BERNARD BARTON. Repr.
        Poems (1821).

211   A Sketch of the Progress of Vocal Science in England. 293-99. R. M. BACON, prob. Bacon, the
        editor of the Quarterly Musical Magazine, published
        Elements of Vocal Science in 1824 (reviewed in the
        London, No. 1317). His address is listed in the
        Taylor Commonplace Book, and his connection with
        the London seems to have begun with Scott and continued through Taylor's editorship. The Taylor
        Commonplace Book assigns this article to a
        "Handel," but this appears to be a pseudonym. In
        a letter to Taylor of 21 March 1823, formerly
        among the Brooke-Taylor MSS and summarized in a
        descriptive list of the MSS, Hessey mentions
        Bacon's "articles." These articles may have been
        the monthly "Report of Music."

212   Mr. Weathercock's Private Correspondence. Signed:
        Janus Weathercock. 299-301. T. G. WAINEWRIGHT.
        Signature.

213   Sonnet, To the Author of the Poems published under
        the name of Barry Cornwall. Signed: ****. 302.
        CHARLES LAMB. Taylor, London; repr. Works, V.

214   To R. S. Knowles, Esq. On his Tragedy of Virginius
        /verse7. 302. CHARLES LAMB. Signed; repr. Works,
        V.

215   A Visit to the Republic of San Marino, in May 1820.
        303-05. Untraced, perhaps Charles Macfarlane on
        subject and style.

216 Critical Notices of New Books: I. Three Months passed in the Mountains East of Rome. 306-11. JOHN SCOTT, prob. Editorial comment shows a knowledge of Rome. II. The Brothers, by C. A. Elton. 311-15. JOHN SCOTT. Taylor, London; III. Lamia, Isabella, the Eve of Saint Agnes, and other Poems, by John Keats. 315-21. JOHN SCOTT. Taylor, London.

217 The Drama, No. IX. Signed: L. 321-25. WILLIAM HAZLITT. Repr. Works, XVIII.

218 Address Spoken, in the Character of the Comic Muse, by Miss Kelly /verse/. 325-26. J. H. REYNOLDS. Attr. Dobell, Sidelights, 188, from comments of Robinson, Diary, 6 April 1833.

219 Report of Music, No. VIII. 326-29. Untraced, perhaps R. M. Bacon. See No. 211.

220 Literary and Scientific Intelligence. 329-33. JOHN SCOTT. Scott/Baldwin Letters.

221 Historical and Critical Summary of Intelligence. 333-42. JOHN SCOTT. See No. 85.

222 Monthly Register. 342-60. JOHN SCOTT. See No. 31. Signed contributions by MARK BEAUFOY, J. M. RICHARDSON, WOLFE and EDMONDS.

VOLUME II. NUMBER X
OCTOBER 1820

223 The Lion's Head. 362-64. JOHN SCOTT. See No. 157.

224 Oxford in the Vacation. Signed: Elia. 365-69. CHARLES LAMB. Signature; repr. Essays.

225 Old Stories, No. II: Guido, the Witless; The Parrot of the Visitandines. 369-73.

226 Table Talk, No. IV: On the Present State of Parliamentary Eloquence. Signed: T. 373-84. WILLIAM HAZLITT. Repr. Works, XVII.

227 The Garden. Suggested by the German of Bindemann /verse/. 384. Untraced, perhaps W. H. Leeds who was contributing German translations.

21

228   The Cider Cellar. Signed: Pomarius. 384-88. B. W. PROCTER. Taylor, London; Hughes, who makes this identification on a manuscript letter in his possession.

229   Lichtenberg's Descriptions of Hogarth's Works, No. II: Rake's Progress. 388-402. W. H. LEEDS. Leeds/Turner Letters. See No. 208.

230   The Ape. Signed: **** /verse/. 402-03. CHARLES LAMB. Repr. Works, V.

231   Ochlenschäger's Correggio. 403-06. W. H. LEEDS. Leeds/Turner Letters.

232   Sonnet. The Leaves are Falling. Signed: M. M. 407. Untraced, and though Hughes suggests M. R. Mitford, there is no evidence outside of the initials to support his claim; M. M. Busk has also been suggested as she did publish poetry under that signature in other periodicals.

233   Lodoiska and her Daughter. A Romance by Madame de la Motte-Fouqué. 407-14. W. H. LEEDS. Leeds/Turner Letters.

234   On the Character and Writings of James Shirley, No. III. Signed: K.Q.AE. 415-20. JOHN PAYNE COLLIER. N. L. of S. MS 1706/158.

235   Star-Gazing. /verse/. Signed: P. 421. P. G. PATMORE. Taylor, London.

236   On the Connexion between the Character and Poetry of Nations. Signed: R. H. 421-26. REGINALD HEBER. Attr. Brooks, Dissertation.

237   The Abbot, by the Author of Waverley. 427-37. JOHN SCOTT. Attr. Zeitlin, p. 241.

238   The Collector, No. VII. 437. JOHN SCOTT, prob. See No. 17.

239   The Drama, No. X. Signed: M. 438-43. Untraced, perhaps J. H. Reynolds who later wrote this feature.

240   Report of Music, No. IX. 443-46. Untraced, perhaps R. M. Bacon. See No. 211.

241   Gleanings from the Foreign Journals. 446-47. JOHN SCOTT or W. H. LEEDS. See No. 23.

242 Literary and Scientific Intelligence. 448-50. JOHN SCOTT. Scott/Baldwin Letters.

243 Historical and Critical Summary of Intelligence. 451-56. JOHN SCOTT. See No. 85.

244 Monthly Register. 456-72. JOHN SCOTT. See No. 31. Signed contributions by MARK BEAUFOY, J. M. RICHARDSON, WOLFE and EDMONDS.

VOLUME II. NUMBER XI
NOVEMBER 1820

245 The Lion's Head. 474-76. JOHN SCOTT. See No. 157. Includes Sonnet signed C. W., by CORNELIUS WEBB; signature.

246 The Literature of the Nursery. 477-83. JOHN SCOTT. Editorial admission in No. 289, p.3.

247 Christ's Hospital Five and Thirty Years Ago. Signed: Elia. 483-90. CHARLES LAMB. Signature; repr. Essays.

248 Old Stories, No. III: The Page faithful to Death. 490-96.

249 Sonnet, written on leaving Leeds. Signed: T. 496. B. W. PROCTER. Taylor, London.

250 Helvellyn [verse]. Signed: W. 497. B. W. PROCTER. Taylor, London; repr. Watts, Poetical Album.

251 The Fairest. From the German [verse]. 498. Untraced, perhaps W. H. Leeds who was contributing German translations.

252 Il Conte di Carmagnola [concludes No. 209]. 499-509. GIOVANNI BERCHET. Attr. Hughes.

253 Blackwood's Magazine. 509-21. JOHN SCOTT. Scott's admission in No. 316, insert.

254 The Protestant Church of France. 521-27. Untraced, perhaps George Croly on subject.

255 Venus de Medicis [verse]. 527.

256 Lines written in Santa Croce, at the Tomb of Alfieri. 527. JOHN SCOTT. Attr. Brooks, Dissertation.

257　To--/verse/. 528.

258　A Promenade on the Prado at Madrid. 528-30. JOHN BOWRING. Attr. Brooks, Dissertation.

259　The Fisherman's Rebellion. Signed: M. 531-41. CHARLES MACFARLANE. N. L. of S. MS 1706/104.

260　Croly's Angel of the World. 542-48. P. G. PATMORE. N. L. of S. MS 1706/104.

261　Stoke Hills /verse/. 548-49. BERNARD BARTON. Repr. Minor Poems.

262　The Society, Scenery and Antiquities of Sicily. 550-57. JOHN SCOTT, prob. Subject and style.

263　Report of Music, No. X. 557-60. Untraced, perhaps R. M. Bacon. See No. 211.

264　Gleanings from Foreign Journals. 560-63. JOHN SCOTT or W. H. LEEDS. See No. 23.

265　Literary and Scientific Intelligence. 563-67. JOHN SCOTT. Scott/Baldwin Letters.

266　Historical and Critical Summary of Intelligence. 568-75. JOHN SCOTT. See No. 85.

267　Monthly Register. 575-92. JOHN SCOTT. See No. 31. Signed contributions by MARK BEAUFOY, J. M. RICHARDSON, WOLFE and EDMONDS.

VOLUME II.　NUMBER XII
DECEMBER 1820

268　The Lion's Head. 595-96. JOHN SCOTT. See No. 157. Contains Elia's reply to G. D.'s criticism, by CHARLES LAMB. Signature.

269　Table Talk, No. V: On the Pleasures of Painting. Signed: T. 597-607. WILLIAM HAZLITT. Repr. Works, VIII.

270　Exmouth Wrestling. 608-18. J. H. REYNOLDS. Attr. Jones, 437; repr. Jones. Reynolds had written on other sporting subjects such as boxing. There are references to the law and he was a solicitor; Devonshire was known to him and his wife came from Exeter. Keats Circle (I, 55) quotes a letter from Reynolds to Taylor dated "Exmouth 21 September

1820" and in the article the writer says "I was induced ... in September last, to pass a fortnight at Exmouth." In both the letter and the article there are almost identical references to the sunsets and the wind.

271 Osmyn, a Persian Tale /verse_/. 618-22.

272 The Quakers /verse_/. Signed: T. R. 622.

273 The Two Races of Men. Signed: Elia. 623-25. CHARLES LAMB. Signature; repr. Essays.

274 Our Arrears. 626-37. JOHN SCOTT. Zeitlin, p. 241; supported by context and style. An editorial review of books: I. Patronage, a Poem. 627-28. II. America, an Epistle in Verse. 629-31. III. Redwald, by Louisa Stuart Costello. 631-32. IV. The Memoirs of Henry Hunt. 632-37.

275 A newly discovered Letter on the Maid of Orleans. 637-40. Perhaps supplied by the Watkins who sent Locke's letter. See No. 150.

276 Traditional Literature, No. I. 641-47. ALLAN CUNNINGHAM. Hogg, Life of Allan Cunningham, 229.

277 Letters of Foote, Garrick, &c. 647-52. B. W. PROCTER. Attr. Butterworth, 15.

278 Sonnet. Signed: C. W. 653. CORNELIUS WEBB. Signature; repr. Lyric Leaves.

279 Sonnet, Written while Travelling. Signed: B. 653. B. W. PROCTER. Signature; style.

280 Sonnet. Signed: C. S. 653. Untraced, perhaps initials stand for Charles Strong.

281 On Population...answer to Mr. Malthus...By Wm. Godwin. 654-60. WILLIAM HAZLITT. Attr. Brooks, Dissertation.

282 Sketch of the Progress of Vocal Science in England, No. II. 660-65. R. M. BACON, prob. See No. 211.

283 Sonnet. Signed: M. M. 665. See No. 232.

284 The Mohock Magazine. 666-85. JOHN SCOTT. Scott's admission in No. 316, insert.

285 The Drama, No. XI. Signed: W. H. 685-90. WILLIAM HAZLITT. Repr. Works, XVIII.

286 Literary and Scientific Intelligence. 690-92.
     JOHN SCOTT. Scott/Baldwin Letters.

287 Historical and Critical Summary of Intelligence.
     692-97. JOHN SCOTT. See No. 85.

288 Monthly Register. 697-712. JOHN SCOTT. See No.
     31. Signed contributions by MARK BEAUFOY, J. M.
     RICHARDSON, WOLFE and EDMONDS.

VOLUME III. NUMBER XIII
JANUARY 1821

289 The Lion's Head. 2-4. JOHN SCOTT. See No. 157.

290 New Year's Eve. Signed: Elia. 5-8. CHARLES
     LAMB. Signature; repr. Essays.

291 With a Lampe for Mie Ladie Faire /verse7. Signed:
     MAIΩN. 8. GEORGE CROLY. Repr. Catiline.

292 The Travels and Opinions of Edgeworth Benson,
     Gentleman, No. I. 9-26. JOHN SCOTT. Haydon,
     Correspondence, II, 68, identifies Scott as
     Benson.

293 Traditional Literature, No. II. 26-32. ALLAN
     CUNNINGHAM. Taylor, London; Hogg, Life of Allan
     Cunningham, 229.

294 On Riding on Horse-Back, No. I. Signed: Mazeppa.
     33-36. P. G. PATMORE. N. L. of S. MS 1706.

295 The Shirt of the Happy Man, from Casti /verse7.
     37-38. Untraced, perhaps John Payne Collier, who
     in 1850 published a translation from the Italian
     of Casti, the work that suggested this poem.

296 Table Talk, No. VI: On the Look of a Gentleman.
     Signed: T. 39-45. WILLIAM HAZLITT. Repr. Works,
     XII.

297 Withered Violets /verse7. 46. WILLIAM READ.
     Repr. Sketches from Dover Castle.

298 The Rainbow /verse7. 46-47.

299 Sonnet. Signed: B. 47. B. W. PROCTER. Signature; style.

300 Sonnet, Written in the Woods of Bolton Abbey, Yorkshire. Signed: B. 47. B. W. PROCTER. Signature; repr. Galignani.

301 Lines written for a Young Lady's Pocket Book, near the Ruins of Horace's Villa. 48. JOHN SCOTT. Attr. Brooks, Dissertation.

302 Letter from John O'Groats to the Editor, Enclosing Specimens of a Poem. Signed: N. 48-50. JAMES HARLEY. Repr. Nonsense Verse.

303 Living Authors, No. IV, Lord Byron. 50-61. JOHN SCOTT. Scott's admission in No. 253, p. 515. In the first paragraph of the present article, the author admits writing the first in this series.

304 The Literary Pocket Book, or, Companion for the Lover of Nature and Art. 62-66. JOHN SCOTT, prob. Consists mainly of editorial comment; style.

305 Town Conversation, No. I. 66-77. JOHN SCOTT. Attr. Zeitlin, p. 241.

306 Miller Redivivus, No. I: Mrs. Rose Grob. Signed: H. 78-81. HORACE SMITH. Repr. Gaieties and Gravities, II.

307 The Apotheosis of Homor. An Explanation of an Ancient Bas-Relief. 81-83. JOHN CONRATH. Signed. First two paragraphs are editorial introduction by JOHN SCOTT.

308 The Drama, No. XII. Signed: A. 83-87. P. G. PATMORE. Signature used elsewhere by Patmore, e.g., No. 167. The articles from January to March were all signed A. Patmore fled to France following Scott's duel and the April Drama is probably by Talfourd.

309 Belzoni's Narrative of his Operations and Recent Discoveries in Egypt and Nubia. 87-91. JOHN SCOTT. Attr. Brooks, Dissertation.

310 The Earthquake, A Tale. 91-96. JOHN SCOTT. Context reveals anti-Blackwood views and writer amid editorial duties.

311 Melmoth the Wanderer, by the Author of Bertram. 96. JOHN SCOTT, prob. Style.

312 Report of Music, No. XI. 96-99. Untraced, perhaps R. M. Bacon. See No. 211.

313 Literary and Scientific Intelligence. 99-101.
JOHN SCOTT. Scott/Baldwin Letters.

314 Monthly Register. 101-20. JOHN SCOTT. See No.
31. Starting with this number, Historical and
Critical Summary of Intelligence is incorporated
under this heading. Signed contributions by MARK
BEAUFOY, J. M. RICHARDSON, WOLFE and EDMONDS.

VOLUME III. NUMBER XIV
FEBRUARY 1821

315 The Lion's Head. 123-24. JOHN SCOTT. See No.
157.

316 Statement, &c. 8 pages inserted. JOHN SCOTT. Context. Includes letters and notes by J. G. LOCKHART, HORACE SMITH and P. G. PATMORE concerning the Scott/Lockhart controversy.

317 Memnon's Head, with Stanzas. Signed: H. 125-28.
HORACE SMITH. Repr. Gaieties and Gravities, III.

318 Table Talk, No. VII: On Reading Old Books. Signed:
T. 128-34. WILLIAM HAZLITT. Repr. Works, XII.

319 A recent Visit to the Abbey of La Trappe. Signed:
G. H. P. 135-40.

320 A Legend of Ischia /verse/. 141-43. Untraced,
perhaps John Scott. In the second of his Living
Authors series, No. 66, Scott states that he spent
three days on the island of Ischia in 1819, and
from his description in the article it seems likely
that he wrote this poem.

321 On the Songs of the People of Gothic, or Teutonic
Race. 143-53. Untraced, perhaps George Croly. He,
John Bowring, and W. H. Leeds all had an interest
in German literature and any one of them could have
written this.

322 The Signs of the Times, No. I. 153-61. JOHN
SCOTT. Morning Chronicle, 30 Jan. 1821.

323 Mrs. Battle's Opinions on Whist. Signed: Elia.
161-65. CHARLES LAMB. Signature; repr. Essays.

324 Verses to Longman, Hurst, Rees, Orme and Brown, On
their Publication of Wordsworth's Excursion. 165.
BERNARD BARTON. N. L. of S. MS 1706.

325   Traditional Literature, No. III /verse/. 166-73.
      ALLAN CUNNINGHAM. Taylor, London; repr. Marmaduke
      Maxwell. Not all of the items in this series were
      reprinted by Cunningham.

326   The Travels and Opinions of Edgeworth Benson, No.
      II. 173-82. JOHN SCOTT. See No. 292.

327   On Pulpit Oratory, No. I. Introduction; with re-
      marks on the Rev. Robert Hall. Signed: Ω.
      182-88. T. N. TALFOURD. Repr. Critical and Mis-
      cellaneous Writings.

328   Kenilworth; a Romance. 188-200. JOHN SCOTT, prob.
      Almost all quotation and the critical comments
      resemble his earlier views on Walter Scott; style.

329   Miller Redivivus, No. II: Nehemiah Muggs /verse/.
      200-02. HORACE SMITH. Repr., with variations,
      Gaieties and Gravities, II.

330   Letters of Garrick, Foote &c. /continued from No.
      277/. Signed: X. 202-05. B. W. PROCTER. Attr.
      Butterworth, 15.

331   Town Conversations, No. II. 206-11. JOHN SCOTT.
      Attr. Zeitlin, p. 241.

332   The Drama, No. XIII. Signed: A. 211-16. P. G.
      PATMORE. Signature; see No. 308.

333   Report of Music, No. XII. 217-19. Untraced, per-
      haps R. M. Bacon. See No. 211.

334   Literary and Scientific Intelligence. 219-22.
      JOHN SCOTT. Scott/Baldwin Letters.

335   Monthly Register. 223-40. JOHN SCOTT. See No.
      31. Signed contributions by MARK BEAUFOY, J. M.
      RICHARDSON, WOLFE and EDMONDS.

VOLUME III. NUMBER XV
MARCH 1821

336   The Lion's Head. 243. Untraced, perhaps William
      Hazlitt, who probably wrote this item for the
      April and May numbers. See Howe, 286 and Baker,
      407. Scott had died the previous month.

337 The Statue of Theseus, and the Sculpture Room of Phidias. With a Plate. Signed: H. 245-50. HORACE SMITH. Repr. Gaieties and Gravities, II.

338 Death--Posthumous Memorials--Children, with Lines on the Death of an Infant. Signed: A Father. 250-55. HORACE SMITH. Repr. Gaieties and Gravities, II.

339 Traditional Literature, No. IV. 255-63. ALLAN CUNNINGHAM. Taylor, London; Hogg, Life of Allan Cunningham, 229.

340 A Chapter on Ears. Signed: Elia. 263-66. CHARLES LAMB. Signature; repr. Essays.

341 To Helene /verse/. Signed: Guilliame. 267. GEORGE DARLEY. Repr. Poetical Works.

342 Lines. 267. BERNARD BARTON. Signed.

343 Stanzas. Signed: N. 268. JAMES HARLEY. Signature is as in No. 302.

344 From the German /verse/. 269. Untraced, perhaps W. H. Leeds who was contributing German translations.

345 On Riding on Horse-back, No. II. Signed: Mazeppa. 269-72. P. G. PATMORE. N. L. of S. MS 1706.

346 The Ambrosian Codex of Homer, with Ancient Paintings. 273-75.

347 A New Opera, by Rossini entitled Maometto Secondo. 276-80. CHARLES MACFARLANE, prob. He writes of Rossini in his Reminiscences and says he knew the composer, as did the writer of this item. Macfarlane lived in Naples from where this is dated.

348 Miller Redivivus, No. III: Nehemiah Muggs /verse/. 280-82. HORACE SMITH. Repr. Gaieties and Gravities, II.

349 Sketches in Lisbon. 282-90. Untraced, perhaps John Bowring.

350 The Collector, No. VIII. 290.

351 Table Talk, No. VIII: On Personal Character. Signed: T. 291-98. WILLIAM HAZLITT. Repr. Works, XII.

352 On the Present State of Religious Parties in Germany. 299-303. Untraced, perhaps George Croly on subject and style.

353 Sonnet to Bernard Barton. 303. In a letter in the N. L. of S. Barton states this was by "a female friend."

354 Derwent-Water and Skiddaw /verse/. Signed: B. 304-05. B. W. PROCTER. Repr. Watts, Poetical Album.

355 Stanzas, Written, after viewing one evening, from Yarmouth Jetty, the Sea in a luminous state. 305. B. W. PROCTER. Attr. Brooks, Dissertation.

356 Pulpit Oratory, No. II. The Rev. John Leifchild. Signed: Ω. 306-11. T. N. TALFOURD. Repr. Critical and Miscellaneous Writings.

357 Town Conversation, No. III. 311-15. JOHN SCOTT. Attr. Zeitlin.

358 Russian Poetry. 316-21. Untraced, perhaps W. H. Leeds who often mentions Russian literature in Gleanings from Foreign Journals and Literary and Scientific Intelligence.

359 A Sketch of the Life of Edward Perrinson, the Poet. 322-29. Contains some verses signed "Thyrsis." Untraced, perhaps John H. Reynolds on style and manner.

360 The Drama, No. XIV. Signed: A. 329-32. P. G. PATMORE. Signature; see No. 308.

361 Gleanings from Foreign Journals. 333-36. W. H. LEEDS. Leeds/Turner Letters.

362 Literary and Scientific Intelligence. 336-38. W. H. LEEDS, prob. In the next number, for April, Gleanings from Foreign Journals is headed by a note which states: "Under the head of Literary Intelligence, in our last Number, we made mention of this comic épopée,--but that article was merely the condensation of a paper which we are now induced to give at length" (III, 413). The reference is to the item which appears under this head on p. 338. Leeds provided the Gleanings from Foreign Journals after Scott's death, and the note above indicates that he also took over the present feature.

363 Report of Music, No. XIII. 338-41. Untraced, perhaps R. M. Bacon. See No. 211.

364 Monthly Register. 341-56. Probably compiled by ROBERT BALDWIN with help from others. Signed contributions from R. HOWARD, J. M. RICHARDSON, WOLFE and EDMONDS.

VOLUME III. NUMBER XVI
APRIL 1821

365 The Lion's Head. 359-60. WILLIAM HAZLITT, prob. See No. 336.

366 All Fools' Day. Signed: Elia. 361-63. CHARLES LAMB. Signature; repr. Essays.

367 Swimming across the Hellespont, Letter from Lord Byron to Mr. Murray. 363-65. LORD BYRON. Signed.

368 Lines on the Death of Princess Charlotte. 365-67. JOSEPH RITCHIE. Attr. Brooks, Dissertation.

369 Sonnet. 367. CHARLES LAMB. Signed; repr. Works, V.

370 Table Talk, No. IX: On People of Sense. Signed: T. 368-74. WILLIAM HAZLITT. Repr. Works, XII.

371 Auto-Biography of John Huggins. Signed: John Huggins. 375-78. HORACE SMITH. Repr. Gaieties and Gravities, III.

372 Atherstone's Last Days of Herculaneum &c. 379-83. Untraced, perhaps George Croly as the subject would probably interest him.

373 The Confessions of F. H. V. H. Delamore Esq. Signed: Henry Francis Vere Harrington Delamore. 383-84. CHARLES LAMB. Attr. Dobell, Sidelights, 92; repr. Works, I.

374 A Quaker's Meeting. Signed: Elia. 384-87. CHARLES LAMB. Signature; repr. Essays.

375 Consolation, To a Friend on the Loss of his Child /verse/. 387. JOSEPH RITCHIE. Attr. Brooks, Dissertation.

376 Albion /verse/. 388. JOSEPH RITCHIE. Repr. Watts, Poetical Album, under the title "A Farewell to England."

377 Traditional Literature, No. V. 389-95. ALLAN
     CUNNINGHAM. Taylor, London; Hogg, Life of Allan
     Cunningham, 229.

378 Sketches on the Road. 395-404. CHARLES MACFAR-
     LANE. Attr. Butterworth, 16. Taylor mentions
     this series as by "McF" in his Commonplace Book.

379 The Collector, No. IX. 405-06.

380 Mr. Charles Lloyd's Poems. 406-13. T. N. TAL-
     FOURD. Repr. Critical and Miscellaneous Writings.

381 Gleanings from Foreign Journals. 413-19. W. H.
     LEEDS. Leeds/Turner Letters.

382 Letter from a Roué. 419-23. Signed: A Roué. T.
     G. WAINEWRIGHT, prob. Attr. Dobell, Sidelights,
     31, though Hughes doubts it.

383 Goethe, on Manzoni's Tragedy of Il Conte di
     Carmagnola. 423-26. GIOVANNI BERCHET. Attr.
     Hughes.

384 Town Conversation, No. IV. 426-32. Death of Mr.
     John Keats. Signed: L. 426-27. B. W. PROCTER.
     Taylor, London Mercury, 260; Armour, Barry Corn-
     wall, 357. Southey's Vision of Judgement. 428-
     30. Perhaps Charles Lamb, attr. Bauer; or William
     Hazlitt, attr. Brooks, Dissertation. The rest of
     the pieces under this head were perhaps by T. N.
     Talfourd, who had told M. R. Mitford on 16 April
     1821 that he had been offered the editorship (see
     Watson, TLS).

385 The Drama, No. XV. 433-37. T. N. TALFOURD, prob.
     Resemblance of this to No. 380 and Crabb
     Robinson's note in Diary, 27 Dec. 1820.

386 The British Institution. 437-44. T. G. WAINE-
     WRIGHT. Leeds/Turner Letters; Curling, 380.

387 Literary and Scientific Intelligence. 444-47. W.
     H. LEEDS. See No. 362.

388 Report of Music, No. XIV. 448-51. Untraced, per-
     haps R. M. Bacon. See No. 211.

389 Monthly Register. 452-72. ROBERT BALDWIN, prob.
     See No. 364. Signed contributions by R. HOWARD,
     J. M. RICHARDSON, WOLFE and EDMONDS.

VOLUME III. NUMBER XVII
MAY 1821

390 The Lion's Head. 474-76. WILLIAM HAZLITT, prob. See No. 336. Contains a note by CHARLES LAMB on F. H. V. H. Delamore. Also a poem, "Epithalamium," by BROOK BRIDGES PARLBY; editorial comment.

391 A May Dream. Signed: Theta. 477-83. B. W. PROCTER. Attr. Butterworth, 15.

392 Living Authors, No. V: Crabbe. 484-90. WILLIAM HAZLITT. Repr. Works, XI.

393 A Brief Memoir of William Meyrick, with some of his Poems. Signed: W. R. 490-92. Untraced, perhaps initials stand for William Read.

394 The Old and the New Schoolmaster. Signed: Elia. 492-97. CHARLES LAMB. Signature; repr. Essays.

395 Verses to the Memory of a Young Friend. Signed: B. B. 497. BERNARD BARTON. Repr. Poetic Vigils.

396 To Mary /verse/. 498. BERNARD BARTON. Signed.

397 Sonnet. Signed: M. M. 498. See No. 232.

398 Emily, A dramatic Sketch. 499-505. M. R. MITFORD. Repr. Dramatic Works, II.

399 Etchings of Different Kinds of Men, No. I: The Humorous Man. Signed: C. W. 505-08. CORNELIUS WEBB. Repr. Posthumous Papers.

400 Major Schill, from a Manuscript Journal. Signed: ɵɤ. 509-14. GEORGE CROLY. Attr. Butterworth, 16-17.

401 On the Writings of Mr. Maturin, and more particularly his Melmoth. 514-24. WILLIAM HAZLITT. Attr. Brooks, Dissertation.

402 Spring /verse/. Signed: Rustica. 525.

403 Life /verse/. Signed: E. R. 525-26. Untraced, perhaps initials stand for Eugenius Roche.

404 Sonnet on the Death of the Poet J. Keats. 526. JOHN TAYLOR. Attr. Blunden, Keats's Publisher, 25. Steele in K-SJ states that the sonnet is included as anonymous in the copy of Housman's Collection of English Sonnets interleaved by James Hessey and

now in the Houghton Library, Harvard.

405 Table Talk, No. X: On Antiquity. Signed: T. 527-33. WILLIAM HAZLITT. Repr. Works, XII.

406 Edinburgh. Signed: Tom Young. 533-35.

407 The Lament /verse/. Signed: M. M. 536. See No. 232.

408 The Guitar /verse/. 536.

409 Mr. Haydon's Picture of Christ's Agony in the Garden. With a Plate. 537-39. WILLIAM HAZLITT. Repr. Works, XVIII.

410 Paris in 1815, A Poem by The Rev. George Croly. 540-44. T. N. TALFOURD. Attr. Hughes; Bauer, 225.

411 Hazlitt's Table Talk. 545-50. T. N. TALFOURD. N. L. of S. MS 1706.

412 Lord Bryon's Marino Faliero &c. 550-54. WILLIAM HAZLITT. Repr. Works, XIX.

413 Old Stories, No. IV. Truth not to be Told at all Times, or the Moral Enchanter. 555-59.

414 The Drama, No. XVI. 559-62. J. H. REYNOLDS. Attr. Hughes. Talfourd was now contributing drama articles to New Monthly and thus unlikely to do this.

415 Town Conversation, No. V. 563-65. Untraced, perhaps T. N. Talfourd. See No. 384.

416 Literary and Scientific Intelligence. 565-67. W. H. LEEDS, prob. See No. 362.

417 Report of Music, No. XV. 568-70. Untraced, perhaps R. M. Bacon. See No. 211.

418 Monthly Register. 570-88. ROBERT BALDWIN, prob. See No. 364. Signed contributions by R. HOWARD, J. M. RICHARDSON, WOLFE and EDMONDS.

VOLUME III. NUMBER XVIII
JUNE 1821

419   The Lion's Head. 591-92. Possibly by Robert
      Baldwin or J. H. Reynolds, but more likely John
      Taylor, as the notes suggest a new editor. Con-
      tains the poem "The Request" by JOHN CLARE; con-
      text and repr. Village Minstrel, I.

420   Pope, Lord Byron, and Mr. Bowles. 593-607.
      WILLIAM HAZLITT. Repr. Works, XIX.

421   The Shriek of Prometheus /verse/. Signed: H. 608-
      11. HORACE SMITH. Repr. Gaieties and Gravities,
      III.

422   My Relations. Signed: Elia. 611-14. CHARLES
      LAMB. Signature; repr. Essays.

423   Song. Signed: C. W. 614. CORNELIUS WEBB. Repr.
      Lyric Leaves.

424   Traditional Literature, No. VI. 615-22. ALLAN
      CUNNINGHAM. Taylor, London; Hogg, Life of Allan
      Cunningham, 229.

425   Count Julius, a Dramatic Sketch. Signed: Φορμιο.
      622-27. GEORGE CROLY. Attr. Coles, 219.

426   Letter from Mr. Humphrey Nixon, De Omnibus Rebus et
      Quibusdam Aliis. Signed: Humphrey Nixon. 628-32.
      Untraced, perhaps J. H. Reynolds on style and con-
      text.

427   Legal Lyrics. Signed: One, &c. 632-33. J. H.
      REYNOLDS, prob. Signature similar to that used in
      No. 747; style. N. L. of S. MS 1706/167 has a
      letter dated 7 July 1821 from Mrs. Davies, wife of
      the publisher, William Davies, to William Black-
      wood, offering to secure for the latter the writer
      of this item. She describes him as "of highly
      respectable connections and large literary ac-
      quaintance--he is a clever young man and very
      indefatigable in researches of every kind." Al-
      though she does not name the writer, it was pro-
      bably Reynolds.

428   To the Memory of Emma Fuller /verse/. Signed: B.
      634-35. BERNARD BARTON. Repr. Minor Poems.

429   Horace's Ode to the Bandusian Fountain. 635.
      CHARLES A. ELTON. Introduced with a signed letter.

430 Horses. Signed: Chevalier. 636-37. Untraced, perhaps T. G. Wainewright, attr. Hughes as conjecture. P. G. Patmore has also been suggested.

431 On Southey's Histories of Religious Sects. Signed: A Dissenter. 637-41. Untraced, perhaps John Taylor. In Writings, III, 129, De Quincey describes Taylor as "a religious dissenter."

432 Song of the Parguinotes. Signed: J. A. G. 641. J. A. GALIFFE, prob. Galiffe wrote books which he signed with this signature.

433 The Dying Soldier /verse/. Signed: J. A. G. 642. J. A. GALIFFE, prob. Signature as in No. 432.

434 Captain Parry's Journal. 642-48.

435 Miller Redivivus, No. IV: Nehemiah Muggs /verse/. 648-50. HORACE SMITH. Not reprinted but a continuation of No. 348.

436 Gleanings from Foreign Journal. 651-55. W. H. LEEDS. Leeds/Turner Letters.

437 Letters from Edinburgh, No. II. Signed: T. Y. 655-59.

438 A Selection of Irish Melodies, by Thomas Moore. 659-63. HARTLEY COLERIDGE. Attr. Brooks, Dissertation.

439 Second Letter from a Roué. 663-69. T. G. WAINEWRIGHT. Attr. Dobell, Sidelights, 31. See No. 382.

440 The Drama, No. XVII. 669-74. J. H. REYNOLDS. Attr. Hughes.

441 Report of Music, No. XVI. 675-77. Untraced, perhaps R. M. Bacon. See No. 211.

442 Necrological Table of Literary and Eminent Public Characters for 1820. 678-83. JOHN TAYLOR. Attr. Blunden, Keats's Publisher, 129. The editorial note that heads this feature states the intention to compile such a table yearly.

443 Literary and Scientific Intelligence. 683-86. W. H. LEEDS, prob. See No. 362.

444 Monthly Register. 686-704. JOHN TAYLOR, prob.
On 23 May 1821, T. N. Talfourd told M. R. Mitford
that "Taylor & Hessey will conduct the mechanism
of the work & leave the rest to regular Correspondents who will furnish certain portions"
(Watson, TLS). As announced in the Lion's Head
for this month (No. 419) "arrangements have been
completed for the future Editorship of the London
Magazine." This was, of course, John Taylor. The
Monthly Register had been Scott's responsibility.
It is likely that Taylor conducted this feature
during his editorship. Others, such as Charles
Phillips and probably Thomas Hood, contributed
various items. Signed contributions by R. HOWARD,
J. M. RICHARDSON, WOLFE and EDMONDS.

VOLUME IV.   NUMBER XIX
JULY 1821

445 The Lion's Head. 3-4. THOMAS HOOD. Hood conducted this feature while he was sub-editor, but
others, primarily John Taylor, made contributions.

446 Warwick Castle. 5-13. J. H. REYNOLDS. Wrapper
of the London gives this as by Edward Herbert, one
of Reynolds's pseudonyms; Reynolds.

447 On Gray's Opinion of Collins, with a Sonnet from
Constanzo. Signed: Noemon. 13-16. H. F. CARY.
Cary, Memoir, II, 72.

448 Sonnet. (Milton visits Galileo in Prison).
Signed: B. 16. B. W. PROCTER. Signature; style.

449 The Heroes of Naples. A new Ballad. 17-18.
THOMAS HOOD. Attr. Brooks, Dissertation.

450 Traditional Literature, No. VII. 19-28. ALLAN
CUNNINGHAM. Taylor, London; Hogg, Life of Allan
Cunningham, 229.

451 Mackery End, in Hertfordshire. Signed: Elia. 28-
30. CHARLES LAMB. Signature; repr. Essays.

452 Sketches on the Road, No. II. 31-34. CHARLES
MACFARLANE. Attr. Butterworth, 16. For entries
that appeared in 1822, Taylor Commonplace Book has
"Sketches on the Road" by "McF--".

453 Rodomontades Espagnoles. 35-38.

454   Thoughts and Images /verse/. 39-40. JAMES MONT-
      GOMERY. Signed; repr. Poetical Works, I.

455   On the Songs of the People of Gothic or Teutonic
      Race. 41-47. See No. 321.

456   Alphabet Studies, and Chinese Imitations. 47-48.

457   Fugitive Literature, with Ballads. Signed: Lauch-
      lin Galloway. 49-56. THOMAS CUNNINGHAM. Taylor
      Commonplace Book.

458   The Garden of Florence, and other Poems; by John
      Hamilton. 57-61. RICHARD WOODHOUSE. Reynolds.

459   Sketch of the Progress of Vocal Science in England,
      No. III. 61-65. R. M. BACON, prob. See No. 211.

460   Exhibition of the Royal Academy. Signed: Cornelius
      van Vinkbooms. 66-76. T. G. WAINEWRIGHT. Signa-
      ture, as identified in No. 864, p. 45, where Waine-
      wright, as Janus, admits to articles by C. V. V.

461   Ballad. 76. JOHN CLARE. Signed; repr. Rural
      Muse.

462   Letters from Edinburgh, No. III. Signed: T. Y.
      77-80.

463   The Drama, No. XVIII. 80-85. J. H. REYNOLDS.
      Reynolds.

464   To Hope, A Poem. 85-86. THOMAS HOOD. Broderip,
      Memorials, I, 9; repr. Poetical Works.

465   Lamb's Translation of Catullus. 86-90. J. H. REY-
      NOLDS. Reynolds.

466   Report of Music, No. XVII. 90-93. Untraced, per-
      haps R. M. Bacon. See No. 211.

467   Literary and Scientific Intelligence. 93-96. W.
      H. LEEDS, prob. See No. 362.

468   Monthly Register. 97-116. JOHN TAYLOR, prob. See
      No. 444. From De Quincey, Writings (III, 143), it
      is clear that CHARLES PHILLIPS was contributing the
      abstracts of foreign and domestic occurrences which
      are included under this heading until No. 594.
      Signed contributions by R. HOWARD, WOLFE and ED-
      MONDS, and J. M. RICHARDSON.

VOLUME IV.   NUMBER XX
AUGUST 1821

469   The Lion's Head. 119-20. THOMAS HOOD. See No. 445. Contains the poem "Beauty is Truth, Truth Beauty," by RICHARD WOODHOUSE; Reynolds.

470   Continuation of Dr. Johnson's Lives of the Poets, No. I: Thomas Warton. 121-26. H. F. CARY. Taylor, London; repr. Lives of the English Poets.

471   Zariadres and Odatis. A Grecian Story. 127-28. H. F. CARY. Taylor Commonplace Book; Cary, Memoir, II, 73.

472   Sonnet. To a Twin-Sister who died in Infancy. 128. JOHN CLARE. Signed.

473   Traditional Literature, No. VIII. 129-36. ALLAN CUNNINGHAM. Taylor, London; Hogg, Life of Allan Cunningham, 229.

474   Epistle to Elia /verse/. Signed: Olen. 137-40. C. A. ELTON. Repr. Boyhood.

475   Sketches on the Road, No. III. 140-48. CHARLES MACFARLANE. Taylor Commonplace Book; Butterworth, 16.

476   The Lawyer:--a Picture, in two Cantos. 148-51. CHARLES LAMB, prob. Attr. Jerrold, Thomas Hood and Charles Lamb, 179-84. Hood, Reynolds, and Woodhouse have also been suggested less persuasively.

477   Jews, Quakers, Scotchmen and other Imperfect Sympathies. Signed: Elia. 152-56. CHARLES LAMB. Signature; repr. Essays.

478   Travels of Cosmo the Third, Grand Duke of Tuscany, through England in 1669. 156-60. H. F. CARY. Cary, Memoir, II, 73.

479   The Buccaneer. A Tale for Gentle and Simple. 161-67.

480   Song to Twilight. Signed: P. P. 167. GEORGE DARLEY. Signature; Taylor Commonplace Book.

481   To The Sun /verse/. 168-72. BERNARD BARTON. Signed; repr. Minor Poems.

482   The Tyrol Wanderer. Signed: Nepos. 172-76.

483   Table Talk, No. XI: On a Landscape of Nicolas Poussin. Signed: T. 176-79. WILLIAM HAZLITT. Repr. Works, VIII.

484   On Sadoleti's Dialogue on Education, with a Poem from Fracastorio. 180-83. H. F. CARY. Taylor Commonplace Book; Cary, Memoir, II, 73.

485   The Coronation. Signed: Ed. Herbert. 184-96. J. H. REYNOLDS. Reynolds; Procter, Charles Lamb, 152.

486   The Drama, No. XIX. 196-202. J. H. REYNOLDS. Reynolds.

487   Report of Music, No. XVII. 202-04. Untraced, perhaps R. M. Bacon. See No. 211.

488   Literary and Scientific Intelligence. 205-09. W. H. LEEDS, prob. See No. 362.

489   Monthly Register. 209-32. JOHN TAYLOR, prob. See No. 444. Signed contributions by WOLFE and EDMONDS, and J. M. RICHARDSON.

VOLUME IV.   NUMBER XXI
SEPTEMBER 1821

490   The Lion's Head. 235-36. THOMAS HOOD. See No. 445. Contains a letter from Edward Herbert, by J. H. REYNOLDS: Signature. Also contains a poem, "The Champion's Farewell," by J. H. REYNOLDS; Reynolds.

491   Traditional Literature, No. IX. 237-46. ALLAN CUNNINGHAM. Taylor, London; Hogg, Life of Allan Cunningham, 229.

492   English Eating. Signed: V. 246-49. W. QUIN, prob. Taylor Commonplace Book has "On Eating" by Quin and the titles of the articles which surround it appeared in August and September 1821. John Taylor also used the signature "V" in No. 568.

493   Influence of Scenery on Poetic Character. Burns. Signed: R. 250-52. Untraced, perhaps Eugenius Roche; also perhaps James Rice, attr. Hughes.

494   The Antiquary. Signed: Thurma. 253-56. C. W. DILKE. Dilke, I, 15 where the signature is identified, but mistaken as Thurusa.

495   Theodore and Bertha, A Dramatic Sketch. 256-65.
      M. R. MITFORD. Repr. Dramatic Works, II.

496   On Spenser's supposed Acquaintance with Shakespeare. 265-68. JOHN TAYLOR. Taylor, London Mercury, 262.

497   Leisure Hours, No. I: On Homer's Battle of the Frogs and Mice. Signed: An Idler. 269-73. C. A. ELTON. B. M. Egerton MS 2246/111.

498   Farewell to Mary /verse/. 273. JOHN CLARE. Signed; repr. Rural Muse.

499   Epitaphs. 274-77. ALLAN CUNNINGHAM. Taylor Commonplace Book.

500   Méditations Poétiques, par M. Alphonse de Lamartine. 277-78. H. F. CARY. Taylor Commonplace Book; Cary, Memoir, II, 73.

501   The Old Benchers of the Inner Temple. Signed: Elia. 279-84. CHARLES LAMB. Signature; repr. Essays.

502   C. Van Vinkbooms, his Dogmas for Dilettanti, No. I: Recollections in a Country Church-yard. 285-93. T. G. WAINEWRIGHT. Lamb, Letters, II, 323.

503   Confessions of an English Opium-Eater, being an Extract from the Life of a Scholar. 293-312. THOMAS DE QUINCEY. Repr. Confessions.

504   Love in a Mist /verse/. 313. Untraced, perhaps B. W. Procter. The style is very much like that of Thomas Hood, but the epithet "cruel kind" used in this poem occurs twice in Procter's "A Song" in the number for June 1822 (No. 692).

505   Gleanings from Foreign Journals. 313-16. W. H. LEEDS. Leeds/Turner Letters.

506   Report of Music, No. XIX. 316-19. Untraced, perhaps R. M. Bacon. See No. 211.

507   The Drama, No. XX. 319-23. J. H. REYNOLDS. Reynolds.

508   A New Hymn-Book. 323-25. J. H. REYNOLDS. Reynolds.

509   Literary and Scientific Intelligence. 325-26. W. H. LEEDS, prob. See No. 362.

510   Monthly Register. 326-48. JOHN TAYLOR, prob.
      See No. 444. Signed contributions by WOLFE and
      EDMONDS, and J. M. RICHARDSON.

VOLUME IV.   NUMBER XXII
OCTOBER 1821

511   The Lion's Head. 351-52. THOMAS HOOD. See No.
      445. Contains a note of THOMAS DE QUINCEY on the
      chronology of the Confessions; context.

512   Confessions of an English Opium-Eater, being an
      Extract from the Life of a Scholar, Pt. II. 353-
      79. THOMAS DE QUINCEY. Repr. <u>Confessions</u>.

513   Estephania de Gantelmes, a Tale of the Middle Ages.
      379-84. H. F. CARY. Taylor Commonplace Book;
      Cary, <u>Memoir</u>, II, 73.

514   Witches, and other Night-Fears. Signed: Elia.
      384-87. CHARLES LAMB. Signature; repr. <u>Essays</u>.

515   Leisure Hours, No. II: The Battle of the Frogs
      and Mice, In a New Translation. 388-93. C. A.
      ELTON. B. M. Egerton MS 2246/111.

516   Madame de Stael. 394-400. Untraced, perhaps
      George Croly on style.

517   Sonnet. A Reflection on Summer. 400. JOHN CLARE.
      Signed.

518   Traditional Literature, No. X. 401-11: ALLAN
      CUNNINGHAM. Taylor, <u>London</u>; Hogg, <u>Life of Allan
      Cunningham</u>, 229.

519   Song, imitated from the Italian. 411. H. F. CARY.
      Cary, <u>Memoir</u>, II, 73.

520   On the Songs of the People of Gothic or Teutonic
      Race. 412-17. See No. 321.

521   The Poet /verse/. Signed: S. 417. JOHN TAYLOR.
      Steele, 69, but see also Brooks, <u>MLN</u>, 450; and
      Wasserman, <u>MLN</u>, 454.

522   C. Van Vinkbooms, his Dogmas for Dilettanti, No. II.
      Giulio Romano. 418-25. T. G. WAINEWRIGHT. Lamb,
      <u>Letters</u>, II, 323.

523   The Hermit, a Fragment from an unpublished Poem.

Signed: Ωτος. 425. GEORGE CROLY. Taylor Commonplace Book.

524 The Drama, No. XXI. 426-29. J. H. REYNOLDS. Attr. Hughes.

525 Report of Music, No. XX. 429-31. Untraced, perhaps R. M. Bacon. See No. 211.

526 The Cook's Oracle. 432-39. J. H. REYNOLDS. Reynolds; Hood, Works, VII, 379; repr. Jones.

527 Song. Signed: Y. 439.

528 Gleanings from Foreign Journals. 440-41. W. H. LEEDS. Leeds/Turner Letters.

529 Literary and Scientific Intelligence. 441-44. W. H. LEEDS, prob. See No. 362.

530 Monthly Register. 444-64. JOHN TAYLOR, prob. See No. 444. Signed contributions by WOLFE and EDMONDS, and J. M. RICHARDSON.

VOLUME IV.   NUMBER XXIII
NOVEMBER 1821

531 The Lion's Head. 465-68. THOMAS HOOD. See No. 445. Contains "Elia to his Correspondents" by CHARLES LAMB; signature. A letter from "Old Mortality" on No. 499, perhaps by Allan Cunningham. "Ode to Dr. Kitchener" by THOMAS HOOD; repr. Poetical Works.

532 Grace Before Meat. Signed: Elia. 469-72. CHARLES LAMB. Signature; repr. Essays.

533 On the Songs of Thibaut, King of Navarre. 472-75. H. F. CARY, Taylor Commonplace Book; repr. Early French Poets.

534 On Parties in Poetry. Signed: Thersites. 476-81. HARTLEY COLERIDGE. Taylor Commonplace Book; repr. Essays and Marginalia, I.

535 Leisure Hours, No. III: A Dialogue of the Living. On the Homeric Poematia. Signed: An Idler. 481-84. C. A. ELTON. B. M. Egerton MS 2246/111.

536 Sonnet. 484. JOHN CLARE. B. M. Egerton MS 2245/374.

537   Table Talk, No. XII: On Consistency of Opinion.
      Signed: T. 485-92. WILLIAM HAZLITT. Repr.
      Works, XVII.

538   The Departure of Summer /verse7. Signed: Incog.
      493-95. THOMAS HOOD. Repr. The Plea.

539   Sketches on the Road, No. IV. 495-98. CHARLES
      MACFARLANE. Attr. Butterworth, 16; Taylor
      Commonplace Book.

540   Traditional Literature, No. XI. 499-507. ALLAN
      CUNNINGHAM. Taylor, London; Hogg, Life of Allan
      Cunningham, 229.

541   Verses written in an Album. Signed: Olen. 507.
      C. A. ELTON. Signature; Taylor Commonplace Book.

542   A Sentimental Journey, from Islington to Waterloo
      Bridge, in March 1821. Signed: Incog. 508-15.
      THOMAS HOOD. Broderip, I, 9.

543   Warner's Church of England Theology. Mock Manu-
      script Sermons. 516-17. J. H. REYNOLDS. Rey-
      nolds's copy of the London is marked "J. H. R."
      in pencil at the beginning of this review.

544   Life of Holty. Signed: X.x. 518-26. CHARLES
      PHILLIPS, prob. Brooks in PQ suggests S. T. Cole-
      ridge as the author, but admits the style is unlike
      his. "Authentic Anecdotes of the Late Dr. Barrett"
      in the number for Jan. 1822 (No. 585) is also
      signed X.x.; see note to that item where it is con-
      tended that Charles Phillips used this signature.

545   Sonnet,--A Dream. 526. JOHN KEATS. Signed.
      Printed previously in Leigh Hunt's Indicator for
      28 June 1820. This is the only item by Keats
      found in the London, yet an advertisement for the
      magazine bound up by Taylor and Hessey at the end
      of a copy of Allan Cunningham's Sir Marmaduke
      Maxwell (1822) states "poems" were contributed by
      Keats. B. W. Procter supports this claim as does
      Cambridge History of English Literature (1932, XII,
      160). On the wrappers of the London for March 1822
      a statement is printed that John Keats contributed
      original poetry between July and December 1821.

546   Edward Herbert's Letters to the Family of the
      Powells, No. II: Greenwich Hospital. Signed: Ed-
      ward Herbert. 527-38. J. H. REYNOLDS. Signature;
      Reynolds; repr. Jones.

547   Letter to Cornelius Van Vinkbooms, Esq. On the
      Exeter Exhibition of Paintings. Signed: Senex.
      538-39. J. H. REYNOLDS, prob. Curling thinks
      this is by T. G. Wainewright, but the letter is
      dated from Exeter and shows a knowledge of Exeter
      personalities which Reynolds would have possessed.
      This month he may well have been in Exeter visit-
      ing his fiancée.

548   A Visit to John Clare, with a Notice of his New
      Poems. Signed: ***. 540-48. JOHN TAYLOR.
      Taylor, London.

549   The Drama, No. XXII. 549-55. J. H. REYNOLDS.
      Reynolds. The context states that the article is
      not by the usual dramatic critic and as sub-
      editor Thomas Hood is likely to have filled any
      gaps, but Reynolds's copy of the London is marked
      "J. H. R."

550   Report of Music, No. XXI. 555-58. Untraced, per-
      haps R. M. Bacon. See No. 211.

551   Literary and Scientific Intelligence. 558-59.
      W. H. LEEDS, prob. See No. 362.

552   Monthly Register. 560-82. JOHN TAYLOR, prob.
      See No. 444. Signed contributions by WOLFE and
      EDMONDS, and J. M. RICHARDSON.

              VOLUME IV.   NUMBER XXIV
                  DECEMBER 1821

553   The Lion's Head. 583-86. THOMAS HOOD. See No.
      445. Contains letter signed X.Y.Z. by THOMAS DE
      QUINCEY; signature.

554   The Early French Poets. Clement Marot. 587-93.
      H. F. CARY. Repr. Early French Poets.

555   Traditional Literature, No. XII. 594-603. ALLAN
      CUNNINGHAM. Taylor, London; Hogg, Life of Allan
      Cunningham, 229.

556   My First Play. Signed: Elia. 603-05. CHARLES
      LAMB. Signature; Taylor Commonplace Book; repr.
      Essays.

557   John Paul Frederick Richter. Signed: Grasmeriensis
      Teutonizans. 606-12. THOMAS DE QUINCEY. Leeds/
      Turner Letters; Lowndes, 2027.

558   The Happy Life of a Parish Priest in Sweden. From
        Richter. 613-15. THOMAS DE QUINCEY. Leeds/
        Turner Letters; Lowndes, 2027.

559   Last Will and Testament--The House of Weeping.
        From Richter. 615-20. THOMAS DE QUINCEY. Leeds/
        Turner Letters; Lowndes, 2027.

560   Table Talk, No. XIII: On the Spirit of Partisan-
        ship. Signed: T. 620-26. WILLIAM HAZLITT.
        Repr. Works, XVII.

561   Continuation of Dr. Johnson's Lives of the Poets,
        No. II. Sir William Jones. 626-38. H. F. CARY.
        Taylor, London; repr. Lives of the English Poets.

562   Leisure Hours, No. IV: Bacchus, or the Pirates.
        From the Homeric Hymns. Signed: An Idler. 639-43.
        C. A. ELTON. B. M. Egerton MS 2246/111.

563   A Boiled Pig /verse/. Signed:***. 643-44. Un-
        traced, perhaps Thomas Hood on style.

564   Sketches on the Road, No. V. 644-51. CHARLES
        MACFARLANE. Taylor Commonplace Book; Butterworth,
        16.

565   Westminster Abbey. Signed: Thurma. 651-54. C.
        W. DILKE. Taylor Commonplace Book; Dilke, I, 15.
        See No. 494.

566   C. Van Vinkbooms, his Dogmas for Dilettanti, No.
        III. The Amateur's Boudoir, or a Visit to Janus.
        655-64. T. G. WAINEWRIGHT. Lamb, Letters, II,
        323.

567   Imitations of Psalms XLII and XLIII. Signed: M.
        664-65. JAMES MONTGOMERY. Signature is dated
        from Sheffield where Montgomery lived; Taylor
        Commonplace Book; repr. Songs of Zion.

568   Sonnet. Signed: V. 665. JOHN TAYLOR. Steele,
        69.

569   The Drama, No. XXIII. 666-72. J. H. REYNOLDS.
        Reynolds. Thomas Hood may have contributed some-
        thing here.

570   Report of Music, No. XXII. 672-73. Untraced, per-
        haps R. M. Bacon. See No. 211.

571   Popular Retrospect of the Progress of Philosophy
        and Science. Signed: R. 674-78. Brooks, PQ,

suggests S. T. Coleridge; Hughes suggests James Rice; Eugenius Roche is another possibility.

572 Monthly Register. 679-98. JOHN TAYLOR, prob. See No. 444. Signed contributions by WOLFE and EDMONDS, and J. M. RICHARDSON.

VOLUME V. NUMBER XXV
JANUARY 1822

573 The Lion's Head. 1-4. THOMAS HOOD. See No. 445. Contains poem, "Please to Ring the Belle," by THOMAS HOOD; Broderip, I, 9 and repr. Whims and Oddities.

574 The Twelve Tales of Lyddalcross. 5-21. ALLAN CUNNINGHAM. Repr. Traditional Tales, II.

575 Dream-Children; A Reverie. Signed: Elia. 21-23. CHARLES LAMB. Signature; repr. Essays.

576 Continuation of Dr. Johnson's Lives of the Poets, No. III: Christopher Anstey. 24-27. H. F. CARY. Taylor, London; repr. Lives of the English Poets.

577 Beauties of the Living Dramatists, a Scene from Virtue's Harvest Home. 27-33. JOHN POOLE. Taylor Commonplace Book; repr. Christmas Festivities.

578 Osmyn, A Persian Tale, Part II /verse7. 33-36.

579 The Early French Poets: Antoine Heroet, and Mellin de Saint Gelais. 37-42. H. F. CARY. Repr. Early French Poets.

580 Hymn to Spring. 43. JOHN CLARE. Signed.

581 Leisure Hours, No. V. On the English Standard Heroic: with some Remarks on the French Drama. Signed: An Idler. 44-49. C. A. ELTON. B. M. Egerton MS 2246/111.

582 Neapolitan Priests. 49-51. Untraced, perhaps Charles Macfarlane. Page 207 of Macfarlane, Reminiscences, resembles the end of this article.

583 On Imitation. Signed: Cogin. 51-52. THOMAS HOOD. Jerrold, Thomas Hood, 100.

584 Dramatic Fragment. Signed: ***. 53. CHARLES LAMB. Repr. Works, V, in "John Woodvil."

585 Authentic Anecdotes of the late Rev. Dr. Barrett, Vice Provost of Trinity College, Dublin. Signed: X.x. 53-60. CHARLES PHILLIPS, prob. The writer says he was at Trinity-College when Barrett was librarian. Charles Phillips, the Irish barrister, who was a contributor to the London (see No. 594 below), was at Trinity from 1802 to 1806, and Barrett was librarian there until he became Vice-Provost in 1807. Phillips, who was a member of the Irish Bar, was called to the English Bar in 1821, but is likely to have been in Dublin in November of that year.

586 Sketches on the Road, No. VI. 60-66. CHARLES MACFARLANE. Taylor Commonplace Book; Butterworth, 16.

587 Sardanapalus, The Two Foscari, and Cain, By Lord Byron. 66-71. T. N. TALFOURD. Attr. Coles, 226.

588 Ode of Casimir to his Lyre. Signed: Olen. 71. C. A. ELTON. Signature.

589 Letters from London to a Friend in Edinburgh, No. I. 72-80.

590 The Pirate. By the Author of Waverley. 80-90. WILLIAM HAZLITT. Repr. Works, XIX.

591 The Drama. 90-95. J. H. REYNOLDS. Reynolds; repr. Jones. Beginning with this issue, this heading is no longer followed by a number in the London.

592 Report of Music. 95-97. Untraced, perhaps R. M. Bacon. See No. 211. Beginning with this issue, this heading is no longer followed by a number in the London.

593 Literary and Scientific Intelligence. 97. W. H. LEEDS, prob. See No. 362.

594 Abstract of Foreign and Domestic Occurrences. 98-100. CHARLES PHILLIPS. De Quincey, Collected Writings, III, 143, where he says of the London: "And so well were all departments provided for that even the monthly abstract of politics, brief as it necessarily was, had been confided to the care of Phillips, the celebrated Irish barrister." The monthly abstract would have been written by Phillips during Taylor and Hessey's editorship, since Scott did this part of the magazine during his editorship. Bauer thinks Phillips ceased to

write this column in 1823. She's probably wrong, for in a letter to his brother James (1 Aug. 1825), John Taylor, proposing a new periodical work, states that Phillips "might do the Political" (Bakewell MSS).

595 Monthly Register. 1-18. JOHN TAYLOR, prob. See No. 444. Beginning with this number, the Register is paginated separately, though continuous from month to month through each volume. Signed contribution by J. M. RICHARDSON.

VOLUME V.   NUMBER XXVI
FEBRUARY 1822

596 The Lion's Head. 101-04. THOMAS HOOD. See No. 445. Contains a Glossary to the difficult Scotch words in the Second Tale of Lyddalcross (No. 604 below), provided, as the context makes clear, by ALLAN CUNNINGHAM. A poem, "To a Critick," signed "Anthony Rushtowne," by THOMAS HOOD; repr. Works, I. Also contains three unidentified poems: "Death" signed H. B. M.; "A Vision" signed H. L.; "The Soldier's Bride" signed Zara.

597 Continuation of Dr. Johnson's Lives of the Poets, No. IV. Oliver Goldsmith. 105-12. H. F. CARY. Repr. Lives of the English Poets.

598 On the Poetical Use of the Heathen Mythology. Signed: Thersites. 113-20. HARTLEY COLERIDGE. Taylor Commonplace Book; repr. Essays and Marginalia.

599 Specimen of a Translation of Valerius Flaccus. 121-24. H. F. CARY. Cary, Memoir, II, 73.

600 Pleasant and Unpleasant People. Signed: Thurma. 125-28. C.W. DILKE. Dilke, I, 15. See No. 494.

601 Stanzas to ****. 128. JOHN CLARE. Signed; repr. Shepherd's Calendar.

602 The Seven Foresters of Chatsworth, an Ancient Derbyshire Ballad. 129-36. ALLAN CUNNINGHAM. Taylor, London; repr. Traditional Tales, II.

603 Beauties of the Living Dramatists, No. II. A Scene from Britain's Glory. 137-41. JOHN POOLE. Repr. Christmas Festivities.

604 The Twelve Tales of Lyddalcross, Tale Second. 142-52. ALLAN CUNNINGHAM. Taylor, London; repr. Traditional Tales, II.

605 A Hermitage, a Poem. Signed: J. M. 152. JAMES MONTGOMERY. Repr. Poetical Works.

606 On the Elgin Marbles. The Ilissus. Signed: W. H. 153-56. WILLIAM HAZLITT. "By the Author of Table Talk" on the contents page; repr. Works, XVIII.

607 From an Unpublished Play. 156. GEORGE SOANE. Taylor Commonplace Book, under the title "Scene from an Unfinished Drama."

608 The Early French Poets: Hugues Salel and Olivier de Magny. 157-60. H. F. CARY. Repr. Early French Poets.

609 Sonnet. Signed: R. 160. JAMES RICE. Attr. Hughes.

610 Homer's Hymn to Pan. Leisure Hours, No. VI. Signed: An Idler. 161-63. C.A. ELTON. Signature.

611 Superstition's Dream, a Poem. 163-65. JOHN CLARE. Letters, 194; repr. Shepherd's Calendar.

612 Bradgate Park, the Residence of Lady Jane Grey, With Stanzas. Signed: E. H. 166-74. J. H. REYNOLDS. Procter, Charles Lamb, 152; repr. Jones.

613 On Some of the Old Actors. Signed: Elia. 174-79. CHARLES LAMB. Signature; repr. Essays.

614 The Drama. 179-84. J. H. REYNOLDS. Reynolds.

615 On a Free Paper Currency, Payable in Gold Ad Valorem. 185-93. JOHN TAYLOR. Taylor, London Mercury, 264.

616 Report of Music. 193-95. Untraced, perhaps R. M. Bacon. See No. 211.

617 Literary and Scientific Intelligence. 196-97. W. H. LEEDS, prob. See No. 362.

618 Abstract of Foreign and Domestic Occurrences. 197-200. CHARLES PHILLIPS. See No. 594.

619   Monthly Register. 19-36. JOHN TAYLOR, prob. See
      No. 444 and No. 595. Signed contributions by
      WOLFE and EDMONDS, and J. M. RICHARDSON.

                    VOLUME V.   NUMBER XXVII
                          MARCH 1822

620   The Lion's Head. 201-04. THOMAS HOOD. See No.
      445. Contains poem, "Faithless Sally Brown," by
      THOMAS HOOD; Broderip, Memorials, I, 9 and repr.
      Whims and Oddities. Morgan, in K-SJ, 88, claims
      that part of this poem was written by J. H. Reynolds.

621   On Witchcraft, Part I. Signed: R. 205-15. Untraced, perhaps James Rice. Attr. Hughes.
      Brooks, PQ, suggests S. T. Coleridge, but the
      evidence is not strong. The inaccurate Alaric A.
      Watts told William Blackwood that J. H. Reynolds
      was the author, but little reliance can be placed
      on his attributions.

622   The Approach of Spring /verse_7. 216-18. JOHN
      CLARE. Signed; repr. Shepherd's Calendar.

623   Additions to Lord Orford's Royal and Noble
      Authors, No. I. 218-21. PHILIP BLISS. Gibson/
      Hindle, 173.

624   Narrative of a Voyage to New South Wales. Signed:
      B. F. 221-28. BARRON FIELD. Signature; Field,
      a contributor to the London, was in New South
      Wales at this time.

625   Peter Klaus, The Legend of the Goatherd.--Rip Van
      Winkle. 229-30. Thomas De Quincey and J. C. Hare
      have been suggested, but Washington Irving's
      address is included among those in the Taylor
      Commonplace Book, suggesting he may have contributed to the London. The author of "Rip Van
      Winkle" could be the most likely contributor of
      this analogue to the story.

626   The Early French Poets. Joachim du Bellay. 231 -
      36. H. F. CARY. Repr. Early French Poets.

627   The Green Room. The Letters of Edward Herbert, No.
      III. Signed: Edward Herbert. 236-43. J. H.
      REYNOLDS. Signature; repr. Jones.

628   The Twelve Tales of Lyddalcross. Tale Third.
        243-52. ALLAN CUNNINGHAM. Taylor, London; repr.
        Traditional Tales, II.

629   Beauties of the Living Dramatists, No. III: The
        River-rock, or the Crimson Hermits. Signed: P*.
        253-64. JOHN POOLE. Repr. Christmas Festivities.

630   Continuation of Dr. Johnson's Lives of the Poets,
        No. V: Joseph Warton. 264-69. H. F. CARY.
        Taylor, London; repr. Lives of the English Poets.

631   The Sea of Death. A Fragment /verse/. Signed:
        ***. 269-70. THOMAS HOOD. Repr. The Plea.

632   The Spirit of Poesy, a Poem. 270-71. Untraced,
        perhaps Bernard Barton as it seems in his style.

633   Sketches on the Road, No. VII. 271-75. CHARLES
        MACFARLANE. Taylor Commonplace Book; Butterworth,
        16.

634   Old Song. Sonnet. Signed: R---. 275. Untraced,
        but William Read, Eugenius Roche and James Rice
        have been suggested.

635   The Dying Poet's Farewell /verse/. Signed: H.
        276. HORACE SMITH. Repr. Gaieties and Gravities,
        III.

636   The Lyrics of Horace: Translated by the Rev.
        Francis Wrangham. 277-81. Untraced, perhaps C.
        A. Elton or John Taylor. Alaric Watts, a most
        unreliable authority, says the translations from
        Horace in the London are by Taylor; they are by
        Elton, but Watts may have had this review of
        Wrangham's Horace in mind.

637   Distant Correspondents. Signed: Elia. 282-85.
        CHARLES LAMB. Signature; repr. Essays.

638   On Black Cats. Signed: ΑΙΛΟΥΡΟΦΙΛΟΣ. 285-87.
        HARTLEY COLERIDGE. Repr. Essays and Marginalia.

639   Report of Music. 287-89. Untraced, perhaps R.
        M. Bacon. See No. 211.

640   Sonnet. 289. JOHN TAYLOR. Steele, 69.

641   The Drama. 290-94. J. H. REYNOLDS. Attr. Hughes;
        Jones, 437.

642   A Bachelor's Soliloquy /verse/. 294. J. H. REY-
        NOLDS. Attr. Hughes; Reynolds was married in 1822

and this is in his style.

643 Literary and Scientific Intelligence. 295-96. W. H. LEEDS, prob. See No. 362.

644 Abstract of Foreign and Domestic Occurrences. 297-300. CHARLES PHILLIPS. See No. 594.

645 Monthly Register. 37-54. JOHN TAYLOR, prob. See No. 444 and 595. Signed contributions by WOLFE and EDMONDS, and J. M. RICHARDSON.

VOLUME V.   NUMBER XXVIII
APRIL 1822

646 The Lion's Head. 303-04. THOMAS HOOD. See No. 445.

647 The Old Actors. Signed: Elia. 305-11. CHARLES LAMB. Signature; repr. Essays.

648 To Celia /verse/. 311. THOMAS HOOD. Broderip, I, 9; repr. Poetical Works.

649 Continuation of Dr. Johnson's Lives of the Poets, No. VI. James Beattie. 312-21. H. F. CARY. Repr. Lives of the English Poets.

650 The Twelve Tales of Lyddalcross, Tale the Fourth. 321-30. ALLAN CUNNINGHAM. Taylor, London; repr. Traditional Tales, II.

651 The Early French Poets: Remy Belleau, and Jan Antoine de Baïf. 331-36. H. F. CARY. Repr. Early French Poets.

652 The Devil's Ladder. From the German of Aloise Schreiber. 337-40. Untraced, but Thomas De Quincey has been suggested by Hughes, and J. C. Hare by Brooks, Dissertation.

653 Homer's Hymn to Ceres. Leisure Hours, No. VII. Signed: An Idler. 340-49. C. A. ELTON. Signature; B. M. Egerton MS 2246/111.

654 The Old White Hat--and the Old Grey Mare. 350-59. HORACE SMITH. Repr. Gaieties and Gravities, III.

655 Brief Observations upon Brevity. Signed: Tom Thumb the Great. 359-62. HARTLEY COLERIDGE. Repr. Essays and Marginalia.

656   Beauties of the Living Dramatists, No. IV. La
      Belle Assemblée. Signed: P*. 362-68. JOHN
      POOLE. Repr. Christmas Festivities.

657   The Rose in January. A German Tale. 369-75.
      Untraced, perhaps H. Crabb Robinson. The author
      says he was friendly with Wieland in the latter's
      old age and the circumstances fit Robinson.

658   To an Absentee /verse/. Signed: Incog. 375.
      THOMAS HOOD. Broderip, I, 9; repr. The Plea.

659   On Witchcraft, No. II. Signed: R. 376-87. See
      No. 621.

660   Additions to Lord Orford's Royal and Noble
      Authors, No. II. 387-90. PHILIP BLISS. Gibson/
      Hindle, 173.

661   Report of Music. 390-94. Untraced, perhaps R. M.
      Bacon. See No. 211.

662   The Drama. 395-97. J. H. REYNOLDS. Reynolds.

663   Abstract of Foreign and Domestic Occurrences. 397-
      400. CHARLES PHILLIPS. See No. 594.

664   Monthly Register. 55-74. JOHN TAYLOR, prob. See
      No. 444 and No. 595. Signed contributions by WOLFE
      and EDMONDS, and J. M. RICHARDSON.

                VOLUME V.   NUMBER XXIX
                       MAY 1822

665   The Lion's Head. 403-04. THOMAS HOOD. See No.
      445. Contains poem, "Moral Relections written on
      the Cross of St. Paul's," by THOMAS HOOD; Broderip,
      I, 9 and repr. Whims and Oddities.

666   The Praise of Chimney-Sweepers: a May-Day Effusion.
      Signed: Elia. 405-08. CHARLES LAMB. Signature;
      repr. Essays.

667   Additions to Lord Orford's Royal and Noble Authors,
      No. III. 409-12. PHILIP BLISS. Gibson/Hindle,
      173.

668   As I came down through Cannobie. An Old Jacobite
      Song. Signed: C. 412. ALLAN CUNNINGHAM. Repr.
      Songs of Scotland, III.

669   A Sketch of the Life of Patrick Henry, the Orator
        of Virginia. 413-21. Untraced, perhaps John
        Taylor, as the last paragraph appears to be edi-
        torial in tone.

670   The Stag-eyed Lady, a Moorish Tale [verse].
        Signed: Incog. 422-25. THOMAS HOOD. Broderip,
        I, 9; repr. Whims and Oddities.

671   Fine Arts--Edinburgh. Williams's Views in Greece,
        &c. Signed: W. H. 425-27. WILLIAM HAZLITT.
        Keynes, 112.

672   Mr. Martin's Pictures and the Bonassus. Signed:
        Winifred Lloyd. 427-28. THOMAS HOOD. Broderip,
        I, 9.

673   The First Canto of Ricciardetto: Translated from
        the Italian of Forteguerri by Lord Glenbervie.
        429-33. Untraced, perhaps H. F. Cary or Charles
        Strong, as this would be a subject of interest to
        them.

674   Continuation of Dr. Johnson's Lives of the Poets,
        No. VII. Richard Owen Cambridge. 433-36. H. F.
        CARY. Repr. Lives of the English Poets.

675   Don Giovanni the XVIII. 436-43. J. H. REYNOLDS.
        Attr. Hughes.

676   To the Cowslip [verse]. 444. JOHN CLARE. Signed;
        repr. Shepherd's Calendar.

677   On the Elgin Marbles. Signed: W. H. 445-55.
        WILLIAM HAZLITT. This is a continuation of No.
        606 and the contents page for that number states,
        "by the Author of Table Talk"; repr. Works, XVIII.

678   War Song. 456. JAMES MONTGOMERY. Signed; repr.
        Poetical Works, III.

679   The Early French Poets. Jan de la Peruse. 456-57.
        H. F. CARY. Repr. Early French Poets.

680   The Twelve Tales of Lyddalcross, Tale the Fifth.
        458-67. ALLAN CUNNINGHAM. Taylor,. London; repr.
        Traditional Tales, II.

681   Sonnet. To Nature. 467. JOHN CLARE. B. M.
        Egerton MS 2245/7, Hessey's letter to Clare of 29
        April 1822.

682   Letter from Janus Weathercock, Esq. Signed: Janus Weathercock. 468-70. T. G. WAINEWRIGHT. Signature.

683   Notices of the Fine Arts. 470-72. Untraced, perhaps Thomas Hood. On p. 471 the author refers to Winifred Lloyd whose name appears in the same issue (no. 672). Only someone on the editorial staff would be likely to see "Mrs. Lloyd's" letter before it was published and Hood wrote the letter given over her name.

684   On Witchcraft, No. III. Signed: R. 472-80. See No. 621.

685   The Drama. 481-84. J. H. REYNOLDS. Reynolds.

686   Some Passages in the Life of Mr. Adam Blair, Minister of the Gospel at Cross-Meikle. 485-90. J. H. REYNOLDS. Reynolds.

687   Report of Music. 490-92. Untraced, perhaps R. M. Bacon. See No. 211.

688   Abstract of Foreign and Domestic Occurrences. 493-96. CHARLES PHILLIPS. See No. 594.

689   Monthly Register. 75-94. JOHN TAYLOR, prob. See No. 444 and No. 595. Signed contributions by WOLFE and EDMONDS, and J. M. RICHARDSON.

VOLUME V.   NUMBER XXX
JUNE 1822

690   The Lion's Head. 499-500. THOMAS HOOD. See No. 445. Contains "Sonnet to the Bat."

691   The Early French Poets. Pierre de Ronsard. 501-15. H. F. CARY. Repr. Early French Poets.

692   A Song. Signed: B. 516. B. W. PROCTER. Signature; style.

693   Sketch of the City of Naples. 517-24. CHARLES MACFARLANE. Footnote on p. 517 states that this is by the writer of "Sketches on the Road," which is attributed to Macfarlane by Butterworth, 16, and the Taylor Commonplace Book.

694   Lovely Woman. A Scottish Song. Signed: C. 524. ALLAN CUNNINGHAM. Signature; style.

695   The Princess of Moonland, an owre true Tale
      /verse/. 525-31. J. H. REYNOLDS. Attr. Hughes.
      Jerrold, Thomas Hood and Charles Lamb, p. 206,
      suggests Hood or Reynolds, or perhaps both in
      collaboration. The style of the poem seems most
      like that of Reynolds, whereas the footnotes might
      well have been supplied by Hood.

696   Life, Death and Eternity /verse/. 531. JOHN
      CLARE. Repr. Poems, I.

697   A Complaint of the Decay of Beggars in the Metro-
      polis. Signed: Elia. 532-36. CHARLES LAMB.
      Signature; repr. Essays.

698   Catullus, with New Translations. Leisure Hours,
      No. VIII. Signed: An Idler. 536-39. C. A.
      ELTON. Signature; two of the songs translated
      here were repr. Boyhood.

699   Tales of Lyddalcross: Tale Sixth. 539-49. ALLAN
      CUNNINGHAM. Taylor, London; repr. Traditional
      Tales, II.

700   Janus Weathercock's Reasons against writing an
      Account of "The Exhibition." Signed: J. W.
      549-56. T. G. WAINEWRIGHT. Signature.

701   Song. 556. JOHN CLARE. Signed on the contents
      page.

702   Polyhymnia. By Mr. Montgomery. 557-59. Un-
      traced, perhaps John Taylor as the comments are
      editorial.

703   Continuation of Dr. Johnson's Lives of the Poets,
      No. VIII. William Julius Mickle. 559-64. H. F.
      CARY. Repr. Lives of the English Poets.

704   Sketch of the Life of Patrick Henry, the Orator of
      Virginia. 564-71. See No. 669, of which this is
      a continuation.

705   A Voice from St. Helena. 572-77.

706   The Russian Tragedy. 577-80.

707   The Drama. 580-82. J. H. REYNOLDS. Reynolds.

708   Report of Music. 583-88. Untraced, perhaps R. M.
      Bacon. See No. 211.

709   Necrological Table for 1821. 588-93. JOHN TAYLOR.
      Blunden, Keats's Publisher, 129. See No. 442.

710   Abstract of Foreign and Domestic Occurrences. 594-98. CHARLES PHILLIPS. See No. 594.

711   Monthly Register. 95-112. JOHN TAYLOR, prob. See No. 444 and No. 595. Signed contributions by WOLFE and EDMONDS, and J. M. RICHARDSON.

VOLUME VI.   NUMBER XXXI
JULY 1822

712   The Lion's Head. 3-4. THOMAS HOOD. See No. 445. Contains verses, "Come, take thy pencil," sent by a "Chelsea Anacreon."

713   Wanderings in June /verse/. 5-9. JOHN CLARE. Signed; repr. Shepherd's Calendar.

714   The Inconstant Lady, A Sonnet. Signed: L. 9. JOHN TAYLOR. Steele, 69.

715   On the Life and Writings of William Mason. In Continuation of Dr. Johnson's Lives of the Poets. 10-20. H. F. CARY. Taylor, London; repr. Lives of the English Poets.

716   Parting /verse/. Signed: E. 20. HARTLEY COLERIDGE. Signature.

717   On Magazine Writers. Signed: P. 21-27. P. G. PATMORE. Signature.

718   The Downfall of Dalzell /verse/. 27-29. ALLAN CUNNINGHAM. Signed on contents page; repr. Songs of Scotland.

719   On Wine.. Signed: F. R. 29-33. Untraced, perhaps Cyrus Redding. He was a contributor to the London, and in 1821/22 he was collecting material for his book on wine. This may well have been a trial article.

720   Detached Thoughts on Books and Reading. Signed: Elia. 33-36. CHARLES LAMB. Signature; repr. Last Essays. Contains poem, "The Two Boys," by MARY LAMB.

721   Beauties of the Living Dramatists, No. V. Processions. Signed: P*. 37-48. JOHN POOLE. Repr. Christmas Festivities.

722   The Falls of Ohiopyle. 48-52. W. H. AINSWORTH. Ellis, II, 349; repr. December Tales.

723 Sonnet, to the Nightingale. Signed: *****. 52. JOHN CLARE. Signature; style.

724 A Voice from St. Helena. 53-60.

725 The Early French Poets. Estienne Jodelle. 60-63. H. F. CARY. Repr. Early French Poets.

726 The Haunted House. 63-71. ALLAN CUNNINGHAM. Contents page states this is a "Tale of Lyddalcross."

727 The Delicate Intricacies. 72-76. T. G. WAINEWRIGHT. "By Janus Weathercock" on contents page; Curling, 381.

728 Hymn to the Morning. From the Latin of Flaminio. 77-78. H. F. CARY. Cary, Memoir, II, 73.

729 Sketch of the City of Naples, Leter II. 78-84. CHARLES MACFARLANE. See No. 693.

730 Song. Signed: A. S. 84. Untraced, perhaps the initials stand for Augustus Skottowe, the poet.

731 The Drama. 85-90. J. H. REYNOLDS. Attr. Hughes.

732 Report of Music. 90-93. Untraced, perhaps R. M. Bacon. See No. 211.

733 Abstract of Foreign and Domestic Occurrences. 93-96. CHARLES PHILLIPS. See No. 594.

734 Monthly Register. 1-16. JOHN TAYLOR, prob. See No. 444 and No. 595. Signed contributions by WOLFE and EDMONDS, and J. M. RICHARDSON.

VOLUME VI.   NUMBER XXXII
AUGUST 1822

735 The Lion's Head. 99-100. THOMAS HOOD. See No. 445. Contains "Reprints of Elia" attributed to CHARLES LAMB by Lucas in Works, I, 431.

736 English Smugglers. Harry Woodriff. Signed: G. S. 101-13. GEORGE SOANE. Signature: Hood, Hood's Own, 550.

737 The Sick Man's Summer Evening /verse/. 113.

738   Marshal Soult and his Murillos. Signed: H. 114-16. HORACE SMITH. Repr. Gaieties and Gravities, III.

739   Sonnets. To the Sky-Lark and A Still Place. Signed: B. 116. B. W. PROCTER. Repr. Flood of Thessaly.

740   Confessions of a Drunkard. Signed: Elia. 117-21. CHARLES LAMB. Signature; repr. Last Essays, 1st. ed. and Works, I.

741   On the Spirit of Youth in the Young and the Old. Signed: R. A. 121-24. RICHARD AYTON. Repr. Essays and Sketches.

742   Defence of the Claims of Propertius. Signed: An Idler. 125-32. C. A. ELTON. Signature.

743   The Mariner's Song. 132. ALLAN CUNNINGHAM. Signed; Taylor Commonplace Book.

744   An Inquiry why Candles invariably burn blue in the Presence of a Ghost. Signed: H. 133-35. HORACE SMITH. Repr. Gaieties and Gravities, III.

745   The Tea-Garden. Signed: W. 136-40. CYRUS REDDING. Boase/Courtney, II, 558.

746   Lycus, the Centaur. From an Unrolled Manuscript of Apollonius Curius [verse]. 141-47. THOMAS HOOD. Repr. The Plea.

747   Ode to a Sparrow alighting before the Judge's Chambers, in Serjeants' Inn, Fleet Street. Signed: Gent. One &c. 148. J. H. REYNOLDS. Reynolds.

748   Additions to Lord Orford's Royal and Noble Authors, No. IV. 149-51. PHILIP BLISS. Gibson/Hindle, 173.

749   To Elia [verse]. 151. JOHN CLARE. Taylor Commonplace Book; repr. Poems, I.

750   Narrative of Nathan Adamson, Student of Divinity. 152-63. ALLAN CUNNINGHAM. Fitzgerald, 95.

751   The Inside of a Stage Coach. Letters of Edward Herbert, No. IV. Signed: Edward Herbert. 163-66. J. H. REYNOLDS. Signature; Reynolds; repr. Jones.

752   The English Universities. 166-72. A. H. NIEMEYER. Headnote to article states that this is a translation of a part of Dr. Niemeyer's Travels, the

second volume of which was published in 1821. The
circumstances in the headnote make it clear that
this is A. H. Niemeyer (1754-1828) of Halle. The
translator is not known, though it may have been
John Bowring, T. De Quincey, or W. H. Leeds.

753 The Funeral of Eleanor. A Ballad. 172-73. H.
F. CARY. Taylor Commonplace Book; Cary, Memoir,
II, 73.

754 Halidon Hill, by Sir Walter Scott. Signed: C.
174-81. JAMES SMITH. Taylor Commonplace Book
has Smith's name in pencil.

755 Report of Music. 181-85. Untraced, perhaps R. M.
Bacon. See No. 211.

756 The Drama. 185-87. Untraced, perhaps Thomas
Hood. As Reynolds, the regular contributor of
this feature, was preparing for his marriage, Hood,
the sub-editor, was likely to have filled the gap.

757 Abstract of Foreign and Domestic Occurrences. 187-
92. CHARLES PHILLIPS. See No. 594.

758 Monthly Register. 17-32. JOHN TAYLOR, prob. See
No. 444 and No. 595. Signed contributions by
WOLFE and EDMONDS, and J. M. RICHARDSON.

VOLUME VI.   NUMBER XXXIII
SEPTEMBER 1822

759 The Lion's Head. 195-96. THOMAS HOOD. See No.
445. Contains poem, "Fare Thee Well," signed
"Theodosius," by THOMAS HOOD; repr. Works, I.

760 The Phrenological System of Drs. Gall and Spurzheim, with an Engraving. 197. JOHN TAYLOR.
Blunden, Keats's Publisher, 129.

761 Observations on Phrenology. 198-204. GEORGE
COMBE. Chilcott, 152 and 226.

762 The Early French Poets. Philippe Desportes. 204-
08. H. F. CARY. Taylor Commonplace Book; repr.
Early French Poets.

763 Elegies of Propertius, Arethusa to Lycotas--Tale
of Tarpeia. Leisure Hours, No. IX. 209-12. C.
A. ELTON. B. M. Egerton MS 2246/111; repr. Boyhood.

764　　The Malvern Hills. Signed: U. 213-17. CYRUS REDDING. Boase/Courtney, II, 558.

765　　A Sketch from Nature /verse/. Signed: *****. 217. JOHN CLARE. Signature. Hughes, who thought this poem by Clare, dismissed the ascription by citing Mrs. Emmerson's letter to Clare (B. M. Egerton MS 2246/111): "I am glad you still indulge in Sonnet Writing, and thank you for owning to me your three sweet children in the 'London'." But since there are four identified sonnets by Clare in this number (Nos. 772, 774, 778 and 782), Mrs. Emmerson's mention of "three" is not good evidence for denying this sonnet to Clare.

766　　Additions to Lord Orford's Royal and Noble Authors, No. V. 218-20. PHILLIP BLISS. Gibson/Hindle, 173.

767　　It's Hame and it's Hame /verse/. 220. ALLAN CUNNINGHAM. Signed.

768　　Popular Superstitions of the Swedes. 221-23.

769　　Sketch of the City of Naples, No. III. 224-28. CHARLES MACFARLANE. Taylor Commonplace Book, which continues to refer to Macfarlane's contributions as "Sketches on the Road." See No. 693.

770　　King Bruce's Bowl, a Dramatic Legend of Galloway. 229-41. ALLAN CUNNINGHAM. Fitzgerald, 95.

771　　On the Life and Writings of John Armstrong. In Continuation of Dr. Johnson's Lives of the Poets. 241-44. H. F. CARY. Repr. Lives of the English Poets.

772　　Sonnet. 244. JOHN CLARE. Repr. Poems, I.

773　　A Dissertation upon Roast Pig. Signed: Elia. 245-48. CHARLES LAMB. Signature; repr. Essays.

774　　Forest Flowers /verse/. 248. JOHN CLARE. Repr. Rural Muse.

775　　The Memoir of a Hypochondriac. 249-61. B. W. PROCTER. Taylor Commonplace Book.

776　　A Bachelor's Complaint of the Behaviour of Married People. Signed: Elia. 261-64. CHARLES LAMB. Signature; repr. Essays.

777 Memoirs of Sir Charles Sedley. Signed: LL.D. 265-72. Untraced, but John Bowring and Octavius Gilchrist were both LL.D. and perhaps one of them wrote this. Gilchrist is the more likely, as he appeared to be more interested in this period than Bowring.

778 Sonnet. 272. JOHN CLARE. Signed; repr. Rural Muse as "The Happiness of Ignorance."

779 Report of Music. 273-76. Untraced, perhaps R. M. Bacon. See No. 211.

780 Hymn to the Sun. 276. THOMAS HOOD. Repr. The Plea.

781 Atrabilious Reflections Upon Melancholy. Signed: E. 277-78. HARTLEY COLERIDGE. Repr. Essays and Marginalia, I.

782 The Ass /verse/. 278. JOHN CLARE. Repr. Rural Muse.

783 The Drama. 279-81. Untraced, perhaps Thomas Hood. As Reynolds was on his honeymoon this month, Hood most likely filled in as drama critic.

784 Abstract of Foreign and Domestic Occurrences. 281-86. CHARLES PHILLIPS. See No. 594.

785 Literary and Scientific Intelligence. 287-88. W. H. LEEDS, prob. See No. 362.

786 Monthly Register. 33-48. JOHN TAYLOR, prob. See No. 444 and No. 595. Signed contributions by WOLFE and EDMONDS, and J. M. RICHARDSON.

VOLUME VI. NUMBER XXXIV
OCTOBER 1822

787 The Lion's Head. 291-92. THOMAS HOOD. See No. 445.

788 French Pretensions. 293-304. Untraced, perhaps Horace Smith who was living in France at this time.

789 The Two Peacocks of Bedfont /verse/. Signed: Ovid. 304-08. THOMAS HOOD. Repr. The Plea. In his article for the London Magazine (Jan. 1823), VII, 50, T. G. Wainewright calls Hood "our new Ovid."

790 Luke Lorance, the Cameronian. Signed: Nalla. 309-21. ALLAN CUNNINGHAM. Signature. "Nalla" is an anagram for "Allan," the explanation for which is given in Elton, Boyhood, 134.

791 On the Diversity of Opinions with regard to Likenesses in Portraits. Signed: R. A. 321-24. RICHARD AYTON. Repr. Essays and Sketches.

792 Eustace de Rimbaumont, a Ballad. 325-26. H. F. CARY. Cary, Memoir, II, 73.

793 Memoirs of the Life and Writings of Tobias Smollett; In Continuation of Dr. Johnson's Lives of the Poets. 327-35. H. F. CARY. Repr. Lives of the English Poets.

794 Sonnet: Sun-Rise. 335. JOHN CLARE. Taylor Commonplace Book; repr. Poems, I.

795 On the Poetry of Nonnus, with a Translation of the Story of Ampelus. Signed: Vida. 336-40. C. A. ELTON. Repr. Boyhood.

796 Sonnet: Sun-Set. 340. JOHN CLARE. Taylor Commonplace Book; repr. Rural Muse.

797 Les Machabees, ou le Martyre. 341-42. H. F. CARY. Cary, Memoir, II, 74.

798 Ferdinand Mendez Pinto. Signed: S. 343-48. HORACE SMITH. Repr. Gaieties and Gravities, III.

799 Charlie Stuart, A Jacobite Song. Signed: C. 348. ALLAN CUNNINGHAM. Signature; Taylor Commonplace Book, where it is given to "A.C."

800 The Old Actors. Signed: Elia. 349-51. CHARLES LAMB. Signature; repr. Essays.

801 The Memoir of a Hypochondriac (concluded). 352-61. B. W. PROCTER. Taylor Commonplace Book.

802 The Early French Poets. Jean Bertaut. 361-67. H. F. CARY. Repr. Early French Poets.

803 The Siege of Vienna. By Hans Kellerman. Signed: G. S. 367-73. GEORGE SOANE. Signature; Hood, Hood's Own, 550.

804 The Drama. 373-77. Untraced, perhaps J. H. Reynolds or George Darley.

805 Report of Music. 378-80. Untraced, perhaps R. M. Bacon. See No. 211.

806 Literary and Scientific Intelligence. 381. W. H. LEEDS, prob. See No. 362.

807 Abstract of Foreign and Domestic Occurrences. 382-84. CHARLES PHILLIPS. See No. 594.

808 Monthly Register. 49-64. JOHN TAYLOR, prob. See No. 444 and No. 595. Signed contributions by WOLFE and EDMONDS, and J. M. RICHARDSON.

VOLUME VI.   NUMBER XXXV
NOVEMBER 1822

809 The Lion's Head. 387-88. THOMAS HOOD. See No. 445. Contains poem, "Farewell to Italy," signed A.B.M., by A. B. JAMESON (née MURPHY); repr. Diary of an Ennuyée. And poem, "Now the Loud Cry," signed Nimrod, by THOMAS HOOD; repr. Whims and Oddities.

810 The Cockpit Royal. Edward Herbert's Letters to the Family of the Powells, No. V. Signed: Edward Herbert. 389-402. J. H. REYNOLDS. Signature; repr. Jones.

811 The Last of Autumn /verse/. 403-05. JOHN CLARE. Signed; Taylor Commonplace Book; repr. Shepherd's Calendar.

812 Fonthill Abbey. Signed: W. H. 405-10. WILLIAM HAZLITT. "By the Author of Table-Talk" on contents page; Taylor Commonplace Book; repr. Works, XVIII.

813 Walking Stewart. 410-13. J. H. REYNOLDS. Taylor Commonplace Book, where it is given to "J. H. R."

814 The Early French Poets. Maurice Sceve and Guillaume des Autels. 413-19. H. F. CARY. Repr. Early French Poets.

815 On the Life and Writings of Richard Jago; In Continuation of Dr. Johnson's Lives of the Poets. 419-20. H. F. CARY. Repr. Lives of the English Poets.

816 The Tale of Allan Lorburne, Mariner. Signed: Nalla. 421-36. ALLAN CUNNINGHAM. Signature; Fitzgerald, 95.

817   Bracebridge-Hall, by the Author of the Sketch-
      Book. 436-39. JAMES SMITH. Taylor Commonplace
      Book.

818   Story of Ampelus, from the Dionysiacs of Nonnus
      (concluded). Signed: Vida. 440-44. C. A. ELTON.
      Signature; repr. Boyhood.

819   The Academy of Taste for Grown Gentlemen, or the
      Infant Connoisseur's Go-Cart. Signed: Janus
      Weathercock. 445-53. T. G. WAINEWRIGHT.
      Signature.

820   Modern Gallantry. Signed: Elia. 453-55. CHARLES
      LAMB. Signature; repr. Essays.

821   Song: Awake, my Love. Signed: C. 455-56. ALLAN
      CUNNINGHAM. Signature; repr. Songs of Scotland,
      IV.

822   On the Moral Influence of Etiquette and Parade.
      Signed: R. A. 456-60. RICHARD AYTON. Taylor
      Commonplace Book; repr. Essays and Sketches.

823   Sir Marmaduke Maxwell, &c. by Allan Cunningham.
      460-66. WILLIAM HAZLITT. Taylor Commonplace
      Book; Sikes, 162; repr. New Writings.

824   The Drama. 466-73. J. H. REYNOLDS. Reynolds.

825   Report of Music. 473-76. Untraced, perhaps R. M.
      Bacon. See No. 211.

826   The Falling Leaf [verse]. Signed: J. M. 477.
      JAMES MONTGOMERY. Signed on contents page; Taylor
      Commonplace Book.

827   Abstract of Foreign and Domestic Occurrences. 477-
      83. CHARLES PHILLIPS. See No. 594.

828   Literary and Scientific Intelligence. 483-84. W.
      H. LEEDS, prob. See No. 362.

829   Monthly Register. 65-80. JOHN TAYLOR, prob.
      See No. 444 and No. 595. Signed contributions by
      WOLFE and EDMONDS, and J. M. RICHARDSON.

VOLUME VI.   NUMBER XXXVI
DECEMBER 1822

830   The Lion's Head. 487-88. THOMAS HOOD. See No. 445. Contains "Stanzas on Leaving England" signed F.A.B.B. and verses, "The Young Poet Dying at a Distance from Home," signed R. S.

831   Mr. Angerstein's Collection of Pictures. Signed: W. H. 489-94. WILLIAM HAZLITT. "By the Author of Table-Talk" on contents page; repr. Criticism on Art.

832   Sonnet: Midnight. Signed: T. 494. THOMAS HOOD. Broderip, I, 10; repr. Poetical Works.

833   A Few Words on "Christmas." 495-97. B. W. PROCTER. Taylor Commonplace Book, as "Some Thoughts on Christmas."

834   On a Sleeping Child, Two Sonnets. Signed: T. 497. THOMAS HOOD. Reynolds; Broderip, I, 10.

835   A Cockney's Rural Sports. Signed: P*. 498-508. JOHN POOLE. Signature; Taylor Commonplace Book; Lamb, Letters, II, 358.

836   On the Supplemental Iliad of Quintus Calaber. Signed: Vida. 508-12. C. A. ELTON. Signature; verses repr. Boyhood.

837   Confessions of an English Opium-Eater. Appendix. 512-17. THOMAS DE QUINCEY. Repr. Confessions.

838   Presentiment: a Fragment. Signed: Incog. 517-20. THOMAS HOOD. Broderip, I, 10.

839   On the Life and Writings of Erasmus Darwin. In Continuation of Dr. Johnson's Lives of the Poets. 520-28. H. F. CARY. Repr. Lives of the English Poets.

840   The Gentle Giantess. Signed: Elia. 529-30. CHARLES LAMB. Signature; repr. Works, I.

841   Of Cruelty to Animals and "Mr. Martin's Act." Signed: R. A. 530-36. RICHARD AYTON. Repr. Essays and Sketches.

842   Sonnet: To Fancy. Signed: T. 536. THOMAS HOOD. Repr. The Plea.

843 Allan Lorburne, Mariner: Second Tale. Signed: Nalla. 537-48. ALLAN CUNNINGHAM. Signature; Fitzgerald, 95.

844 My Father's House. Signed: W. 549-52. CYRUS REDDING. Boase/Courtney, II, 538.

845 Philosophy. A Poem. Signed: /B/. 552. B. W. PROCTER. Taylor Commonplace Book; Procter/Taylor letters.

846 Additions to Lord Orford's Royal and Noble Authors, No. VI. 553-55. PHILIP BLISS. Gibson/Hindle, 173.

847 The Voyage, a Dramaticle. 556-58. GEORGE DARLEY. Procter, Charles Lamb, 152; repr. Poetical Works; Taylor Commonplace Book has "P P Pickle Herring," one of Darley's pseudonyms.

848 The Old Seaman, a Sketch from Nature. Signed: T. 559-60. THOMAS HOOD. London Magazine (Jan. 1823), VII, 50.

849 The Miscellany. 561-70. As the Procter/Taylor letters make clear, B. W. PROCTER conducted the Miscellany, but many of the items were contributed by others. Friar Bacon, signed Δ : GEORGE DARLEY on signature. To an Unknown /verse/, signed B: B. W. PROCTER on signature and style. Scraps of Criticism: CHARLES LAMB, attr. Dobell, Sidelights, 102; repr. Works, I. Montgomery's "Songs of Zion": mainly extracts, provided perhaps by John Taylor. On Spiders, signed S: untraced perhaps Charles Strong on signature. Sonnet, "I never pass a venerable tree": JOHN CLARE, repr. Rural Muse. On Epitaphs and Monuments, signed G: OCTAVIUS GILCHRIST, prob., on signature. A Wish /verse/, signed C: ALLAN CUNNINGHAM on signature. The Mermaid.

850 The Drama. 570-73. J. H. REYNOLDS. Reynolds.

851 Report of Music. 573-75. Untraced, perhaps R. M. Bacon. See No. 211.

852 Abstract of Foreign and Domestic Occurrences. 575-80. CHARLES PHILLIPS. See No. 594.

853 Monthly Register. 81-96. JOHN TAYLOR, prob. See No. 444 and No. 595. Signed contributions by WOLFE and EDMONDS, and J. M. RICHARDSON.

VOLUME VII. NUMBER XXXVII
JANUARY 1823

854   The Lion's Head. 3-4. THOMAS HOOD. See No. 445.

855   Rejoicings upon the New Year's coming of Age.
Signed: Elia's Ghost. 5-7. CHARLES LAMB. Signature; repr. Last Essays.

856   Of Exaggeration and Matter-of-Fact People. Signed:
R. A. 8-13. RICHARD AYTON. Repr. Essays and Sketches.

857   The Dulwich Gallery. Signed: W. H. 13-19.
WILLIAM HAZLITT. "By the Author of Table-Talk" on contents page; repr. Criticism on Art.

858   A Character of the late Elia, by a Friend. Signed:
Phil-Elia. 19-21. CHARLES LAMB. Signature; repr. Last Essays as the Preface.

859   New Year's Day in Paris. Signed: P*. 22-28. JOHN POOLE. Signature; Morning Chronicle, Jan. 15, 1823; repr. Christmas Festivities.

860   On English Versification. Signed: C. 29-37.
WILLIAM CROWE. King, 171; repr. Treatise.

861   Twelfth Night, or What you will. Signed: Ω. 37-40. B. W. PROCTER. Lamb, Letters, III, 346; Procter/Taylor Letters.

862   Sonnet. An Italian Philosopher to his Friend.
Signed: B. 40. B. W. PROCTER. Signature; style.

863   The Early French Poets. Robert Garnier. 41-45.
H. F. CARY. Repr. Early French Poets.

864   Janus Weatherbound; or the Weathercock Steadfast for Lack of Oil. Signed: ** ***********. 45-52.
T. G. WAINEWRIGHT. Signature in title; Curling, 381.

865   I'll Daut Nae Mair a Posie /verse/. Signed: C.
52. ALLAN CUNNINGHAM. Signature; Morning Chronicle, 15 Jan. 1823.

866   A Visit to the Franciscan Monastery of Sorrento.
53-63. CHARLES MACFARLANE. Note in London Magazine (July 1823), VIII, 13.

867   Translations from the Supplemental Iliad of Quintus Calaber (continued). 63-68. C. A. ELTON.
See No. 836.

868 Sketches from My Life, By Goethe--Fifth Part. 68-73.

869 Christina Swayne. Signed: Nalla. 73-82. ALLAN CUNNINGHAM. Signature.

870 The Maniac /verse/. 83-84. BERNARD BARTON. Signed; repr. Poetic Vigils.

871 Letters to a Young Man whose Education has been Neglected. By the Author of the Confessions of an English Opium-Eater. Signed: X.Y.Z. 84-90. THOMAS DE QUINCEY. Signature; repr. Collected Writings, X.

872 Grimm's German Popular Stories. 91-92. J. H. REYNOLDS. Taylor Commonplace Book, where it is marked "J.H.R."

873 The Miscellany. 93-98. Conducted by B. W. PROCTER, see No. 849. Letter on the Author of "Connubia Florum" by E. HILL: signed. The Fête-Dieu /verse/, signed H. H. The Choice of a Grave by CHARLES LAMB: repr. Works, I. On Dedications, signed Dicatus, by B. W. PROCTER: Procter/Taylor Letters. Fair Innes /verse/, signed H., by THOMAS HOOD: Repr. The Plea. Wilks, by CHARLES LAMB: repr. Works, I. Obituary, signed Gust. Vostermann, by B. W. PROCTER: Procter/Taylor Letters. German Honesty and Simplicity: untraced, perhaps by Richard Ayton. Presence of Mind in a Ghost, by THOMAS HOOD: Works, I, 101.

874 The Drama. 99-103. J. H. REYNOLDS. Reynolds.

875 Report of Music. 103-06. Untraced, perhaps R. M. Bacon. See No. 211.

876 Abstract of Foreign and Domestic Occurrences. 107-13. CHARLES PHILLIPS. See No. 594.

877 Sketch of Foreign Literature. 113-16. Untraced, perhaps W. H. Leeds. This feature is similar in nature to "Gleanings from Foreign Journals" and "Literary and Scientific Intelligence" which Leeds provided for earlier numbers.

878 Monthly Intelligence. 117-20. JOHN TAYLOR, prob. Beginning with this issue, the title "Monthly Register" is dropped and the items formerly included under that title are reduced in number and listed without a general title. The new title is arbitrarily established by the compilers of this

index and includes the kind of tabular items formerly headed "Monthly Register." They are Literary Intelligence, Works Lately Published, Ecclesiastical Preferments, Births, Marriages, and Deaths. As with the "Monthly Register," these items were no doubt provided by the editor, for which see No. 444 and No. 595.

VOLUME VII.   NUMBER XXXVIII
FEBRUARY 1823

879   The Lion's Head. 123-24. THOMAS HOOD. See No. 445. Contains a letter signed J.W.W., by J. W. WILLIAMSON; signature and Rollins, II, 428.

880   A Day of a Persian Jew. Signed: J.W.W. 125-32. J. W. WILLIAMSON. Signature; Rollins, II, 434.

881   Corporal Colville, a Tale with Songs. Signed: Nalla. 132-40. ALLAN CUNNINGHAM. Signature.

882   Valentine's Day. A Homily for the Fourteenth of February. Signed: Ω. 141-45. B. W. PROCTER. Lamb, Letters, III, 347; Procter/Taylor Letters; Taylor Commonplace Book.

883   The Marquis of Stafford's Pictures. Signed: W. H. 145-51. WILLIAM HAZLITT. "By the Author of Table-Talk" on contents page; repr. Criticism on Art.

884   On Honesty. Signed: R. A. 151-56. RICHARD AYTON. Repr. Essays and Sketches.

885   The Literary Police Office, Bow Street. Edward Herbert's Letters to the Family of the Powells, No. VIII. Signed: Ed. Herbert. 157-61. J. H. REYNOLDS. Signature; repr. Jones.

886   The Early French Poets. Robert Garnier, continued. 162-69. H. F. CARY. Repr. Early French Poets.

887   The Bride's Tragedy. 169-72. B. W. PROCTER. Armour, Barry Cornwall, 79; Taylor Commonplace Book.

888   On English Versification, No. II. Signed: C. 173-80. WILLIAM CROWE. King, 171; repr. Treatise.

889   Sonnets addressed to R. S. Jameson. 180-81. HARTLEY COLERIDGE. Signed.

890   The Ruelle, a Dramaticle. 181-87. GEORGE DARLEY. Procter, Charles Lamb, 152; Taylor Commonplace Book has "P P Pickleherring," Darley's pseudonym.

891   Ode. Autumn. Signed: H. 187-88. THOMAS HOOD. Repr. The Plea.

892   Letters to a Young Man whose Education has been Neglected. By the Author of the Confessions of an English Opium-Eater, No. II. Signed: X.Y.Z. 189-94. THOMAS DE QUINCEY. Signature; repr. Collected Writings, X.

893   Sonnet to Elia. 194. BERNARD BARTON. Signed: repr. Poetic Vigils.

894   The Drama. 195-99. J. H. REYNOLDS. Attr. Hughes; Jones, 438.

895   Translations from the Supplemental Iliad of Quintus Calaber (concluded). Signed: Vida. 199-204. C. A. ELTON. Signature; See No. 836.

896   Anecdote of Dr. Franklin, related by Jefferson. 205. THOMAS JEFFERSON. Contributor of the item unknown.

897   Peveril of the Peak, by the Author of Waverley. 205-10. WILLIAM HAZLITT. Taylor, London Mercury, 264; repr. Works, XIX.

898   Poesy. 210-11. JOHN CLARE. Signed: repr. Shepherd's Calendar.

899   The Loves of the Angels. 212-15. J. H. REYNOLDS. Rollins, II, 429.

900   The Miscellany. 215-20. Conducted by B. W. PROCTER, see No. 849. Sonnet--Silence, signed T, by THOMAS HOOD; Broderip, I, 10 and repr. The Plea. Mrs. Siddons's Abridgement of Paradise Lost by J. H. REYNOLDS: Rollins, II, 429. Thoughts on Sculpture, signed T, by THOMAS HOOD: repr. Works, I. Original Letter of General Washington, by GEORGE WASHINGTON: contributor of item unknown. Milton, by CHARLES LAMB: repr. Works, I. Cooke's Exhibition of Drawings and Engravings, by B. W. PROCTER: Procter/Taylor Letters. A Check on Human Pride, by CHARLES LAMB: repr. Works, I. Meikle Sandie Gordon and Wee Sandie Gordon: untraced, perhaps Allan Cunningham on style. Anticipation by an Historian of the Mock Fight in 1814, on the Serpentine: untraced, perhaps B. W. Procter.

901 Report on the Progress of Science. 221-24.
ANDREW FYFE. Rollins, II, 440.

902 Report of Music. 225-27. Untraced, perhaps R. M.
Bacon. See No. 211.

903 View of Public Affairs. 227-33. CHARLES PHILLIPS.
See No. 594. This heading is merely a re-naming
of "Abstract of Foreign and Domestic Occurrences."

904 Sketch of Foreign Literature. 234-36. Untraced,
perhaps W. H. Leeds. See No. 877.

905 Monthly Intelligence. 237-40. JOHN TAYLOR, prob.
See No. 878.

VOLUME VII.   NUMBER XXXIX
MARCH 1823

906 The Lion's Head. 243-44. THOMAS HOOD. See No.
445. Contains a letter from CHARLES LAMB on
Elia's supposed death.

907 On Hunting. Signed: R. A. 245-56. RICHARD AYTON.
Repr. Essays and Sketches.

908 The King of Persia's Female Guards. Signed: J.W.W.
256-59. J. W. WILLIAMSON. Signature; Rollins, II,
428.

909 Sonetti. 259-60. B. SESTINI. Signed; repr.
Poesie di B. Sestini. Contributor of item unknown.

910 Anecdotage, No. I. Miss Hawkins's Anecdotes.
Signed: X.Y.Z. 261-69. THOMAS DE QUINCEY. Signature; Lowndes, 2027; repr. Collected Writings, V.

911 Old China. Signed: Elia. 269-72. CHARLES LAMB.
Signature; repr. Last Essays.

912 On English Versification, No. III. Signed: C.
273-82. WILLIAM CROWE. King, 171; repr. Treatise.

913 Riley Grave-Stones, a Derbyshire Story. Signed:
Nalla. 282-91. ALLAN CUNNINGHAM. Signature;
Taylor Commonplace Book.

914 Dr. Routh's New Edition of Bishop Burnet's History
of His Own Times. 291-96. PHILIP BLISS. Gibson/
Hindle, 255.

915   Olympian Revels, a Dramaticle. 297-306. GEORGE
      DARLEY. Taylor Commonplace Book; Procter,
      Charles Lamb, 152.

916   The Pictures at Windsor Castle. Signed: W. H.
      306-10. WILLIAM HAZLITT. "By the Author of Table-
      Talk" on contents page; repr. Criticism on Art.

917   Arago's Narrative of a Voyage round the World by
      Captain Freycinet. 310-17.

918   A Comment on the Divine Comedy of Dante. 317-24.
      H. F. CARY. Taylor Commonplace Book; Cary, Memoir,
      II, 74.

919   Letters to a Young Man whose Education has been
      Neglected. By the Author of the Confessions of an
      English Opium-Eater, No. III. Signed: X.Y.Z.
      325-35. THOMAS DE QUINCEY. Signature; repr.
      Collected Writings, X.

920   Report of the Progress of Science. 335-41.
      ANDREW FYFE. Rollins, II, 440.

921   Sketch of Foreign Literature. 341-42. Untraced,
      perhaps W. H. Leeds. See No. 877.

922   A Visit to the Franciscan Monastery of Sorrento
      (continued). 343-50. CHARLES MACFARLANE. Note
      in London Magazine (July 1823), VIII, 13.

923   Number of Members in the University of Oxford. 350.

924   Report of Music. 350-53. Untraced, perhaps R. M.
      Bacon. See No. 211.

925   The Drama. 354-58. J. H. REYNOLDS. Attr. Hughes
      and Jones, 438.

926   View of Public Affairs. 358-64. CHARLES PHILLIPS.
      See No. 594 and No. 903.

927   Monthly Intelligence. 365-68. JOHN TAYLOR, prob.
      See No. 878.

VOLUME VII. NUMBER XL
APRIL 1823

928   The Lion's Head. 371-72. THOMAS HOOD. See No.
      445. Contains letter signed X.Y.Z., by THOMAS DE
      QUINCEY: signature. Also a poem, "To Allan

Cunningham," "By the Author of 'The River Derwent'," who is W. B. CLARKE; see London Magazine for Aug. 1822, under "Works Lately Published" (VI, page 22 of Monthly Register).

929   Death of a German Great Man, Herder. Signed: X.Y.Z. 373-80. THOMAS DE QUINCEY. Signature; repr. Collected Writings, IV.

930   Antiquity /verse/. 380-82. JOHN CLARE. Signed; repr. Shepherd's Calendar.

931   A Shipwreck. Signed: R. A. 382-89. RICHARD AYTON. Repr. Essays and Sketches.

932   A Road to Preferment in Persia. 389-95. J. W. WILLIAMSON. Rollins, II, 434.

933   A Comment on the Divine Comedy of Dante (continued). 396-404. H. F. CARY. See No. 918.

934   Ode. Addressed to His Magesty the King of France. Signed: by the Author of the Essays on English Versification. 404. WILLIAM CROWE. Signature; Taylor Commonplace Book.

935   Spanish Romances. Signed: B. 405-10. JOHN BOWRING. Taylor Commonplace Book; repr. Ancient Poetry.

936   Kate of Windiewa's. Signed: Nalla. 410-20. ALLAN CUNNINGHAM. Signature; Taylor Commonplace Book.

937   A Poet's Thanks /verse/. 421. BERNARD BARTON. Signed; repr. Poetic Vigils.

938   Expedition from Pittsburgh to the Rocky Mountains. 422-28.

939   Sonnet. Faith. Signed: B. 428. B. W. PROCTER. Morning Chronicle, 28 Mar. 1823; Taylor Commonplace Book has Barry Cornwall, Procter's pseudonym.

940   On English Versification, No. IV. Signed: C. 429-36. WILLIAM CROWE. King, 171; repr. Treatise.

941   M. Tullii Ciceronis de Re Publica quae supersunt, Edente Angelo Maio. 437-42. H. F. CARY. Taylor Commonplace Book has "HFC"; Cary, Memoir, II, 74.

942   Anglo-German Dictionaries. 442-43. THOMAS DE QUINCEY. Lowndes, 2027; repr. Collected Writings, X.

943   Original Letter from Sir Philip Francis to Mr.
      George Thicknesse. 444. SIR P. FRANCIS, contri-
      buted and introduced by JOHN TAYLOR. Identity of
      Junius, 402, where part of the letter is printed
      in facsimile.

944   Ritson versus John Scott the Quaker. 445-48.
      CHARLES LAMB. "By Elia" on contents page; Letters,
      II, 376; repr. Works, I.

945   Mr. Kemble. 449-60. J. H. REYNOLDS. Rollins, II,
      434; Taylor Commonplace Book has "J.H.R."

946   The Miscellany. 460-63. Conducted by B. W.
      PROCTER. See No. 849. The Flood of Thessaly, The
      Girl of Provence, and Other Poems. By Barry
      Cornwall: J. H. REYNOLDS in Rollins, II, 440. Law
      of the Legislature of South Carolina against
      Duelling. Richardson. Prefigurations of Remote
      Events, signed Z., by THOMAS DE QUINCEY: repr.
      Collected Writings, X. A Song--(for Music), signed
      B., by B. W. PROCTER: Taylor Commonplace Book.
      Blunders.

947   Report of Music. 464-66. Untraced, perhaps R. M.
      Bacon. See No. 211.

948   Report of the Progress of Science. 466-70. ANDREW
      FYFE. Rollins, II, 440.

949   Sketch of Foreign Literature. 470-72. Untraced,
      perhaps W. H. Leeds. See No. 877.

950   The Drama. 473-76. J. H. REYNOLDS. Attr. Jones,
      438; see also Rollins, II, 440.

951   View of Public Affairs. 476-84. CHARLES PHILLIPS.
      See No. 594 and No. 903.

952   Monthly Intelligence. 485-88. JOHN TAYLOR, prob.
      See No. 878.

VOLUME VII.   NUMBER XLI
MAY 1823

953   The Lion's Head. 489-92. THOMAS HOOD. See No.
      445. Contains a signed letter from W. C. MACREADY;
      and a response to it by J. H. REYNOLDS, attr.
      Jones, 438. Also contains a poem, "Elegy on the
      Death of Bow-Fair"; untraced, perhaps a collabora-
      tion of Thomas Hood and J. H. Reynolds, as
      suggested by Hughes.

954 Mr. Schnackenberger; or Two Masters for One Dog. From the German. 493-505. THOMAS DE QUINCEY. Lowndes, 2027; repr. Collected Writings, XII.

955 Account of a New Process in Painting. 505-08. JOHN EAGLES. Taylor Commonplace Book.

956 Stanzas. 508. HARTLEY COLERIDGE. Signed; repr. as "Inania Munera" in Poems.

957 Spanish Romances. No. II. Signed: B. 509-14. JOHN BOWRING. Taylor Commonplace Book; repr. Ancient Poetry.

958 Facetiae Bibliographicae; or The Old English Jesters, No. I. 515-18. PHILIP BLISS. Taylor Commonplace Book; Gibson/Hindle, 173.

959 A Road to Preferment in Persia (concluded). Signed: J.W.W. 519-24. J. W. WILLIAMSON. Taylor Commonplace Book; Rollins, II, 434.

960 A Parthian Peep at Life /verse/. Signed: Ned Ward, Jun. 525-26. J. H. REYNOLDS. Signature; Taylor Commonplace Book.

961 On Beauty, and other Conditions of Face. Signed: R. A. 526-32. RICHARD AYTON. Repr. Essays and Sketches.

962 Spring Song. Signed: E. W. 533. J. H. REYNOLDS. Signature.

963 Poor Relations. Signed: Elia. 533-36. CHARLES LAMB. Signature; repr. Last Essays.

964 The late Earl St. Vincent. 537-40.

965 Lord William. A Scottish Song. Signed: C. 540. ALLAN CUNNINGHAM. Signature; Morning Chronicle, 2 May 1823.

966 The Roses. Translated from the Dutch of Bilderdijk /verse/. 541. H. S. VAN DYK. Attr. Hughes; style.

967 Sonnet, written in Keats's Endymion. Signed: T. 541. THOMAS HOOD. Broderip, I, 10.

968 The Land's End of Cornwall. Signed: Nalla. 542-52. ALLAN CUNNINGHAM. Signature; Taylor Commonplace Book.

969 On the Life and Writings of Alain Chartier. Early French Poets. 552-56. H. F. CARY. Repr. Early French Poets.

970 Letters to a Young Man whose Education has been Neglected. By the Author of the Confessions of an English Opium-Eater, No. IV. Signed: X.Y.Z. 556-58. THOMAS DE QUINCEY. Signature; repr. Collected Writings, X.

971 The Drama. 558-62. J. H. REYNOLDS. Attr. Hughes; Jones, 438.

972 Essays on Petrarch, by Ugo Foscolo. 562-64. H. F. CARY. Cary, Memoir, II, 74.

973 The Miscellany. 564-68. Conducted by B. W. PROCTER. See No. 849. Moral Effects of Revolutions, signed Z, by THOMAS DE QUINCEY: Lowndes, 2027; repr. Collected Writings, X. Sonnet to an Enthusiast, signed T, by THOMAS HOOD: Broderip, I, 10 and repr. A Plea. Signs of the Times, signed A, by RICHARD AYTON: Taylor Commonplace Book. Stanzas to a Young Friend, signed B. B., by BERNARD BARTON: repr. Poetic Vigils. A Sailor's Receipt for tying his Pig-tail--Shaving, &c., signed A, by RICHARD AYTON: signature as above. A Pleasant Climate. A Valentine to--/verse/, signed J. C., by JOHN CLARE: Taylor Commonplace Book and Rollins, II, 443. The Ruling Passion or Habit, by RICHARD AYTON: Taylor Commonplace Book.

------Pages 569 to 572 are omitted in magazine.---------

974 Narrative of a Journey to the Shores of the Polar Sea. 573-79.

975 Report of Music. 579-82. Untraced, perhaps R. M. Bacon. See No. 211.

976 Report of the Progress of Science. 582-87. ANDREW FYFE. Rollins, II, 439 and 440.

977 Sketch of Foreign Literature. 588-90. Untraced, perhaps W. H. Leeds. See No. 877.

978 View of Public Affairs. 590-96. CHARLES PHILLIPS. See No. 594 and No. 903.

979 Monthly Intelligence. 597-600: JOHN TAYLOR, prob. See No. 878.

VOLUME VII. NUMBER XLII
JUNE 1823

980 The Lion's Head. 603-04. THOMAS HOOD. See No. 445. Contains poem, "Lines from the Port-folio of H--," signed Δ, and though Hood says the poem has come from America, the signature was used by GEORGE DARLEY elsewhere, as No. 1347.

981 Spanish Romances. No. III. Signed: B. 605-15. JOHN BOWRING. Signature; repr. Ancient Poetry.

982 The Pictures at Hampton-Court. Signed: W. H. 616-20. WILLIAM HAZLITT. Repr. Criticism on Art.

983 Sonnet addressed to Bernard Barton. 620. JOHN MITFORD. Signed.

984 Facetiae Bibliographicae; or The Old English Jesters. No. II. 621-24. PHILIP BLISS. Gibson/Hindle, 173.

985 On the Tragic Drama of Greece. Introductory to a Series of Scenes from the Greek Tragic Poets. Signed: Vida. 625-33. C. A. ELTON. Taylor Commonplace Book; signature; repr. Boyhood.

986 Angling and Izaak Walton, with an Ode to Master Izaak Walton. Signed: E. W. 633-36. J. H. REYNOLDS. Signature; Taylor Commonplace Book.

987 Sonnet;--Death. Signed: T. 636. THOMAS HOOD. Broderip, I, 10; repr. A Plea.

988 St. Paul's Character of the Ancient Cretans, exemplified by an interesting Story from Polybius. 637-41. WILLIAM CROWE. Taylor Commonplace Book.

989 On Signs, a Ramble. Signed: Crito-Galen. 641-43. B. W. PROCTER. Procter/Taylor Letters, where Procter comments on his article on "Sign posts."

990 Bannocks of Barley. A Song. 643-44. ALLAN CUNNINGHAM. Signed on contents page; editorial note on p. 643. Taylor Commonplace Book has Darley for this item, but it is no doubt an error as the evidence for Cunningham is strong and·consistent.

991 Ode to the Printer's Devil. Signed: Ned Ward, Jun. 644-45. J. H. REYNOLDS. Signature; Taylor Commonplace Book.

992 Mr. Schnackenberger; or, Two Masters for One Dog. From the German (concluded). 646-59. THOMAS DE

QUINCEY. Lowndes, 2027; repr. Collected Writings, XII.

993 Stanzas. 660. HARTLEY COLERIDGE. Signed; repr. Poems.

994 To a Cold Beauty /verse/. Signed: T. 660. THOMAS HOOD. Repr. A Plea.

995 On English Versification. No. V. 661-68. WILLIAM CROWE. King, 171; repr. Treatise.

996 The Flood of Thessaly, The Girl of Provence, and Other Poems. By Barry Cornwall. 669-72. J. H. REYNOLDS. Attr. Jones, 438.

997 Report of Music. 672-75. Untraced, perhaps R. M. Bacon. See No. 211.

998 The Daisy in India, with an Extract from a Letter of Dr. Carey. 675-76. JAMES MONTGOMERY. Signed.

999 The Child Angel:--A Dream. Signed: Elia. 677-78. CHARLES LAMB. Signature; repr. Last Essays.

1000 The Fairy Miller of Croga, With Songs. Signed: Nalla. 678-89. ALLAN CUNNINGHAM. Signature.

1001 Table Talk. By William Hazlitt. Vol. II. 689-93. J. H. REYNOLDS. Taylor Commonplace Book has "J.H.R."

1002 View of Public Affairs. 693-700. CHARLES PHILLIPS. See No. 594 and No. 877.

1003 The Exhibition of the Royal Academy. 700-04. GEORGE DARLEY, prob. Attr. Hughes as conjecture.

1004 Epigram, Written on a Picture, in the Exhibition, called "The Doubtful Sneeze." 704. THOMAS HOOD. Repr. Works, I.

1005 The Drama. 705-06. J. H. REYNOLDS. Attr. Hughes.

1006 Sonnet. Signed: J. C. 706. JOHN CLARE. Signed on contents page.

1007 Retrospective View of the Commerce of Great Britain for the Last Six Months. 706-10. W. H. LEEDS. Taylor Commonplace Book.

1008 Monthly Intelligence. 711-14. JOHN TAYLOR, prob. See No. 878.

VOLUME VIII.   NUMBER XLIII
JULY 1823

1009   The Lion's Head. 3-4. THOMAS HOOD. See No. 445.
       Contains a sonnet, "By a person who never could
       write one," by THOMAS HOOD: attr. Hughes. Also
       a letter signed A. B. by OCTAVIUS GILCHRIST,
       prob.: signature as in No. 185.

1010   Imaginary Conversation between Mr. Southey and
       Professor Porson. 5-9. W. S. LANDOR. Procter,
       Charles Lamb, 153; repr. and enlarged in Imagi-
       nary Conversations.

1011   The Chase:--a Dramaticle. 10-13. GEORGE DARLEY.
       Procter, Charles Lamb, 152.

1012   Visit to the City of Sorrento. 13-20. CHARLES
       MACFARLANE. Morning Chronicle, 2 July 1823.

1013   The Old Margate Hoy. Signed: Elia. 21-25.
       CHARLES LAMB. Signature; repr. Last Essays.

1014   Stanzas. 25. HARTLEY COLERIDGE. Signed; repr.
       Poems.

1015   The Elgin Gallery /verse/. Signed: John Bull.
       26-31. Untraced, perhaps C. A. Elton in subject.
       Taylor Commonplace Book has "John Bull," but this
       appears to be a pseudonym.

1016   Lord Grosvenor's Collection of Pictures. Signed:
       W. H. 32-36. WILLIAM HAZLITT. Repr. Criticism
       on Art.

1017   Stanzas to --. Signed: V. D. 36. H. S. VAN DYK.
       Signature; Taylor Commonplace Book.

1018   On Fame and Monuments. Signed: R. A. 37-43.
       RICHARD AYTON. Repr. Essays and Sketches.

1019   An Heiress in Jeopardy. Signed: Ellen. 43-45.

1020   Poem, From the Dutch of Jacob Westerbaen. Signed:
       V. D. 45-46. H. S. VAN DYK. Taylor Commonplace
       Book; repr. Batavian Anthology.

1021   Sonnet. Signed: Percy Green. 46. JOHN CLARE.
       Signature; Tibble, 205; repr. Rural Muse.

1022   Spanish Romances, No. IV. 47-56. JOHN BOWRING.
       Repr. Ancient Poetry, VIII.

1023　On the Life and Writings of Samuel Johnson, LL.D. In Continuation of Johnson's Lives of the Poets. 57-69. H. F. CARY. Repr. Lives of the English Poets.

1024　The Yorkshire Alehouse. Signed: Nalla. 69-77. ALLAN CUNNINGHAM. Signature.

1025　Report of Music. 77-80. Untraced, perhaps R. M. Bacon. See No. 211.

1026　A Letter to the Dramatists of the Day. 81-86. GEORGE DARLEY. Procter, Charles Lamb, 152. Subsequent articles under this title are signed John Lacy, for which see B. M. Egerton MS 2247/269.

1027　Letters to a Young Man whose Education has been Neglected. By the Author of the Confessions of an English Opium-Eater, No. V. Signed: X.Y.Z. 87-95. THOMAS DE QUINCEY. Signature; repr. Collected Writings, X.

1028　The Progress of Science. 95-98. ANDREW FYFE. Rollins, II, 439 and 440.

1029　Sketch of Foreign Literature. 99-100. Untraced, perhaps W. H. Leeds. See No. 877.

1030　The Drama. 101-02. J. H. REYNOLDS. Attr. Hughes; Jones, 438.

1031　View of Public Affairs. 102-08. CHARLES PHILLIPS. See No. 594 and No. 903.

1032　Monthly Intelligence. 109-12. JOHN TAYLOR, prob. See No. 878.

VOLUME VIII.　NUMBER XLIV
AUGUST 1823

1033　The Lion's Head. 115-16. THOMAS HOOD. See No. 445.

1034　The Dice. From the German. 117-31. THOMAS DE QUINCEY. Lowndes, 2027; repr. Collected Writings, XII.

1035　The Flower-Spirit, A Faëry Tale /verse/. Signed: V. D. 131-33. H. S. VAN DYK. Signature.

1036   A Second Letter to the Dramatists of the Day.
       Signed: John Lacy. 133-41. GEORGE DARLEY. Procter, <u>Charles Lamb</u>, 152; B. M. Egerton MS 2247/269.

1037   Poems from the Dutch of Gerbrand Brederode.
       Signed: V. D. 141-44. H. S. VAN DYK. Taylor
       Commonplace Book; signature; repr. <u>Batavian Anthology</u>.

1038   The Daisy. 144-48. ELIZABETH KENT. Rollins, II, 434.

1039   Two Sonnets to Mary. Signed: Percy Green. 148.
       JOHN CLARE. Signature; Tibble, 206.

1040   The Marriage Act of Olympus. Signed: Hannibal.
       149. Untraced, perhaps Thomas Hood on style.

1041   Visit to the City of Sorrento (continued). 150-57. CHARLES MACFARLANE. See No. 1012.

1042   Spanish Romances, No. V. 158-68. JOHN BOWRING.
       Repr. <u>Ancient Poetry</u>, VIII.

1043   On the Life and Writings of Samuel Johnson, LL.D.
       (concluded). 169-86. H. F. CARY. Repr. <u>Lives of the English Poets</u>.

1044   Orations, &c. By the Rev. Edward Irving. 186-92.
       Untraced, perhaps John Taylor on subject.

1045   Andrew Laurie's Return. Signed: Nalla. 193-205.
       ALLAN CUNNINGHAM. Signature.

1046   Report of Music. 205-09. Untraced, perhaps R. M.
       Bacon. See No. 211.

1047   Sketch of Foreign Literature. 209-11. Untraced,
       perhaps W. H. Leeds. See No. 877.

1048   The Drama. 212-15. J. H. REYNOLDS. Attr.
       Hughes; Jones, 438.

1049   The Progress of Science. 215-18. ANDREW FYFE.
       Rollins, II, 439.

1050   View of Public Affairs. 218-28. CHARLES
       PHILLIPS. See No. 594 and No. 903.

1051   Monthly Intelligence. 228-32. JOHN TAYLOR, prob.
       See No. 878.

VOLUME VIII. NUMBER XLV
SEPTEMBER 1823

1052 The Lion's Head. 235-36. THOMAS HOOD. See No. 445.

1053 Sea-Roamers.--Old Johnny Wolgar. Signed: R. A. 237-47. RICHARD AYTON. Repr. Essays and Sketches.

1054 Nugae Criticae: by the Author of Elia. No. I. Defence of the Sonnets of Sir Philip Sydney. Signed: L. 248-52. CHARLES LAMB. Signature; repr. Last Essays.

1055 Sonnet from the Italian of Filicaja. Signed: C. S. 252. CHARLES STRONG. Repr. Specimens of Sonnets.

1056 Notes from the Pocket-Book of a late Opium-Eater. No. I: Walking Stewart. Signed: X.Y.Z. 253-60. THOMAS DE QUINCEY. Lowndes, 2028; repr. Collected Writings, X.

1057 The Nuns and Ale of Caverswell. A Sketch. 260-62. ALLAN CUNNINGHAM. Lamb, Letters, III, 347.

1058 Greek Tragic Scenes. Aeschylus. From the Agamemnon. Signed: Vida. 262-72. C. A. ELTON. Signature.

1059 Festival at Haarlem, on the Tenth and Eleventh of July Last, in Commemoration of the Invention of Printing. 272-75. Untraced, perhaps H. S. Van Dyk on subject and context.

1060 A Third Letter to the Dramatists of the Day. Signed: John Lacy. 275-83. GEORGE DARLEY. Signature; B. M. Egerton MS 2247/269.

1061 Sonnet written on Seeing a Greek at Vauxhall. 283.

1062 Elegiac Stanzas, written by an Officer long resident in India, on his return to England. 284.

1063 Sir Hugh Heron. Signed: Nalla. 285-99. ALLAN CUNNINGHAM. Signature.

1064 Birth-Day Verses. Translated from the Dutch of Tollens. Signed: V. D. 300. H. S. VAN DYK. Signature.

1065 Charles, Duke of Orleans. Early French Poets. 301-06. H. F. CARY. Repr. Early French Poets.

1066 The Doomed Man. Signed: H. 306-17. THOMAS POOLE. Taylor Commonplace Book.

1067 Report of Music. 317-21. Untraced, perhaps R. M. Bacon. See No. 211.

1068 The Drama. 321-24. J. H. REYNOLDS. Attr. Hughes; Jones, 438. The review of "Presumption or the Fate of Frankenstein" may have been by Edward Foss; see Jerrold, Thomas Hood, 134.

1069 Sketch of Foreign Literature. 324-27. Untraced, perhaps W. H. Leeds. See No. 877.

1070 The Progress of Science. 327-30. ANDREW FYFE. Rollins, II, 439.

1071 View of Public Affairs. 330-41. CHARLES PHILLIPS. See No. 594 and No. 903.

1072 Monthly Intelligence. 341-44. JOHN TAYLOR, prob. See No. 878.

VOLUME VIII.   NUMBER XLVI
OCTOBER 1823

1073 The Lion's Head. 347-48. JOHN TAYLOR, prob. As it contains "Verses on the Death of Bloomfield, the Suffolk Poet" by BERNARD BARTON (repr. Poetic Vigils), with introductory comments to the poem by JOHN TAYLOR; Rollins, II, 449.

1074 Notes from the Pocket-Book of a late Opium-Eater. No. II. Signed: X.Y.Z. 349-56. THOMAS DE QUINCEY. Signature; Lowndes, 2028; repr. Collected Writings, X.

1075 The Negro's Euthanasia. Translated from the Introductory Stanzas to a Greek Prize Ode of Mr. Coleridge. Signed: Olen. 356. C. A. ELTON. Signature.

1076 Pictures at Wilton, Stourhead, &c. Signed: W. H. 357-60. WILLIAM HAZLITT. Repr. Criticism on Art.

1077 A Chit Chat Letter on Men and other Things [verse]. Signed: Ned Ward, Jun. 361-64. J. H. REYNOLDS. Signature; Jones, 439.

1078   Sonnet from the Italian of Gaetana Passerini.
        Signed: C. S. 365. CHARLES STRONG. Signature;
        repr. Specimens of Sonnets.

1079   The Lucrece of France. Signed: Cyril. 365-72.

1080   Greek Tragic Scenes. No. II. Sophocles. From
        the Electra. Signed: Vida. 373-80. C. A. ELTON.
        Signature.

1081   Schiller's Life and Writings. Part I. His Youth.
        381-400. THOMAS CARLYLE. Repr. Life of Schiller.

1082   Letter of Elia to Robert Southey, Esquire.
        Signed: Elia. 400-07. CHARLES LAMB. Signature;
        repr. Works, I.

1083   A Fourth Letter to the Dramatists of the Day.
        Signed: John Lacy. 407-12. GEORGE DARLEY.
        Signature.

1084   Scripture Poetry.--Ruth. Traits of the Female
        Character. Signed: D. 413-17. Untraced, per-
        haps John Taylor, attr. Hughes; or Thomas De
        Quincey, attr. Brooks, Dissertation.

1085   Lord Roland Cheyne. Signed: Nalla. 418-28.
        ALLAN CUNNINGHAM. Signature.

1086   A Sonnet of the Moon. 428. CHARLES BEST. Signed;
        contributor unknown.

1087   The Fate of Hylas. Signed: C. 429-30. B. W.
        PROCTER. Rollins, II, 449 states Procter con-
        tributed 1¼ pages to the Oct. 1823 issue. This
        is the only item which fits this space and Proc-
        ter used this signature elsewhere.

1088   Report of Music. 430-32. Untraced, perhaps R. M.
        Bacon. See No. 211.

1089   The Drama. 432-35. GEORGE DARLEY. Rollins, II,
        448 and 449.

1090   François Villon. Early French Poets. 436-38. H.
        F. CARY. Repr. Early French Poets.

1091   Sketch of Foreign Literature. 439-43. Untraced,
        perhaps W. H. Leeds. See No. 877.

1092   The Progress of Science. 443-46. ANDREW FYFE.
        Rollins, II, 439 and 440.

1093 View of Public Affairs. 446-53. CHARLES PHILLIPS. See No. 594 and No. 903.

1094 Monthly Intelligence. 453-56. JOHN TAYLOR, prob. See No. 878.

VOLUME VIII. NUMBER XLVII
NOVEMBER 1823

1095 The Lion's Head. 459-60. THOMAS HOOD. See No. 445. Contains signed letter from WILLIAM HAZLITT on De Quincey's article on Malthus, No. 1074.

1096 Journal of an Excursion Across the Blue Mountains of New South Wales. Signed: B. F. 461-75. BARRON FIELD. Taylor Commonplace Book; signature; Rollins, II, 450.

1097 Cockney Latin. Signed: Philopatris Londiniensis. 475-76. CHARLES LAMB. Prance, TLS, 92.

1098 Sonnet from the Italian of Pietro Bembo. 447. CHARLES STRONG. Repr. Specimens of Sonnets.

1099 Guy Faux. Signed: Elia. 477-81. CHARLES LAMB. Signature; repr. Works, I.

1100 The Clouds; a Dream. 482-84. H. F. CARY. Cary, Memoir, II, 74.

1101 Spanish Romances. No. VI. 485-92. JOHN BOWRING. Signed on contents page.

1102 Nugae Criticae: By the Author of Elia, No. II. On a Passage in the Tempest. Signed: L. 492-93. CHARLES LAMB. Signature; repr. Works, I.

1103 Notes from the Pocket-Book of a late Opium-Eater. No. III. Signed: X.Y.Z. 493-501. THOMAS DE QUINCEY. Signature; repr. Collected Writings, X.

1104 Early Italian Poets. Guittone D'Arezzo. 501-03. H. F. CARY. Cary, Memoir, II, 74.

1105 Greek Tragic Scenes. No. III. Euripides. From the Orestes. Signed: Vida. 503-08. C. A. ELTON. Signature.

1106 Pictures at Oxford and Blenheim. Signed: W. H. 509-13. WILLIAM HAZLITT. Repr. Criticism on Art.

1107 Old Corehead's Fireside. 513-16. ALLAN CUNNINGHAM. Signed.

1108 The King of Hayti. From the German. 517-29. THOMAS DE QUINCEY. Lowndes, 2027; repr. Collected Writings, XII.

1109 A Fifth Letter to the Dramatists of the Day. Signed: John Lacy. 530-38. GEORGE DARLEY. Signature.

1110 Sketch of Foreign Literature. 538-40. Untraced, perhaps W. H. Leeds. See No. 877.

1111 Phrenology. 541-44. In a letter to Hessey of Oct. 20, 1823, Taylor refers to this article as by Hessey's "Scotch Friend," in Rollins, II, 450.

1112 Report of Music. 545-48. Untraced, perhaps R. M. Bacon. See No. 211.

1113 The Drama. 549-52. GEORGE DARLEY. Rollins, II, 459.

1114 The Progress of Science. 553-57. ANDREW FYFE. Rollins, II, 439.

1115 View of Public Affairs. 557-65. CHARLES PHILLIPS. See No. 594 and No. 903.

1116 Monthly Intelligence. 565-68. JOHN TAYLOR, prob. See No. 878.

VOLUME VIII.   NUMBER XLVIII
DECEMBER 1823

1117 The Lion's Head. 569-74. THOMAS HOOD. See No. 445. Contains a letter concerning Hazlitt's communication in No. 1095 from X.Y.Z. by THOMAS DE QUINCEY; signature. Also a sonnet signed "An Unworthy Rector" by Thomas Price or R. Wilks; attr. King, 141. In Lamb's Works (III, 982), Lucas suggests that the paragraph on p. 573, beginning "Can Neptune Sleep?", might be by Charles Lamb.

1118 Ode on the Death of Marco Bozzari. Signed: J. B. 573-76 /misnumbered/. JOHN BOWRING. Signed on contents page.

1119   On Modern French Poetry, with Translations. 577-86. C. A. ELTON. Translations repr. Boyhood.

1120   Measure of Value. Signed: X.Y.Z. 586-88. THOMAS DE QUINCEY. Signature; Lowndes, 2027; repr. Collected Writings, IX.

1121   Facetiae Bibliographicae; or, The Old English Jesters. No. III. 589-93. PHILIP BLISS. Gibson/Hindle, 173.

1122   Spanish Romances. No. VII. 593-96. JOHN BOWRING. Signed on contents page.

1123   Serenade. (From an unpublished Poem.) Signed: V. D. 596. H. S. VAN DYK. Signature.

1124   Recent Poetical Plagiarisms and Imitations. 597-604. HENRY TAYLOR. Taylor, Autobiography, I, 62.

1125   Song. 604. JOSIAH CONDER. Signed; repr. Star in the East.

1126   Sonnet. 605. JOSIAH CONDER. Signed: repr. Star in the East.

1127   Additions to the Lord Orford's Royal and Noble Authors. No. VII. 605-11. PHILIP BLISS. Gibson/Hindle, 173.

1128   Scene from the Medea of Euripides. Signed: K. 611-13. Untraced, perhaps C. A. Elton. Attr. Hughes, who refers to Elton's article on Euripides, No. 1105. But Elton is not known to have used this signature. H. S. Van Dyk contributed items over this signature, and this could be his.

1129   Amicus Redivivus. Signed: Elia. 613-15. CHARLES LAMB. Signature; repr. Last Essays.

1130   Rhodes's Peak Scenery. 616-17. Untraced, perhaps Allan Cunningham on subject and style.

1131   Don Saavedra: a Dramatic Story. 617-20. Untraced, perhaps J. S. Knowles.

1132   The Curse of Coldengame. Signed: Nalla. 621-34. ALLAN CUNNINGHAM. Signature.

1133   To His Mistress's Lips. Translated from Gabriello Chiabrera. Signed: N.O.H.J. 634-35. JOHN PAYNE COLLIER. Signature used by Collier in No. 1174, with I. substituted for J.

1134 Note to Elia, on the "Passage in the Tempest."
Signed: Laelius. 635-36. JOHN PAYNE COLLIER.
Attr. Hughes.

1135 The Drama. 637-43. J. H. REYNOLDS. Attr.
Hughes; Jones, 439.

1136 Early Italian Poets. Lapo Gianni. 643-44. H.
F. CARY. Cary, Memoir, II, 74.

1137 A Sixth Letter to the Dramatists of the Day.
Signed: John Lacy. 645-52. GEORGE DARLEY. Signature.

1138 Specimens of Sonnets from the most eminent Poets
of Italy. Signed: S. 652-53. CHARLES STRONG.
Repr. Specimens of Sonnets.

1139 Report of Music. 654-57. Untraced, perhaps R. M.
Bacon. See No. 211.

1140 The Progress of Science. 657-60. ANDREW FYFE.
Rollins, II, 439.

1141 View of Public Affairs. 660-68. CHARLES
PHILLIPS. See No. 594 and No. 903.

1142 Retrospective View of the Commerce of Great Britain, for the last Six Months. 669-73. W. H.
LEEDS. Taylor Commonplace Book.

1143 Monthly Intelligence. 674-76. JOHN TAYLOR, prob.
See No. 878.

VOLUME IX. NUMBER XLIX
JANUARY 1824

1144 The Lion's Head. 3-4. THOMAS HOOD. See No. 445.
Contains a poem, "Cupid's Revenge. Translated
from Benedetto Menzini," signed N.O.H.I. by JOHN
PAYNE COLLIER; signature for which see No. 1174.

1145 Historico-Critical Inquiry into the Origin of the
Rosicrucians and the Free-Masons. Signed: X.Y.Z.
5-13. THOMAS DE QUINCEY. Signature; Lowndes,
2027; repr. Collected Writings, XIII.

1146 The Son and Heir. Signed: Cyril. 14-21.

1147 Recollections of Italy. 21-26. MARY SHELLEY.
Nitchie, 63.

1148 Fresnaie Vauquelin. Early French Poets. 26-32. H. F. CARY. Repr. Early French Poets.

1149 Specimens of Sonnets from the most eminent Poets of Italy. Signed: S. 33-34. CHARLES STRONG. Repr. Specimens of Sonnets.

1150 The Indifference of Nature. From the French of Chênedollé. 35. Untraced, perhaps H. F. Cary, who was doing the series on French poets.

1151 Stanzas to the Memory of Richard Allen. Signed: Edward Ward, Jun. 35-36. J. H. REYNOLDS. Signature; Jones, 439.

1152 Schiller's Life and Writings. Part II. 37-59. THOMAS CARLYLE. Repr. Life of Schiller.

1153 Stanzas from the Italian of Lorenzo de Medici. Signed: B. 59. BERNARD BARTON. Repr. Poetic Vigils.

1154 Postscript to the Letters to Dramatists. Signed: John Lacy. 60-64. GEORGE DARLEY. Signature.

1155 Letters to the Country. No. I. Signed: Richard Chatterton. 64-70.

1156 Another Bode for Bodenton. Signed: Nalla. 71-83. ALLAN CUNNINGHAM. Signature.

1157 Spanish Romances. No. VIII. JOHN BOWRING. 84-92. Signed on contents page.

1158 The Drama. 92-96. J. H. REYNOLDS. Attr. Hughes; Jones, 439.

1159 Report of Music. 96-99. Untraced, perhaps R. M. Bacon. See No. 211.

1160 Sketch of Foreign Literature. 99-101. Untraced, perhaps W. H. Leeds. See No. 877.

1161 View of Public Affairs. 101-09. CHARLES PHILLIPS. See No. 594 and No. 903.

1162 Monthly Intelligence. 109-12. JOHN TAYLOR, prob. See No. 878.

VOLUME IX.   NUMBER L
FEBRUARY 1824

1163   The Lion's Head. 115-16. THOMAS HOOD. See No. 445.

1164   Analects from John Paul Richter. By the Author of the Confessions of an English Opium-Eater. 117-21. THOMAS DE QUINCEY. Signature in title; repr. Collected Writings, XI.

1165   A Walk to Paestum, Lucosia &c. 122-32. CHARLES MACFARLANE. Attr. Hughes, which is supported by subject and style.

1166   Specimen of popular Poetry from the Old Sclavonico-Polish Dialect. 132-33. JOHN BOWRING. Signed on contents page.

1167   Memoir and Remains of Charles Forster Featherstonhaugh. 133-39. The headnote informs the reader that this article was compiled from the papers of a C. F. FEATHERSTONHAUGH, but the contributor is unknown.

1168   The Nightingale. From the Dutch of Maria Tesselschade Visscher. 140. H. S. VAN DYK. Printed from Batavian Anthology.

1169   Historico-Critical Inquiry into the Origin of the Rosicrucians and the Free-Masons (continued). 140-51. THOMAS DE QUINCEY. Lowndes, 2027; repr. Collected Writings, XIII.

1170   Song of the Maidens. Signed: C. 151-52. ALLAN CUNNINGHAM. Signed on contents page; repr. Songs of Scotland, I; Morning Chronicle, 30 Jan. 1824.

1171   Translations from the Modern French Poets. Casimir de la Vigne. Signed: Lacento. 153-62. C. A. ELTON. Repr. Boyhood.

1172   The Quarterly Review on Tithes. 162-64. JOHN TAYLOR. Attr. Hughes, which is supported by subject and style.

1173   A Pen and Ink Sketch of a late Trial for Murder. Signed: Edward Herbert. 165-85. J. H. REYNOLDS. Signature; Morley, H. C. Robinson on Books, I, 302.

1174   The Dedication prefixed by Goethe to his Poems.
        Signed: N.O.H.I. 186-88. JOHN PAYNE COLLIER.
        Collier, 20.

1175   From the Polish of Zimorowicz. Signed: B. 188.
        JOHN BOWRING. Signature; style.

1176   Memoirs of Rossini. 189-93. Untraced, perhaps
        Charles Macfarlane, who knew Rossini and who
        often wrote on Italian subjects in the London.

1177   The Adventures of Hajji Baba, of Ispahan. 193-97.
        Untraced, perhaps John Taylor as the article is
        mainly editorial comment and quotation.

1178   The Drama. 197-202. J. H. REYNOLDS. Attr.
        Hughes; Jones, 439.

1179   Prose by a Poet. 202-04.

1180   Specimens of Sonnets from the most eminent Poets
        of Italy. 205-07. CHARLES STRONG. Repr.
        Specimens of Sonnets.

1181   Report of Music. 207-11. Untraced, perhaps R. M.
        Bacon. See No. 211.

1182   Sketch of Foreign Literature. 211-14. Untraced,
        perhaps W. H. Leeds. See No. 877.

1183   View of Public Affairs. 214-21. CHARLES
        PHILLIPS. See No. 594 and No. 903.

1184   Monthly Intelligence. 221-24. JOHN TAYLOR, prob.
        See No. 878.

VOLUME IX.   NUMBER LI
MARCH 1824

1185   The Lion's Head. 227-28. THOMAS HOOD. See No.
        445.

1186   Re-Establishment of the Jesuits in Naples. 229-
        36. CHARLES MACFARLANE. Attr. Hughes, which is
        supported by subject and style.

1187   German Epigrams. Signed: B. 237-39. JOHN BOW-
        RING. Morning Chronicle, 2 April 1824, sup.

1188   Facetiae Bibliographicae; or The Old English
        Jesters. No. VI. 239-41. PHILIP BLISS. Gib-
        son/Hindle, 173.

1189   Dream upon the Universe. By John Paul Richter.
       Signed: X.Y.Z. 242-44. THOMAS DE QUINCEY. Sig-
       nature; repr. Collected Writings, XI.

1190   Captain W. H. Smyth's Memoir descriptive of
       Sicily and its Islands. 245-51.

1191   Amadis Jamyn. Early French Poets. 251-52. H.
       F. CARY. Repr. Early French Poets.

1192   On Ghosts. Signed: Σς. 253-56. MARY SHELLEY.
       Beddoes, 23.

1193   Historico-Critical Inquiry into the Origin of the
       Rosicrucians and the Free-Masons. 256-61.
       THOMAS DE QUINCEY. Lowndes, 2027; repr. Collected
       Writings, XIII.

1194   The Pirate's Treasure. Signed: H. 261-71.
       THOMAS POOLE. An advertisement in the Morning
       Chronicle, for March 1, 1824, states that this
       piece is by the same author as "The Doomed Man,"
       No. 1066.

1195   Sonnet to M.F.M. 271.

1196   On the Author of the "Connubia Florum." 272.
       JONATHAN STOKES. Signed.

1197   A Letter from one of the "Dramatists of the Day,"
       to John Lacy, Esquire. Signed: Terentius
       Secundus. 272-76. B. W. PROCTER. Procter/
       Taylor Letters; Abbott, 45.

1198   Recent Poetical Plagiarisms and Imitations (con-
       tinued). 277-85. HENRY TAYLOR. Taylor, Auto-
       biography, I, 62.

1199   Advertisements Extraordinary. 285-89.

1200   A Sabbath among the Mountains. 290-91. ALLAN
       CUNNINGHAM. Attr. Hughes.

1201   The Rhapsodist. Morning. 291-92. GEORGE DARLEY.
       Repr. Poetical Works.

1202   Sonnet. Signed: V. D. 292. H. S. VAN DYK.
       Signature.

1203   Letters to the Country. No. II. Signed: Richard
       Chatterton. 293-99.

1204   Batavian Anthology. 300-04. Untraced, perhaps
       C. A. Elton on style and context.

1205   Report of Music. 304-08. Untraced, perhaps R. M.
       Bacon. See No. 211.

1206   The Services of Mr. Ricardo to the Science of
       Political Economy. Signed: X.Y.Z. 308-10.
       THOMAS DE QUINCEY. Signature; repr. Collected
       Writings, IX.

1207   The Drama. 311-15. J. H. REYNOLDS. Attr.
       Hughes; Jones, 439.

1208   The Deformed Transformed, a Drama; By Lord
       Byron. 315-21. Untraced, perhaps John Taylor.

1209   View of Public Affairs. 321-29. CHARLES
       PHILLIPS. See No. 594 and No. 903.

1210   Sketch of Foreign Literature. 329-31. Untraced,
       perhaps W. H. Leeds. See No. 877.

1211   The Fighting Gladiator /verse/. 332.

1212   Monthly Intelligence. 332-36. JOHN TAYLOR, prob.
       See No. 878

                VOLUME IX.   NUMBER LII
                     APRIL 1824

1213   The Lion's Head. 339-40. JOHN TAYLOR, prob.
       Contains a letter in answer to the reviewer of
       the Batavian Anthology, No. 1204, signed V. D.,
       by H. S. VAN DYK; signature. By this time Hood
       is almost certain to have severed his connection
       as subeditor. Both Taylor and Hessey were active
       in the compilation of the Lion's Head under Hood's
       direction, but Taylor, as the editor, was most
       likely to have continued as principal compiler
       from this point.

1214   Dialogues of Three Templars on Political Economy,
       chiefly in Relation to the Principles of Mr.
       Ricardo. 341-55. THOMAS DE QUINCEY. Lowndes,
       2027; repr. Collected Writings, IX.

1215   Gordon of Brackley. An Ancient Scottish Ballad.
       Signed: C. 355-56. ALLAN CUNNINGHAM. Repr.
       Poems and Songs.

                          96

1216 The Bride of Modern Italy. 357-63. MARY SHELLEY. Beddoes, 23.

1217 German Epigrams. No. II. 364-67. JOHN BOWRING. Morning Chronicle, 2 April 1824, sup.

1218 The Ghost-Player's Guide, or a Hint to Two Great Houses. Signed: Umbra. 368-72.

1219 Lines Written beneath a Picture of Love riding on a Tiger. 372.

1220 On the Madness of Hamlet. 373-80. WILLIAM FARREN. Signed.

1221 The Partition of the Earth. By Schiller. Signed: J.P.C. 380. JOHN PAYNE COLLIER. Collier, 20.

1222 Kant on National Character, in relation to the Sense of the Sublime and Beautiful. Signed: X.Y.Z. 381-88. THOMAS DE QUINCEY. Signature; Lowndes, 2027; repr. Collected Writings, XIV.

1223 Sonnet. Signed: V. D. 388. H. S. VAN DYK. Signature.

1224 Captain W. H. Smyth's Memoir Descriptive of Sicily and its Islands. 389-97.

1225 Facetiae Bibliographicae; or, The Old English Jesters. No. V. 397-400. PHILIP BLISS. Gibson/Hindle, 173.

1226 Pierre Gringore. Early French Poets. 401-05. H. F. CARY. Repr. Early French Poets.

1227 Report of Music. 405-09. Untraced, perhaps R. M. Bacon. See No. 211.

1228 Education. Plans for the Instruction of Boys in Large Numbers. 410-16. THOMAS DE QUINCEY. Lowndes, 2027; repr. Collected Writings, XIV.

1229 Fleet-Street Biography. 417-24. J. H. REYNOLDS. Attr. Hughes.

1230 The Characteristic of the Present Age of Poetry. 424-27. GEORGE DARLEY. Abbott, 46.

1231 The Templars Dialogues on Political Economy. Dialogue the Second. 427-28. THOMAS DE QUINCEY. Lowndes, 2027; repr. Collected Writings, IX.

1232   The Drama. 429-31. J. H. REYNOLDS. Attr.
       Hughes; Jones, 439.

1233   Sonnets from the most eminent Poets of Italy.
       Signed: S. 431-32. CHARLES STRONG. Repr.
       Specimens of Sonnets.

1234   View of Public Affairs. 433-41. CHARLES
       PHILLIPS. See No. 594 and No. 903.

1235   Sketch of Foreign Literature. 441-44. Untraced,
       perhaps W. H. Leeds. See No. 877.

1236   Monthly Intelligence. 444-48. JOHN TAYLOR, prob.
       See No. 878.

           VOLUME IX.   NUMBER LIII
                 MAY 1824

1237   The Lion's Head. 451-52. JOHN TAYLOR, prob.
       See No. 1213.

1238   A Visit Incog: or The Devil in Ireland. 453-61.
       CHARLES PHILLIPS. Attr. Hughes, which is support-
       ed by subject and context.

1239   Observations on "The Ghost-Player's Guide."
       Signed: Horrida Bella. 461-66. THOMAS HOOD.
       Attr. Jerrold, Thomas Hood, 261.

1240   The Rhapsodist. Noon. 446-68. GEORGE DARLEY.
       Repr. Poetical Works.

1241   John Lacy's Reply to the Letter of Terentius
       Secundus. Signed: John Lacy. 469-73. GEORGE
       DARLEY. Signature.

1242   Captain Parry's Second Voyage of Discovery. 474-
       84.

1243   The Two Ravens. An Old Scottish Ballad. Signed:
       C. 484. ALLAN CUNNINGHAM. Repr. Songs of
       Scotland, I.

1244   On the Madness of Ophelia. 485-88. WILLIAM FAR-
       REN. Signed.

1245   Abstract of Swedenborgianism: by Immanuel Kant.
       489-92. THOMAS DE QUINCEY. Lowndes, 2027; repr.
       Collected Writings, XIV.

1246	Sketches of Paul Jones. 492-99. Untraced, perhaps Allan Cunningham. He may have been collecting material for his novel, Paul Jones, which appeared in 1826.
1247	On the Death of an Infant. From the Dutch of Dirk Smits. Signed: V. D. 500. H. S. VAN DYK. Signature.
1248	Stanzas to M. F. M. 500.
1249	Advice to a Young Essayist. 501-03. GEORGE DARLEY. Taylor, London Mercury, 266.
1250	Education. Plans for the Instruction of Boys in Large Numbers (continued). 503-15. THOMAS DE QUINCEY. Lowndes, 2027; repr. Collected Writings, XIV.
1251	The Nightingale and the Thorn. 516. GEORGE DARLEY. Repr. Poetical Works.
1252	Facetiae Bibliographicae; or, The Old English Jesters. No. VI. 517-20. PHILIP BLISS. Gibson/Hindle, 173.
1253	Mexican Wonders; A Peep into the Piccadilly Museum. Signed: Jacob Goosequill. 521-22. GEORGE DARLEY. In a letter of Apr. 12, 1823 to Marian Neail, Darley calls himself "Goosequill": in Abbott, 32.
1254	On Walter Savage Landor's Imaginary Conversations. Signed: J. C. H. 523-41. J. C. HARE. Procter, Charles Lamb, 153.
1255	Song. 541.
1256	Report of Music. 542-46. Untraced, perhaps R. M. Bacon. See No. 211.
1257	Dialogues of the Three Templars on Political Economy, chiefly in Relation to the Principles of Mr. Ricardo. 547-66. THOMAS DE QUINCEY. Lowndes, 2027; repr. Collected Writings, IX.
1258	The Drama. 567. J. H. REYNOLDS. Attr. Hughes; Jones, 439.
1259	View of Public Affairs. 568-75. CHARLES PHILLIPS. See No. 594 and No. 903.
1260	Monthly Intelligence. 575-78. JOHN TAYLOR, prob. See No. 878.

VOLUME IX.   NUMBER LIV
JUNE 1824

1261   The Lion's Head. 581-82. JOHN TAYLOR, prob. See No. 1213.

1262   Memoirs of Captain Rock. 583-98. CHARLES PHILLIPS. Attr. Hughes.

1263   The Pirate's Song. Signed: C. 598. ALLAN CUNNINGHAM. Repr. Poems and Songs.

1264   German Epigrams. No. III. Signed: J. B. 599-602. JOHN BOWRING. Signature; Morning Chronicle, 2 April 1824, sup.

1265   Richard the Third, after the Manner of the Ancients. 603-12. Untraced, perhaps C. A. Elton on subject.

1266   Specimens of Sonnets from the most eminent Poets of Italy. 612-14. CHARLES STRONG. Repr. Specimens of Sonnets.

1267   Old Letters. 615-20. H. S. VAN DYK. Repr. The Gondola.

1268   Excerpta Antiquaria: Miscellaneous Antiquities. 620-22. PHILIP BLISS. Gibson/Hindle, 173.

1269   Death /verse7. Signed: X. 622. B. W. PROCTER. Signature.

1270   Rose's Orlando Furioso. 623-28. H. F. CARY. Attr. Bauer, 301.

1271   Paul Jones. To the Editor of the London Magazine. Signed:✠. 629-30. Untraced, perhaps Allan Cunningham. See No. 1246.

1272   The Life of Thomas Chatterton. 631-38. H. F. CARY. King, 190.

1273   Royal Poets. Verses written by King Henry VI and King Henry VIII. 638-41. Untraced, perhaps Philip Bliss. This is a most likely attribution as the article seems a continuation of his Royal and Noble Authors.

1274   Notes from the Pocket-Book of a late Opium-Eater. No. IV. Signed: X.Y.Z. 642-46. THOMAS DE QUINCEY. Signature; repr. Collected Writings, X.

1275 On Hamlet's Soliloquy. "To Be or Not To Be."
647-52. WILLIAM FARREN. Signed.

1276 Conclusion of the Historico-Critical Inquiry into
the Origin of the Rosicrucians and the Free-
Masons. Appendix. Signed: X.Y.Z. 652-62.
THOMAS DE QUINCEY. Signature; repr. Collected
Writings, XIII.

1277 Annual Exhibition of the Royal Academy. 663-71.

1278 The Drama. 671. J. H. REYNOLDS. Attr. Hughes;
Jones, 439.

1279 Report of Music. 672-76. Untraced, perhaps R. M.
Bacon. See No. 211.

1280 View of Public Affairs. 676-86. CHARLES
PHILLIPS. See No. 594 and No. 903.

1281 Retrospect of the Commerce of Great Britain for
the last Six Months. 686-91. W. H. LEEDS. Taylor Commonplace Book.

1282 Monthly Intelligence. 691-94. JOHN TAYLOR, prob.
See No. 878.

VOLUME X. NUMBER LV
JULY 1824

1283 The Lion's Head. 3-4. JOHN TAYLOR, prob. See
No. 1213. Contains poem, "An Address to Sleep,"
signed D. L. R----n. by D. L. RICHARDSON: attr.
Turnbull.

1284 Lilian of the Vale. 5-15. GEORGE DARLEY.
Abbott, 61.

1285 Schiller's Life and Writings, Part III. 16-25.
THOMAS CARLYLE. Repr. Life of Schiller.

1286 Notes from the Pocket-Book of a late Opium-Eater.
No. V. 25-28. THOMAS DE QUINCEY. Signature in
title; repr. Collected Writings, X.

1287 On English Versification. No. VI. 29-35. WIL-
LIAM CROWE. Repr. Treatise.

1288 Time. Signed: X. 35. B. W. PROCTER. Signature.

1289 The Cuckoo /verse/. Signed: C. 36. ALLAN CUNNINGHAM. Signed on contents page.

1290 Captain Cochrane's Pedestrian Journey through Russia and Siberia. 36-41.

1291 John A'Schaffelaar. Translated from the Dutch of Tollens. Signed: V. D. 42-44. H. S. VAN DYK. Signature.

1292 Forest Legends. No. I. The Archer of Ulvescroft. 44-51. CHARLES STRONG. The second item to appear under this title, No. 1423, is signed S, a signature used by Strong.

1293 The Last Day of Summer /verse/. Signed: B. C. 52-53. B. W. PROCTER. Signature.

1294 A Plea for Female Genius. Signed: Surrey. 53-55.

1295 Sonnet. Signed: J. C. 55. JOHN CLARE. Signed on contents page.

1296 Specimens of Sonnets from the most eminent Poets of Italy. 55-57. CHARLES STRONG. Repr. Specimens of Sonnets.

1297 Godwin's History of the Commonwealth. 57-60. Untraced, perhaps John Taylor on style.

1298 Facetiae Bibliographicae; or, The Old English Jesters. No. VII. 61-64. PHILIP BLISS. Gibson/Hindle, 173.

1299 More Ghost-Playing: Banquo's Spirit brought to Book. 65-69.

1300 Redgauntlet. 69-78.

1301 Stanzas. Signed: B. C. 78. B. W. PROCTER. Signature.

1302 On the Madness of Lear. 79-84. WILLIAM FARREN. Signed.

1303 Report of Music. 84-88. Untraced, perhaps R. M. Bacon. See No. 211.

1304 The Drama. 89-91. J. H. REYNOLDS. Rollins, II, 459. In the Athenaeum, p. 548, Dobell suggests the piece on Munden is by Thomas Hood, though Lucas reprints it as a doubtful piece by Lamb, Works, I.

1305 Podagrae Encomion; or Praise of the Gout. Signed: E. D. 91-95. Untraced, perhaps George Darling on subject.

1306 Sketch of Foreign Literature. 95-99. Untraced, perhaps W. H. Leeds. See No. 877.

1307 View of Public Affairs. 100-09. CHARLES PHILLIPS. See No. 594 and No. 903.

1308 Monthly Intelligence. 109-12. JOHN TAYLOR, prob. See No. 878.

VOLUME X. NUMBER LVI
AUGUST 1824

1309 The Lion's Head. 115-16. JOHN TAYLOR, prob. See No. 1213. Contains a letter signed Jerry Sneak, possibly by Thomas Hood; the prefatory note facetiously comments on the signature, "which we suppose is the English for Horrida Bella," for which see No. 1239. Also contains poem, "An Address to the Echo," by E. V. RIPPINGILLE: B. M. Egerton MS 2246/366.

1310 Robert Burns and Lord Byron. 117-22. ALLAN CUNNINGHAM. Taylor Commonplace Book; Hogg, Life of Allan Cunningham, 237.

1311 Excerpta Antiquaria: Miscellaneous Antiquities. 122-24. PHILIP BLISS. Gibson/Hindle, 173.

1312 Dreams: Felon's Hill--Windy Hovel--The Violets. 125-31.

1313 A Storm [verse]. Signed: B. 131-32. B. W. PROCTER. Signature.

1314 Old English Drama:--The Second Maiden's Tragedy. Signed: John Lacy. 133-39. GEORGE DARLEY. Signature; Taylor Commonplace Book; Procter, Charles Lamb, 152.

1315 Tropical Recollections: The Indian's Tale. 139-43. H. S. VAN DYK. Repr. The Gondola; Taylor Commonplace Book has "VD."

1316 The Idler's Epistle to John Clare. Signed: An Idler. 143-45. C. A. ELTON. Taylor Commonplace Book; repr. Boyhood.

1317   Elements of Vocal Science. 145-48. H. S. VAN
       DYK. Taylor Commonplace Book has "VD."

1318   Schiller's Life and Writings, Part III continued.
       149-63. THOMAS CARLYLE. Repr. Life of Schiller.

1319   On a Picture /verse/. Signed: B. 163. B. W.
       PROCTER. Signature.

1320   Sonnet. The Return of Time. Signed: --L. 163.
       JOHN BULL. Taylor Commonplace Book. This may be
       a pseudonym.

1321   Stanzas to --. Signed: K. 164. H. S. VAN DYK.
       Signature, as in No. 1398; Taylor Commonplace
       Book has "VD."

1322   The Power of Beauty. A Syrian Tale. 165-76.

1323   Ballad. 176-77. H. S. VAN DYK. Taylor Common-
       place Book has "VD."

1324   On the Cookery of the French. Signed: Timothy
       Walkinshaw. 178-79. A Mr. HAY. Taylor Common-
       place Book.

1325   Le Cuisinier Francais versus Dr. Kitchiner.
       Signed: Σ. 179-80. GEORGE DARLEY. Signature
       as in No. 1391.

1326   Journal of an Excursion to the Five Islands and
       Shoal Haven on the Coast of New South Wales.
       Signed: B. F. 181-84. BARRON FIELD. Taylor
       Commonplace Book; Morning Chronicle, 31 July
       1824; repr. Geographical Memoirs.

1327   Female Genius. Signed: Julius. 184-88. GEORGE
       DARLEY. Taylor Commonplace Book.

1328   Sonnet. Signed: R. S. W. 188. Untraced, perhaps
       W. S. Rose on signature.

1329   Goethe. 189-97. THOMAS DE QUINCEY. Lowndes,
       2027; repr. Collected Writings, XI.

1330   The Drama. 197-201. J. H. REYNOLDS. Rollins,
       II, 459.

1331   On Clenches. Signed: N. 201. JAMES BROUGHTON.
       Taylor Commonplace Book.

1332   Report of Music. 202-05. Untraced, perhaps R. M.
       Bacon. See No. 211.

1333 Important Intelligence from New South Wales. Discovery of Brisbane River. 205-06. BARRON FIELD. Article states by a "gentleman just arrived from New South Wales" and Field arrived in England on 18 June from that country.

1334 Sketch of Foreign Literature. 206-09. Untraced, perhaps W. H. Leeds. See No. 877.

1335 View of Public Affairs. 209-17. CHARLES PHILLIPS. See No. 594 and No. 903.

1336 Monthly Intelligence. 217-20. JOHN TAYLOR, prob. See No. 878.

VOLUME X.   NUMBER LVII
SEPTEMBER 1824

1337 The Lion's Head. 223-24. JOHN TAYLOR, prob. See No. 1213. Contains a sonnet by J. BOUDEN: signed.

1338 Blakesmoor in H--shire. Signed: Elia. 225-28. CHARLES LAMB. Signature; repr. Last Essays. Contains the poem "Helen" by MARY LAMB, repr. from Lamb's John Woodvil, 1802 (Works, V).

1339 Song. 228. H. S. VAN DYK. Taylor Commonplace Book has "VD."

1340 South America. Captain Basil Hall's Journal. 229-38.

1341 The Lawyer. 238-41. EDWARD DUBOIS. Taylor Commonplace Book.

1342 A Dream of Orpheus /verse_7. Signed: Olen. 241-50. C. A. ELTON. Taylor Commonplace Book; signature; repr. Boyhood.

1343 Narrative of a Voyage from New South Wales. Signed: B. F. 251-56. BARRON FIELD. Taylor Commonplace Book; signature; repr. Geographical Memoirs.

1344 Elegy. 256. C. A. ELTON. Taylor Commonplace Book.

1345 The Portrait Painter. Signed: P. P. 257-59. GEORGE DARLEY. Attr. Hughes; supported by signature for Peter Pickleherring, and style.

1346   Schiller's Life and Writings. Part III concluded. 259-69. THOMAS CARLYLE. Repr. Life of Schiller.

1347   Nugae Philosophicae. No. I. Signed: Δ. 269-72. GEORGE DARLEY. Taylor Commonplace Book.

1348   The Oramas. Signed: Jacob Goosequill. 273-77. GEORGE DARLEY. Signature, for which see No. 1253.

1349   Sonnet. Caesar. 277.

1350   Burchell's Travels in Southern Africa. 277-84.

1351   Facetiae Bibliographicae; or, The Old English Jesters. No. VIII. 285-89. PHILIP BLISS. Gibson/Hindle, 173.

1352   Vauxhall Meminiscences /verse7. Signed: Ned Ward, Jun. 289-91. J. H. REYNOLDS. Signature; Taylor Commonplace Book.

1353   Goethe (continued). 291-307. THOMAS DE QUINCEY. Lowndes, 2027; repr. Collected Writings, XI.

1354   Hearts' Ease /verse7. 308. H. S. VAN DYK. Attr. Hughes on MS authority.

1355   Contrasted Scenes. 308-11. H. S. VAN DYK. Repr. The Gondola.

1356   Sonnet. 311. JOHN BULL. Taylor Commonplace Book. This may be a pseudonym.

1357   The Drama. 312-13. GEORGE DARLEY. Rollins, II, 459n.

1358   Report of Music. 313-17. Untraced, perhaps R. M. Bacon. See No. 211.

1359   Sketch of Foreign Literature. 318-22. Untraced, perhaps W. H. Leeds. See No. 877.

1360   View of Public Affairs. 322-29. CHARLES PHILLIPS. See No. 594 and No. 903.

1361   Monthly Intelligence. 330-32. JOHN TAYLOR, prob. See No. 878.

VOLUME X.   NUMBER LVIII
OCTOBER 1824

1362   The Lion's Head. 333-34. JOHN TAYLOR, prob. See No. 1213.

1363   Reply to Blackwood. 335-36. JOHN TAYLOR. Editorial; Rollins, I, 137n.

1364   Personal Character of Lord Byron. Signed: R. N. 337-47. HENRY SOUTHERN. Taylor, London Mercury, 265.

1365   Beauties of the Innuendo. Signed: S. D. S. 348-49.

1366   Macadamization. Signed: Billy O'Rourke. 350-52. GEORGE DARLEY. Attr. Tibble, 453, which was supported by Turnbull.

1367   Walladmor: Sir Walter Scott's German Novel. 353-82. THOMAS DE QUINCEY. Leeds/Turner Letters; repr. Collected Writings, XIV.

1368   On Dying for Love. 382-84. H. S. VAN DYK. Attr. Hughes on MS authority.

1369   Idea of a Universal History on a Cosmo-Political Plan, by Immanuel Kant. 385-93. THOMAS DE QUINCEY. Lowndes, 2027; repr. Collected Writings, IX.

1370   Memento Mori, inscribed on a Tombstone. 393. GEORGE DARLEY. Repr. Poetical Works; Taylor Commonplace Book has "P," one of Darley's signatures.

1371   The Life and Remains of the Rev. Edward Daniel Clarke,. LL.D. 393-98. Untraced, perhaps John Taylor on subject.

1372   Raising the Dead. 398-400. GEORGE DARLEY. Attr. Hughes; supported by context and style.

1373   Washington Irving's New Work. 401-06.

1374   Facetiae Bibliographicae; or, The Old English Jesters. No. IX. 406-08. PHILIP BLISS. Gibson/Hindle, 173.

1375   Now am I happier than a King! /verse/. 408.

1376　Walk to Paestum, Leucosia. &c. Part II. 409-16. CHARLES MACFARLANE. Attr. Hughes; supported by subject and style.

1377　On the Death of a Young Girl. 416. GEORGE DARLEY. Repr. Poetical Works; Taylor Commonplace Book has "P," one of Darley's signatures.

1378　Montgomery's Mistress. Signed: C. 417. ALLAN CUNNINGHAM. Repr. Poems and Songs.

1379　The late Major-General Macquarie. Signed: A. H. 417-19.

1380　The Drama. 420-22. GEORGE DARLEY. Rollins, II, 459n.

1381　Hymn to the Monad. Signed: S. 426-27. CHARLES STRONG. Signature.

1382　Report of Music. 427-30. Untraced, perhaps R. M. Bacon. See No. 211.

1383　Sketch of Foreign Literature. 430-33. Untraced, perhaps W. H. Leeds. See No. 877.

1384　View of Public Affairs. 433-41. CHARLES PHILLIPS. See No. 594 and No. 903.

1385　Monthly Intelligence. 441-44. JOHN TAYLOR, prob. See No. 878.

VOLUME X.　NUMBER LIX
NOVEMBER 1824

1386　The Lion's Head. 447-48. JOHN TAYLOR, prob. See No. 1213.

1387　Conversations of Lord Byron. 449-62. HENRY SOUTHERN. Procter, Charles Lamb, 153.

1388　My Harp. From Hoelty. 462. H. S. VAN DYK, prob. Van Dyk's other translations of Hoelty are much the same.

1389　Original Letter of James Thomson. 463-64. Submitted by CHARLES LAMB. Headnote to letter; repr. Works, I.

1390　Memoirs of St. Henry. 465-72.

1391 Nugae Philosophicae. No. II. On Reverie.
Signed: Σ. 472-76. GEORGE DARLEY. Taylor Commonplace Book.

1392 Excerpta Antiquaria; or Miscellaneous Antiquities. 476-80. PHILIP BLISS. Gibson/Hindle, 173.

1393 Captain Jackson. Signed: Elia. 481-83. CHARLES LAMB. Signature; repr. Last Essays.

1394 M. Benjamin Constant--De la Religion. 483-91. STENDHAL. Gunnell, 280.

1395 'Tis Past--The Fond--The Fleeting Dream. 491. Untraced, perhaps John Clare as the poem is in his manner and style.

1396 The Portrait Painter (No. II). Signed: P.P. 492-95. GEORGE DARLEY. Attr. Hughes; supported by signature and style.

1397 Stanzas. 496. H. S. VAN DYK. Attr. Hughes.

1398 Karl and his Horse Nicolaus. Signed: K. 497-501. H. S. VAN DYK. Repr. The Gondola.

1399 The Life of William Hayley. 502-12. H. F. CARY. Taylor Commonplace Book; King, 110.

1400 Song of the Stars to the Earth. From the German of Gr. Von Stolberg. 512. Untraced, perhaps John Bowring on subject.

1401 Scripture Poetry, the Finding of Moses. Signed: D. 513-16. Untraced, perhaps John Taylor. Subject and style. The signature as in No. 1084 which he probably wrote.

1402 Walk to Paestum, Leucosia, &c. (concluded). 517-21. CHARLES MACFARLANE. Attr. Hughes.

1403 Bullock's Mexico. 521-28.

1404 The Revelation of Beauty /verse/. Signed: S. 528. CHARLES STRONG. Signature.

1405 A Page or Two on a Preface to a New Translation of Dante's Inferno. 529-31. Untraced, perhaps H. F. Cary on subject.

1406 Clotilda of Kynast, A Silesian Legend /verse/. 531-33.

1407 The Drama. 534-35. GEORGE DARLEY. Rollins, II, 459n.

1408 Sketch of Foreign Literature. 535-38. Untraced, perhaps W. H. Leeds. See No. 877.

1409 Report of Music. 539-42. Untraced, perhaps R. M. Bacon. See No. 211.

1410 View of Public Affairs. 543-53. CHARLES PHILLIPS. See No. 594 and No. 903.

1411 Monthly Intelligence. 553-56. JOHN TAYLOR, prob. See No. 878.

VOLUME X.   NUMBER LX
DECEMBER 1824

1412 Address. /n.p./. HENRY SOUTHERN, prob. This is an advertisement for the new series, to begin in January, of which Southern was editor.

1413 The Lion's Head. 559-60. JOHN TAYLOR, prob. See No. 1213.

1414 The Fanariotes of Constantinople. 561-70. HENRY SOUTHERN. Procter, Charles Lamb, 153.

1415 The Errors of Ecstasie. 571-76. B. W. PROCTER, prob. Abbott, 16, though he does express some doubt.

1416 The Old Oak. Translated from the Danish. Signed: G. O. B. 576. GEORGE BORROW. Repr. Romantic Ballads.

1417 Sonnet. 577.

1418 The Canadas--Emigration. 577-87.

1419 The Land of Logres. 588-89. H. F. CARY. Cary, Memoir, II, 74.

1420 Original Letter of Evelyn's. 589-92. JOHN EVELYN. Contributor unknown, but prob. Henry Southern.

1421 On De Beranger and De la Martine and other French Poets of the Modern School. Signed: Lacento. 593-98. C. A. ELTON. Verses repr. Boyhood.

1422　In my Bower so bright. 599. GEORGE DARLEY. Repr. Poetical Works.

1423　Forest Legends. No. II. Bradgate in the Seventeenth Century. Signed: S. 599-606. CHARLES STRONG. Signature.

1424　Fair Annie of Lochroyan. A Traditional Version of the Ancient Romantic Ballad. Signed: C. 607-08. ALLAN CUNNINGHAM. Morning Chronicle, 2 Dec. 1824; repr. Songs of Scotland.

1425　The Life of Henry Kirke White. 608-10. H. F. CARY. King, 190.

1426　French School of Painting. Signed: Y. 611-17. Untraced, perhaps W. Y. Ottley.

1427　The Lost Walking-Stick. Signed: R. R. 617-24.

1428　Notes from the Pocket-Book of a late Opium-Eater. Signed: X.Y.Z. 625-33. THOMAS DE QUINCEY. Signature; repr. Collected Writings, X.

1429　The Parisian Aristocracy. 633-35. STENDHAL. Gunnell, 280.

1430　Theatricals of the Day. Signed: John Lacy. 635-41. GEORGE DARLEY. Signature.

1431　Report of Music. 641-44. Untraced, perhaps R. M. Bacon. See No. 211.

1432　The Drama. 644-48. GEORGE DARLEY. Rollins, II, 459n.

1433　View of Public Affairs. 649-57. CHARLES PHILLIPS. See No. 594 and No. 903.

1434　Retrospect of the Commerce of Great Britain for the Last Six Months. 657-61. W. H. LEEDS. Taylor Commonplace Book.

1435　Monthly Intelligence. 662-64. JOHN TAYLOR, prob. See No. 878.

NEW SERIES. VOLUME I. NUMBER I
JANUARY 1825

1436   The Thames Quay, with a Plan. 1-6. HENRY SOUTH-
       ERN. Attr. Hughes; editorial reference to this
       in No. 1506.

1437   The Vagrant Act. 7-15. J. H. REYNOLDS. Attr.
       Hughes; style and other similarities to No. 885.

1438   To the Nightingale, Written in the Woods of
       Bolton Abbey /verse7. Signed: Umbroso. 16. B.
       W. PROCTER. Attr. Hughes; style and subject
       similar to "Sonnet, Written in the Woods of Bolton
       Abbey," No. 300.

1439   Biographical Memoir of Mr. Liston. 17-22.
       CHARLES LAMB. Lamb, Letters, II, 452; repr.
       Works, I.

1440   The Fallen Star /verse7. 22-23. GEORGE DARLEY.
       Repr. Complete Poetical Works.

1441   Theatricals. Signed: P. Pickle. 23-28. GEORGE
       DARLEY. Signature.

1442   A Vision of Horns. Signed: Elia. 29-32. CHARLES
       LAMB. Signature; repr. Works, I.

1443   Rail-ways. 33-37. THOMAS GRAY, prob. In a
       letter to Taylor of 13 July 1824, Gray advocates
       railways as an improved means of transportation:
       Brooke-Taylor MSS. This article is a follow-up
       to the letter.

1444   Sonnet. 37.

1445   Stern at Calais and Montreuil. Signed: P*. 38-
       46. JOHN POOLE. Signature; repr. Christmas
       Festivities.

1446   Advice to Various Persons. Signed: A Philanthro-
       pist. 46-49.

1447   Letters from Paris, by Grimm's Grandson. No. I.
       Signed: P.N.D.G. 49-60. STENDHAL. Gunnell,
       280; repr. Courrier Anglais, V.

1448   The Tenth Nemean Ode of Pindar. 60-64. H. F.
        CARY. King, 194n; repr. Pindar in English Verse.

1449   The French Cook. 65-71.

1450   Ariosto's Laurel. From His Capitoli Amorosi
        /verse/. Signed: Ουτις. 71-72.

1451   The Street Companion; or the Young Man's Guide
        and the Old Man's Comfort, in the Choice of
        Shoes. By the Rev. Tom. Foggy Dribble. 73-77.
        THOMAS DE QUINCEY. Axon. 267.

1452   Madame Campan's Journal. 77-80. HENRY SOUTHERN.
        Attr. Hughes; attack on the publication practices
        of Henry Colburn.

1453   A Sea-Piece, In Three Sonnets. 81-82. JAMES
        MONTGOMERY. Signed.

1454   Juaniana. Signed: Ardelius. 82-95. GEORGE DAR-
        LEY. Taylor Commonplace Book; the signature,
        which suggests ardelio, a busy body, is an anagram
        for Darley.

1455   To the Editor of the London Magazine. Signed:
        Elia. 95. CHARLES LAMB. Signature; repr. Works,
        I.

1456   Letter to an Old Gentleman whose education has
        been neglected. Signed: Elia. 95-99. CHARLES
        LAMB. Signature; repr. Works, I.

1457   Letter to a Friend in Natchitoches, Southey and
        Medwin's Bryon. Signed: Peter Pith. 100-03.
        HENRY SOUTHERN. Attr. Hughes; reference to this
        item in No. 1994. Some copies of the London do
        not contain the signature, Peter Pith.

1458   Ode to George Colman the Younger, Deputy Licenser
        of Plays. Signed: U.B.D.! 104-06. Jerrold,
        Thomas Hood and Charles Lamb, 149, gives this to
        Hood or J. H. Reynolds, with preference for Hood.

1459   The London Tithe Question. Signed: Philarchaeus.
        106-12. JOHN TAYLOR. Abbott, 35.

1460   Athenaion. 113-15.

1461   Report of Music. 115-20.

1462   The Drama. 120-25. Untraced, perhaps George Dar-
        ley; he was still contributing and had written
        dramatic articles previously.

1463 View of Public Affairs. 125-33. Untraced, perhaps Charles Phillips, who had done this feature for Taylor.

1464 Monthly Intelligence. 133-56. HENRY SOUTHERN, prob. This title, arbitrarily established at No. 878, is continued by the compilers of this index for Southern's editorship. As under Taylor's editorship, this heading includes various kinds of tabular items and information. They are Commerce, Agriculture, University Intelligence, Philosophical Societies, Natural Philosophy, Medicine, Chemistry, Celestial Phenomena, Stock Prices, List of Projected Works, List of Works Published, Theatrical Notices, Births, Deaths, and Marriages. Under Scott and Taylor, these items were provided by the editor (see Nos. 31 and 444), and Southern no doubt provided them during his tenure. H. Crabb Robinson, in his MS diary for 14 December 1824, mentions that Southern was to have "Mr. Thornton" do the monthly review of commerce, included under this head. This was THOMAS THORNTON, Robinson's nephew, and he was probably responsible for this item until March 1828, No. 2082.

NEW SERIES. VOLUME I. NUMBER II
FEBRUARY 1825

1465 Men, Measures and Manners in France, at the opening of the Session of 1825. 157-83. STENDHAL. Repr. Courrier Anglais, IV.

1466 Unitarian Protests: in a Letter to a Friend of that Persuasion Newly Married. Signed: Elia. 183-86. CHARLES LAMB. Signature; repr. Works, I.

1467 Pensive Stanzas to Miss M. A. T---. A Favourite Actress. Signed: Strephon. 186-88. Untraced, perhaps Thomas Hood or J. H. Reynolds, as it is much like their ephemera.

1468 High-ways and By-ways. 189-97. HENRY SOUTHERN. Attr. Hughes.

1469 The Chamber of Psyche /verse/. Signed: A. B. C. 197-98. JOHN NEAL. Signature, for which see Neal, 251.

1470 The British Code of Duel. 198-204. HENRY SOUTHERN. Attr. Hughes.

1471 History of Napoleon and the Grand Army in 1812. By General Comte Philippe de Segur. 205-24. STENDHAL. Repr. Courrier Anglais, IV.

1472 Sonnet. 224. GEORGE DARLEY. Repr. Complete Political Works.

1473 Meddling's Journal. Signed: E. A. 224-30. Hughes thought this by Hood or Reynolds, as it recalls the Odes and Addresses with its reference to Dr. Kitchener's "noted conversations."

1474 Autobiography of Mr. Munden: in a letter to the Editor. Signed: Joseph Munden. 231-32. CHARLES LAMB. Repr. Works, I.

1475 Letter from Abraham Twaddler. Signed: Abraham Twaddler. 233-41. HENRY SOUTHERN. Attr. Hughes; periodical criticism of this kind is continued in No. 1491 on Blackwood's, and the dropping of the letter device, in No. 1589 on the Quarterly.

1476 Le Mois Bubblose, or The A. S. S. Company. 241-46. T. L. PEACOCK, prob. Attr. Felton, 302.

1477 The Art of Advertizing Made Easy. Signed: P. A. Z. 246-53. THOMAS HOOD. Jerrold, Thomas Hood and Charles Lamb, 150.

1478 Academy of Sciences. Statistics. Signed: E. 253-59.

1479 Anthenaion. 259-60.

1480 Mr. Abernethy and the Lancet. Signed: Papinian. 260-65.

1481 Colburniana. 265-69. HENRY SOUTHERN. Attr. Hughes; renewing his attack on Henry Colburn's publication practices, Southern refers to his earlier article, No. 1452.

1482 The New Shepherd's Calendar. An Eclogue on Cox and Kean. Signed: Alexis. 270-72.

1483 Letters from Paris, By Grimm's Grandson. No. II. Signed: P. N. D. G. 272-82. STENDHAL. Gunnell, 280; repr. Courrier Anglais, V.

1484 Report of Music. 283-87.

1485 The Drama. 287-96. Untraced, perhaps George Darley; see No. 1462.

1486   View of Public Affairs. 297-304. Untraced, perhaps Charles Phillips; see No. 1463.

1487   Monthly Intelligence. 304-22. HENRY SOUTHERN, prob. See No. 1464.

NEW SERIES. VOLUME I. NUMBER III
MARCH 1825

1488   On the Profession of the Bar. 323-38. T. N. TALFOURD. Repr. Critical and Miscellaneous Writings.

1489   Letters from Paris, By Grimm's Grandson. No. III. 339-47. STENDHAL. Gunnell, 280; repr. Courrier Anglais, V.

1490   Odes and Addresses to Great People. 347-54. HENRY SOUTHERN. Attr. Hughes; see No. 1917.

1491   Letter from Abraham Twaddler, on the last number of Blackwood. Signed: Abraham Twaddler. 355-64. HENRY SOUTHERN. Attr. Hughes; see No. 1475.

1492   Hymn to Diana. Signed: A Lunatic. 365.

1493   Excerptions from an Idler's Scrap-book. 366-67. C. A. ELTON. "Idler" in the title is one of Elton's signatures.

1494   Reflections in the Pillory. 368-70. CHARLES LAMB. Repr. Works, I.

1495   The London Tithe Question. Signed: Philarchaeus. 371-79. JOHN TAYLOR. Abbott, 35.

1496   Sayings and Doings. Second Series. 379-87.

1497   Sterne at Paris and Versailles. Signed: P*. 387-94. JOHN POOLE. Signature; repr. Christmas Festivities.

1498   Sonnet. 395. GEORGE DARLEY. Repr. Complete Poetical Works.

1499   Old London. 395-402.

1500   The Stranger: A Romance. By the Viscount D'Arlincourt. 403-10. STENDHAL. Gunnell, 280; repr. Courrier Anglais, IV.

1501   Gipsey Song. Signed: Amante. 410.

1502   A Word with Blackwood in his own way: On the
        Posthumous Letters of Charles Edwards, Esq. No.
        IV. In Blackwood's Magazine for December.
        Signed: P. P. 411-17. GEORGE DARLEY. Signature;
        writer identifies himself as "Pickle" on p. 411.

1503   The Last Days of Napoleon. By Dr. Antommarchi.
        418-33. HENRY SOUTHERN. Attr. Hughes.

1504   Memoirs of Madame du Hausset. 434-46. SARAH
        AUSTIN. Ross, Three Generations, I, 46; in
        Courrier Anglais, IV, Martineau mistakenly
        attributes this to Stendhal.

1505   Academy of Science. Signed: A. 447-50.

1506   Surrey Quay. 451. HENRY SOUTHERN. Refers to
        his earlier article on the Thames Quay, No. 1436.

1507   Conversations of Napoleon with Canova in 1810.
        451-60. HENRY SOUTHERN. Attr. Hughes; almost
        completely a translation of notes by ANTONIO
        CANOVA, which were published as a pamphlet in
        Paris, 1824.

1508   Report of Music. 460-65.

1509   View of Public Affairs. 465-72. Untraced, per-
        haps Charles Phillips; see No. 1463.

1510   Monthly Intelligence. 472-90. HENRY SOUTHERN,
        prob. See No. 1464. Signed contribution by
        ROBERT W. MOORE.

          NEW SERIES. VOLUME I. NUMBER IV
                     APRIL 1825

1511   Struggles of a Poor Student through Cambridge.
        Signed: Senior Wrangler. 491-510. SOLOMON
        ATKINSON. Venn.

1512   Barbara S---. Signed: Elia. 511-14. CHARLES
        LAMB. Signature; repr. Last Essays.

1513   Niaseries of the Newspapers. Signed: P. P. 515-
        21. GEORGE DARLEY. Signature.

1514   The Lay of Arion. The Tale of Erigone. Signed:
        Olen. 521-27. C. A. ELTON. Signature.

1515   Tremaine, or the Man of Refinement. 527-38.
        HENRY SOUTHERN. Attr. Hughes; attack on the
        publication practices of Henry Colburn.

1516   Memorabilia of Dr. Parr, By a Friend. 539-54.
        Untraced, perhaps E. H. Barker, who was Parr's
        amanuensis and who, in 1828-29, published
        Parriana.

1517   The First Edition of Hamlet. Signed: J. 555-64.
        JOHN TAYLOR. Abbott, 35.

1518   Voyage en Angleterre et en Écosse, Par Adolphe
        Blanqui. 564-71. HENRY SOUTHERN. Attr. Hughes;
        Southern also reviewed this book in the West-
        minster Review, using some of the same quotations.

1519   Expedition to the Source of St. Peter's River.
        571-85.

1520   Twenty-one Elegiac Stanzas. To the Black Man who
        swept the crossing at the Obelisk, Blackfriars,
        and who lately died of age. Signed: Amen. 585-
        87. Untraced, perhaps Thomas Hood or J. H. Rey-
        nolds on style.

1521   Mr. Campbell's Last Man. 588-90. Untraced, per-
        haps Henry Southern; two-thirds of the article is
        a reprinting of a letter from THOMAS CAMPBELL to
        the Edinburgh Review.

1522   Gymnastics. 590-93.

1523   The Last Peach. Signed: Suspensurus. 593-94.
        CHARLES LAMB. Repr. Works, I.

1524   Italian Opera. 595-600.

1525   Letters from Paris, By Grimm's Grandson. No. IV.
        601-13. STENDHAL. Gunnell, 280; repr. Courrier
        Anglais, V.

1526   Letter from the Mediterranean. 613-18.

1527   Mornings in Albemarle-Street. No. I. 618-26.

1528   Loose Thoughts on Harriette Wilson. 626-31.

1529   Report of Music. 631-37.

1530   Theatrical Register. 637. HENRY SOUTHERN, prob.
        This kind of list would ordinarily be included
        under "Monthly Intelligence" provided by the
        editor.

1531 View of Public Affairs. 638-45. Untraced, perhaps Charles Phillips; see No. 1463.

1532 Monthly Intelligence. 645-62. HENRY SOUTHERN, prob. See No. 1464. Signed contribution by ROBERT W. MOORE.

NEW SERIES. VOLUME II. NUMBER V
MAY 1825

1533 Mr. W. Bankes and Mr. Buckingham. 1-11.

1534 The Opera. 11-16.

1535 Quatrains to the Editor of The Every Day-book. 16. CHARLES LAMB. Signed; repr. Works, V.

1536 Proverbes Dramatiques, Par M. Theodore Leclercq. Signed: N. 17-36. STENDHAL. Gunnell, 280; repr. Courrier Anglais, IV. Hughes attributes the translation of Leclercq's "Le Plus Beau Jour de la Vie" on pp. 21-36 to HENRY SOUTHERN.

1537 Mr. Campbell's University. 36-40. HENRY SOUTHERN. Attr. Hughes; attack on the publication practices of Henry Colburn.

1538 The Three Graves /verse/. · 41. CHARLES LAMB. Repr. Works, V.

1539 Models of Switzerland. Signed: W. S. 41-45.

1540 Examination of a Young Pretender. By the Modern Dilworth. 46-48.

1541 A Convict's Recollections of New South Wales. Written by Himself. 49-67. MELLISH. Signed; Barron Field was perhaps responsible for this reaching the editor.

1542 The Superannuated Man. Signed: J. D. 67-73. CHARLES LAMB. Repr. Last Essays.

1543 Moralities. No. I. The Lawyers. 73-80.

1544 The Playhouses. 81-90.

1545 Gaieties and Gravities. 90-96. HENRY SOUTHERN. Attr. Hughes.

1546 Chess and Chess-Players. By an Ancient Amateur. 97-102.

1547 Lying, in all its Branches. Review of Mrs. Opie's Book. 103-14.

1548 Second Exhibition of the Society of British Artists, in Suffolk-Street. 114-28. Untraced, perhaps Henry Southern, as H. Crabb Robinson calls him an "authority" on art in his MS Diary for 9 November 1824.

1549 The Man of Refinement. 128-31. HENRY SOUTHERN. Attr. Hughes; resumes his attack on Henry Colburn's publication practices and his review of Tremaine, No. 1515.

1550 Letters from Paris. By Grimm's Grandson. No. V. Signed: P. N. D. G. 131-41. STENDHAL. Gunnell, 280; repr. Courrier Anglais, V.

1551 Report of Music. 141-46.

1552 Monthly Intelligence. 147-60. HENRY SOUTHERN, prob. See No. 1464. Signed contribution by ROBERT W. MOORE.

NEW SERIES. VOLUME II. NUMBER VI
JUNE 1825

1553 Continuation of the Struggles of a Senior Wrangler. Signed: N. N. 161-82. SOLOMON ATKINSON. Venn.

1554 Letter from an Absent Contributor on Hazlitt's Spirit of the Age. Signed: P. P. 182-89. GEORGE DARLEY. Signature.

1555 Remonstratory Ode, From the Elephant at Exeter Change, to Mr. Mathews, at the English Opera House. 189-92. J. H. REYNOLDS. Mathews, II, 485.

1556 Observations on Mitford's History of Greece. 193-204.

1557 Scraps from the Correspondence of a Musical Dilettante Travelling in Italy. 204-08.

1558 An Epistle to a Country Cousin /verse/. 208-10. THOMAS HOOD. Attr. Jerrold, Thomas Hood and Charles Lamb, 151.

1559 Wright's Life of Richard Wilson, Esq. R. A. 210-16.

1560 The Wedding. Signed: Elia. 217-21. CHARLES LAMB. Signature; repr. Last Essays.

1561 Don Esteban, or the Memoirs of a Spaniard. 221-24. HENRY SOUTHERN. Attr. Hughes.

1562 Eating and Drinking. The Natural and Medical Dieteticon. 225-39.

1563 Economic Funeral Society. 239-40.

1564 The Claqueurs of Paris. 241-46.

1565 Foolery at Cheltenham. 247-50.

1566 Diary of Henry Teonge. 250-56.

1567 The Fine Arts. Exhibition of the Royal Academy. 256-68. Untraced, perhaps Henry Southern; see No. 1548.

1568 The Music of the Month. 269-71.

1569 Extracts from Mr. Croker's Journal, Kept During a Late Attempt to Discover the Topographical Position of Russell Square. 272-76.

1570 Letters from Paris. By Grimm's Grandson. No. VI. Signed: P. N. D. G. 276-90. STENDHAL. Gunnell, 280; repr. Courrier Anglais, V.

1571 The Opera. 290-293.

1572 Rev. Sydney Smith's Speech on the Catholic Claims. 293-99. SYDNEY SMITH. A recording of his speech, reprinted from the Liverpool Mercury of this month.

1573 The Playhouses. 299-302.

1574 Report of Public Affairs. 303-05. Untraced, perhaps Charles Phillips; see No. 1463.

1575 Monthly Intelligence. 305-18. HENRY SOUTHERN, prob. See No. 1464. Signed contribution by ROBERT W. MOORE.

1576 The London and Edinburgh Chess Match. 319-20.

NEW SERIES. VOLUME II. NUMBER VII
JULY 1825

1577 Italy. Secret History of the last Conclave. Signed: R. P. 321-32. STENDHAL. Gunnell, 280.

1578 To Charles Lamb. Written over a Flask of Sherris /verse/. Signed: C. 332-34. B. W. PROCTER. Repr. English Songs.

1579 Loss of the Kent East Indiaman. 335-39. Editorial note by HENRY SOUTHERN, followed by an eyewitness report of the disaster.

1580 A Thesbian Supper. 340-50.

1581 The Widow Fairlop. Signed: Master Slender. 350-54. Untraced, perhaps B. W. Procter, though this imitation of Lamb may well have been by Thomas Hood or J. H. Reynolds.

1582 The Highlands and Western Isles of Scotland. By John Macculloch. 354-62. HENRY SOUTHERN. Attr. Hughes.

1583 New Cemetery Project and Cemeteries. 363-70.

1584 The Opera. 371-76.

1585 The Convalescent. Signed: Elia. 376-79. CHARLES LAMB. Signature; repr. Last Essays.

1586 To-Day in Ireland. 379-87. HENRY SOUTHERN. Attr. Hughes; opening clause, "while we oppose the quackeries of the press," is an editorial allusion to his criticism of Colburn and various of the journals; Southern owned a copy of the book which he loaned to H. Crabb Robinson--see MS diary for 14 June 1826.

1587 The British Institution. No. I. 387-400.

1588 The Plays of Clara Gazul, with a translation of The Spaniards in Denmark. 401-36. STENDHAL. Gunnell, 280. Hughes attributes the translation on pp. 404-36 to SARAH AUSTIN.

1589 The Quarterly Review, No. LXIII. 437-43. HENRY SOUTHERN. Attr. Hughes; see No. 1475.

1590 Four Sonnets composed during Ascot Race Week, By a Person of Sentiment. 443-45. J. H. REYNOLDS. Jones, 439.

1591 On the Projected Improvements of St. James's Park. 445-57.

1592 Letters from Paris. By Grimm's Grandson. No. VII. Signed: P. N. D. G. 457-68. STENDHAL. Gunnell, 280; repr. Courrier Anglais, V.

1593 The Infant Lyra. 468-71.

1594 The National Stud. A New Project. 471-73.

1595 The Music of the Month. 474-78.

1596 Monthly Intelligence. 478-88. HENRY SOUTHERN, prob. See No. 1464. Signed contribution by ROBERT W. MOORE.

NEW SERIES. VOLUME II. NUMBER VIII
AUGUST 1825

1597 The Modern Athens. 489-510.

1598 The late Editor of the Quarterly Review. 510-15. HENRY SOUTHERN. Attr. Hughes.

1599 The Opera. 516-20.

1600 Moralities. No. II. The Way to Conquer. 521-33.

1601 Broster's System for the Cure of Impediments of Speech. By a Pupil. Signed: G. D. 533-36. GEORGE DARLEY. Darley suffered from an impediment in his speech and was a pupil of Broster. Abbott, p. 48, quotes a letter from John Taylor to his brother of February 1825, stating that Darley had "set off for Edinburgh...to see if Mr. Broster there can cure him of his Impediment."

1602 Spanish Religious Tournaments. 537-42.

1603 Death in the Gallipot. 542-45.

1604 Approved Methods of Setting Houses on Fire. 545-52, 543-44 /misnumbered/.

1605 Wines: No. I. The Wines of England, Germany, Russia, The Cape, &c. 545-55. Untraced, perhaps Cyrus Redding who was preparing his book on wines.

1606 Hackney Coaches. Signed: Jehu. 555-57.

1607   Voyage en Angleterre et en Ecosse. Par M. Amédée Pichot, D. M. 558-66. HENRY SOUTHERN, prob. Style and long quotations indicate the editor, as well as his penchant to review French books, especially by French travellers in England as in No. 1518.

1608   Chess. 566-70.

1609   Letters from Paris. By Grimm's Grandson. No. VIII. Signed: P. N. D. G. 570-82. STENDHAL. Gunnell, 280; repr. Courrier Anglais, V.

1610   Ode to L. E. L. 582-84. Untraced, perhaps Thomas Hood or J. H. Reynolds on style; both are also suggested by Jerrold, Thomas Hood and Charles Lamb, 151.

1611   On Fashions. 585-92. See No. 1624.

1612   Tales of the Crusaders. 593-99.

1613   Imperfect Dramatic Illusion. Signed: Elia. 599-601. CHARLES LAMB. Signature; repr. as "Stage Illusion" in Last Essays.

1614   The Playhouses. 602-05.

1615   Three Original Letters of Dr. Franklin, Hitherto Unpublished. 606-08. BENJAMIN FRANKLIN. Contributor unknown.

1616   The Belzoni Sepulchre. 609-13.

1617   Monthly Intelligence. 614-22. HENRY SOUTHERN, prob. See No. 1464. Signed contribution by ROBERT W. MOORE.

NEW SERIES. VOLUME III. NUMBER IX
SEPTEMBER 1825

1618   The Journal of a Detenu. An Eye-Witness of the Events in Paris during the first four months of 1814. 1-35. T. R. UNDERWOOD. Repr. Journal of a Detenu.

1619   Letter from Rome on the Present State of Italian Literature. Signed: C. D. 36-45. STENDHAL. Gunnell, 281; repr. Courrier Anglais, IV.

1620   Ode to the Anatomie Vivante. 45-48. Untraced,
        perhaps Thomas Hood or J. H. Reynolds as the
        style is that of <u>Odes and Addresses</u>; both are al-
        so suggested by Jerrold, <u>Thomas Hood and Charles
        Lamb</u>, 151.

1621   The British Institution. No. II. 49-69.

1622   The Bricks of Modern Babylon. 69-75.

1623   Wines. No. II. French Wines. 75-88. Untraced,
        perhaps Cyrus Redding who was preparing his book
        on wines.

1624   More Fashions. 88-95. Hughes attributes this to
        Henry Southern, but when Southern discusses the
        subject in No. 1635, he refers to p. 93 of this
        and No. 1611 as by a contributor.

1625   The Sorrows of ** ***. 95-98. Untraced, perhaps
        Charles Lamb, as Dobell, 153-54, suggests,
        though he also admits this could be by Hood.

1626   On the Domestication of Wild Animals. Signed:
        C. 98-116. B. W. PROCTER. Signature as in No.
        1578.

1627   The Complete Servant. By Samuel and Sarah Adams.
        116-20.

1628   Letters from Paris. By Grimm's Grandson. No. IX.
        Signed: P. N. D. G. 120-32. STENDHAL. Gunnell,
        280; repr. <u>Courrier Anglais</u>, V.

1629   The Music of the Month. 132-34.

1630   Tales by the O'Hara Family. 134-36. HENRY
        SOUTHERN, prob. Style; in a MS letter to H. C.
        Robinson of 12 June 1826, Southern mentions he
        cannot locate his copy of this book: Southern
        Letters.

1631   Butleriana. From Unpublished Manuscripts. No. I.
        136-40. HENRY SOUTHERN. See No. 1687.

1632   Monthly Intelligence. 140-44. HENRY SOUTHERN,
        prob. See No. 1464. Signed contribution by
        ROBERT W. MOORE.

NEW SERIES. VOLUME III. NUMBER X
OCTOBER 1825

1633 The Life and Adventures of an Italian Gentleman; containing his travels in Italy, Greece, France, etc. No. I. 145-73. STENDHAL. Gunnell, 281.

1634 Notes on a Note Book. 173-76.

1635 On Fashions in Physic. 177-91. HENRY SOUTHERN. Attr. Hughes; Southern's reference to Lady Bountiful points forward to No. 1686.

1636 Letters from the Continent. No. I. The Netherlands. Signed: H. T. S. 191-206. T. J. HOGG. Repr. Journal of a Traveller.

1637 Civilization. 207-13.

1638 Wines. No. III. Italian, Spanish, Portuguese, &c. 214-28. Untraced, perhaps Cyrus Redding who was preparing his book on wines.

1639 The Ballad of the Living Skeleton. 228-30. Untraced, perhaps Thomas Hood or J. H. Reynolds, one of the authors of Odes and Addresses.

1640 A Tale of Paraguay. 231-36. HENRY SOUTHERN. Attr. Hughes.

1641 The Journal of a Detenu. No. II. 237-56. T. R. UNDERWOOD. Repr. Journal of a Detenu.

1642 The Musician at York. The Yorkshire Festival. Signed: S. 257-72.

1643 Letters from Paris. By Grimm's Grandson. No. X. Signed: P. N. D. G. 273-84. STENDHAL. Gunnell, 280; repr. Courrier Anglais, V.

1644 The Music of the Month. 285-88.

1645 Monthly Intelligence. 289-92. HENRY SOUTHERN, prob. See No. 1464. Signed contribution by ROBERT W. MOORE.

NEW SERIES. VOLUME III. NUMBER XI
NOVEMBER 1825

1646 The Life and Adventures of an Italian Gentleman. No. II. 293-335. STENDHAL. Gunnell, 280.

1647 Extracts of a Correspondence from the North of Germany. Signed: F. V. 336-40.

1648 The British Institution. No. III. 341-56.

1649 National Pride. 356-62.

1650 The Eventful Life of a Soldier. 363-80. HENRY SOUTHERN. Attr. Hughes; articulates the book review policy of the London, especially on pp. 364-65, which is reiterated in the new feature for 1827, Monthly Advice to Purchasers of Books, beginning with No. 1692.

1651 Pythagorean Objections against animal food. Signed: T. H. 380-83. Untraced, perhaps Thomas Hood on signature.

1652 The Journal of a Detenu. No. III. 384-404. T. R. UNDERWOOD. Repr. Journal of a Detenu.

1653 The Playhouses. 405-11.

1654 Letters from Paris. By Grimm's Grandson. No. XI. Signed: P. N. D. G. 412-21. STENDHAL. Gunnell, 280; repr. Courrier Anglais, V.

1655 Letter to Joseph Hume, Esq. M. P. Signed: Navita. 422-25.

1656 Butleriana. No. II. 425-30. HENRY SOUTHERN. See No. 1687.

1657 Original Letters of Dr. Franklin, hitherto Unpublished. No. II. 430-31. BENJAMIN FRANKLIN. Contributor unknown.

1658 Monthly Intelligence. 431-36. HENRY SOUTHERN, prob. See No. 1464. Signed contribution by ROBERT W. MOORE.

NEW SERIES. VOLUME III. NUMBER XII
DECEMBER 1825

1659 Notice to Correspondents. /n.p./ HENRY SOUTHERN. Editorial notice.

1660 The Regrets of a Cantab. Signed: A. H. 437-66. SOLOMON ATKINSON, prob. Style; similar to Nos. 1511 and 1553; though Hughes gives this to Henry Southern on style, his comparison is to the above articles which he mistakenly attributed to Southern; also, the writer addresses the editor.

1661 Extracts of a Correspondence from the North of Germany, No. II. 467-70.

1662 Architecture of Manufactories. Signed: L. I. 471-79.

1663 Original Letters of Dr. Franklin, hitherto unpublished. No. III. 479-480. BENJAMIN FRANKLIN. Contributor unknown.

1664 A Chapter on Spiders. Signed: T. N. 481-84.

1665 The Journal of a Detenu. No. IV. 485-517. T. R. UNDERWOOD. Repr. Journal of a Detenu.

1666 Narrative of the loss of the Kent. 517-27. HENRY SOUTHERN. Attr. Hughes; editorial stricture on author for copying an article which appeared in the London, No. 1579, without acknowledgement.

1667 Letters from Constantinople. 527-32.

1668 Library of the British Museum. 533-36.

1669 Chit-Chat of the Times of Charles II. 536-40. CHARLES BARKER, prob. See No. 1690.

1670 Letters from Paris. By Grimm's Grandson. No. XII. Signed: P. N. D. G. 541-50. STENDHAL. Gunnell, 280; repr. Courrier Anglais, V.

1671 The Playhouses. 550-55.

1672 Flowers of Speech; or the Young Writer's Complete Guide to the Beauties of Style. 556-62. HENRY SOUTHERN. Attr. Hughes.

1673 Annual Souvenir Books. 562-63. HENRY SOUTHERN, prob. Editorial references; he returns to subject in No. 1856.

1674   Authentic Account of the Sicilian Auto-da-fé, celebrated at Palermo in 1724. 563-78.

1675   Monthly Intelligence. 579-84. HENRY SOUTHERN, prob. See No. 1464. Signed contribution by ROBERT W. MOORE.

NEW SERIES. VOLUME IV. NUMBER XIII
JANUARY 1826

1676   Editorial Note. /n.p./. HENRY SOUTHERN. The editor announces the policy of the London to provide "an impartial guide to the purchasers of books" beginning with No. 1692 below.

1677   Greece in 1825. 1-17. HENRY SOUTHERN. Attr. Hughes.

1678   On Italian Literature. No. II. Signed: L. C. D. 18-26. STENDHAL. Gunnell, 281; repr. Courrier Anglais, IV.

1679   Narrative of the Imprisonment and Adventures of Joshua Done, in various parts of France. 26-37. JOSHUA DONE. Editorial note identifies writer.

1680   Courtship and Marriage. 37-44.

1681   The Progress of Cant. 45-46. HENRY SOUTHERN, prob. Attr. Hughes; Reid, 48, suggests Charles Lamb, but this doesn't seem likely.

1682   Lord Normanby's Matilda. 47-48. HENRY SOUTHERN. Attr. Hughes; continues his attack on Henry Colburn's publications and the periodicals which support them.

1683   Miss Edgeworth's Harry and Lucy. 49-61. HENRY SOUTHERN, prob. Style and general attitude.

1684   The Life and Adventures of an Italian Gentleman. No. III. 61-76. STENDHAL. Gunnell, 280.

1685   Diary of "a Constant Reader" for the Month of December. 76-86. HENRY SOUTHERN. See No. 1825, where the temporary editor identifies Southern, the regular editor, as the writer of this feature; style; attack throughout on the publication practices of Henry Colburn.

1686 On Dilettante Physic. 87-94. HENRY SOUTHERN. Attr. Hughes; his return to Lady Bountiful promised in No. 1635.

1687 Butleriana, from Unpublished MSS. No. III. 94-98. HENRY SOUTHERN. Comments in headnote, signed "Ed.", show clearly that Southern contributed this series. Hughes was the first to note this series of unpublished manuscripts which are now in the British Museum.

1688 The Music of the Month. 98-102.

1689 A Hint to Whist Players. Signed: Thomas Pam. 102-04. Untraced, perhaps Charles Lamb, though Hughes and Dobell think it only an imitation of Lamb.

1690 Manners of the Court of Charles II. 105-18. CHARLES BARKER, prob. Attr. Hughes; the style is similar to Barker's article on the same subject in The Retrospective Review, VII. This is a follow-up to No. 1669, which was an excerpt from Pepys's Diary and probably sent by Barker.

1691 The Playhouses. 118-21.

1692 Monthly Advice to Purchasers of Books. 121-32. HENRY SOUTHERN. The editorial note that precedes these brief reviews of books reiterates the review policy of No. 1650 and refers to the editorial announcement of this feature in No. 1676.

1693 Table Talk. 133-38. HENRY SOUTHERN. Editorial note explains these excerpts from other publications, chiefly from current books reviewed in the London, "are calculated to make an impression on the mind of the reader."

1694 Monthly Intelligence. 138-44. HENRY SOUTHERN, prob. See No. 1464. Signed contribution by ROBERT W. MOORE.

NEW SERIES. VOLUME IV. NUMBER XIV
FEBRUARY 1826

1695 Letter to Editor. [n.p.]. NEIL CAMPBELL. Signed.

1696   Journal Descriptive of the Route from New York to
       Real del Monte. 145-71. SARAH AUSTIN. Morley,
       H. C. Robinson on Books, I, 332.

1697   The Opera. 171-73.

1698   The Naval Sketch-Book. 173-77. HENRY SOUTHERN.
       Attr. Hughes.

1699   The Duties of a Lady's Maid. Signed: L. I. T.
       177-90. HENRY SOUTHERN. Attr. Hughes.

1700   Music of the Month. 190-92.

1701   The Siege of the Acropolis of Athens in the Years
       1821-22. By an Eye-witness. 193-208.

1702   Diary of "a Constant Reader" for the Month of
       January. 209-24. HENRY SOUTHERN. See No. 1685.

1703   North American Review on Lord Byron's Works and
       Pinkney's Poetry. 224-29. HENRY SOUTHERN.
       Attr. Hughes; editorial policy of reviewing other
       periodicals.

1704   The Cambridge University. Westminster, Edinburgh,
       and Quarterly Reviews. 229-42. HENRY SOUTHERN.
       Attr. Hughes; Southern was himself an alumnus of
       Cambridge and associates himself with the writer
       of No. 1660, to which he refers.

1705   Memoirs of the Margravine of Anspach. Written by
       Herself. 243-53. SARAH AUSTIN. Attr. Hughes.

1706   Adventures of a Young Rifleman. 253-67. HENRY
       SOUTHERN. Attr. Hughes.

1707   Monthly Advice to Purchasers of Books. 267-72.
       HENRY SOUTHERN. See No. 1692.

1708   Table Talk. 273-84. HENRY SOUTHERN. See No.
       1693.

1709   Monthly Intelligence. 284-88. HENRY SOUTHERN,
       prob. See No. 1464. Signed contribution by
       ROBERT W. MOORE.

NEW SERIES. VOLUME IV. NUMBER XV
MARCH 1826

1710 The Cambridge University. Senate-House Examinations for degrees. Signed: W. 289-314. HENRY SOUTHERN. Attr. Hughes; a follow-up to No. 1704.

1711 The Opera. 314-18.

1712 Brambletye House. 318-20. HENRY SOUTHERN. Attr. Hughes.

1713 The Early Life and Education of Counsellor O'D---, The Son of an Irish Peasant. Written by Himself. 321-36. JOHN O'DRISCOLL. H. Crabb Robinson's manuscript Diary for 14 March 1826 gives the full name, O'Driscoll, who wrote on Ireland and Irish history.

1714 The Playhouses. 336.

1715 Sketch of the Remarkable Persons who died in France during 1825. Signed: L'Anonyme Litteraire. 337-42.

1716 Waterton's Wanderings in South America. 343-53. HENRY SOUTHERN. Attr. Hughes.

1717 The Count De St. Germain's Tale. From the Memoirs of the Court of Louis XV. By Madame du Hausset. 354-57. SARAH AUSTIN. Attr. Hughes; the article is almost entirely a translation from a book Mrs. Austin reviewed, No. 1504.

1718 The Times and the Medical Adviser versus Snuff. Signed: T. L. Dustington. 357-68.

1719 Diary of "a Constant Reader" for the Month of February. 369-81. HENRY SOUTHERN. See No. 1685.

1720 Sir Egerton Brydges and the New Monthly Magazine. 382-84. SIR EGERTON BRYDGES. Writer identified in editorial note.

1721 Italian Literature. Signed: A poor Italian. 385-91. ANTONIO PANIZZI, prob. This is a response to the articles on Italian literature, Nos. 1619 and 1678. Panizzi came to England in 1823, studied Italian literature and lectured on it at the Royal Institution in Liverpool in 1825. He was a native of Modena, referred to in the note on p. 391. In the articles to which this responds, Stendhal had attacked Roscoe, Panizzi's friend.

1722 City Sonnets. 392-93.

1723 Chateaubriant's Sketch of Roman History, from Julius Caesar to Augustus. 394-401. CHATEAUBRIAND. Reprinted from the Introduction to his History of France, and probably translated by HENRY SOUTHERN, whose interest in French literature is often manifest in the pages of the London.

1724 Characters from the Unpublished Manuscripts of the Author of Hudibras. 401-06. HENRY SOUTHERN. See No. 1687.

1725 Fraser's Journey to Khorasan. 406-13.

1726 Proceedings in Parliament Relative to the Currency. 413-20. JOHN TAYLOR. Attr. Bauer, 149n.

1727 Sir Thomas Lethbridge and the Edinburgh Review. 421. HENRY SOUTHERN, prob. Style; editorial policy of reviewing other periodicals.

1728 Monthly Advice to the Purchasers of Books. 422. HENRY SOUTHERN. See No. 1692.

1729 Table Talk. 422-34. HENRY SOUTHERN. See No. 1693.

1730 Monthly Intelligence. 435-36. HENRY SOUTHERN, prob. See No. 1464. Signed contribution by ROBERT W. MOORE.

NEW SERIES. VOLUME IV. NUMBER XVI
APRIL 1826

1731 Yankee Notions. Signed: N. 437-50. JOHN NEAL. Neal, 246.

1732 Destruction of an Elephant at Geneva, in May 1820. 450-55.

1733 Klaproth's Asiatic Magazine. 455-66. HENRY SOUTHERN. Attr. Hughes; editorial policy of reviewing other periodicals.

1734 Poetical Distress /verse/. 466-68.

1735 The Life and Adventures of an Italian Gentleman. No. IV. 469-85. STENDHAL. Gunnell, 280.

1736   Journal of a Traveller on the Continent. No. II.
        485-95. T. J. HOGG. Repr. Journal of a
        Traveller.

1737   The Temple of Butterflies. Signed: T. 495-500.

1738   Extracts of a Correspondence from the North of
        Germany. No. III. 501-10.

1739   Account of the Rebellion in the Philippine Islands in the year 1823. 510-18. This title is
        not on contents page.

1740   Diary for the Month of March. 518-30. HENRY
        SOUTHERN. See No. 1685. The phrase, "of a
        Constant Reader," was dropped from the title as
        of this month.

1741   Mr. M'Culloch's Doctrine of Absenteeism, A Study,
        With an Extension to the Subjects of Free Trade
        and Neutral Rights. 530-42.

1742   Williams's Tour in Jamaica. 543-53. HENRY
        SOUTHERN. Attr. Hughes; references in No. 1744,
        p. 560.

1743   Calamities of Irish Law Students. 553-57.

1744   Mathews at Home. 558-60. HENRY SOUTHERN, prob.
        Style; references to Mathews earlier in No. 1457
        and the next month, No. 1748, to Mathews's monopolylogue indicate Southern's interest.

1745   Monthly Advice to Purchasers of Books. 560-62.
        HENRY SOUTHERN. See No. 1692.

1746   Table Talk. 563-74. HENRY SOUTHERN. See No.
        1693.

1747   Monthly Intelligence. 574-76. HENRY SOUTHERN,
        prob. See No. 1464. Signed contribution by
        ROBERT W. MOORE.

            NEW SERIES. VOLUME V. NUMBER XVIII
                        MAY 1826

1748   Diary for the Month of April. 1-18. HENRY
        SOUTHERN. See No. 1685.

1749   Six Months in the West Indies. 18-27. HENRY
        SOUTHERN. Reference in No. 1744, p. 560.

1750 The Last American Novel. 27-31.

1751 The Puffs of the Month; or Colburniana. 31-32.
HENRY SOUTHERN. See No. 1481; attack on the
publication practices of Henry Colburn.

1752 Journal of a Traveller on the Continent. No. III.
33-58. T. J. HOGG. Repr. Journal of a Traveller.

1753 Two Songs: the Music by Mr. J. Barnett, the Nonsense by Mr. T. Campbell. 58-60. HENRY SOUTHERN. Attr. Hughes; a reprinting of the lyrics
by THOMAS CAMPBELL is introduced by an editorial
note on their "inanity."

1754 The Collegians /verse/. Signed: H. O. 60-64.

1755 Ancient Encaustic Painting of Cleopatra, with
an Engraving, on facing page. 65-71. UGO
FOSCOLO. Ottolini, 48.

1756 Yankee Notions. No. II. Signed: N. 71-89.
JOHN NEAL. Neal, 246.

1757 The Three Magazines. 90-94. HENRY SOUTHERN.
Attr. Hughes; editorial policy of reviewing
other periodicals.

1758 Execution of Mr. Berney, at Norwich in 1684. 94-96. An editorial note by HENRY SOUTHERN, followed
by an "extract from an old family manuscript."

1759 Sheridaniana. 97-103. HENRY SOUTHERN. Attr.
Hughes.

1760 History of a Portrait. Signed: W. H. S. S. 104-08.

1761 The Diary of Luc'Antonio Viterbi, kept by himself
during the time he was starving himself to death
in the prisons of Corsica, in the year 1821.
108-15. HENRY SOUTHERN. Long editorial note
followed by an excerpt from Robert Benson's
Sketches in Corsica (1825).

1762 The Last Number of the Quarterly Review. 116-25.
HENRY SOUTHERN. Attr. Hughes; editorial policy
of reviewing other periodicals.

1763 Ways and Means /verse/. 125-26.

1764 Table Talk. 126-41. HENRY SOUTHERN. See No.
1693.

1765   Monthly Intelligence. 141-44. HENRY SOUTHERN, prob. See No. 1464. Signed contribution by ROBERT W. MOORE.

NEW SERIES. VOLUME V. NUMBER XVIII
JUNE 1826

1766   Boccaccio. 145-57. UGO FOSCOLO. Ottolini, 47.

1767   Journal of a Traveller on the Continent. No. IV. 158-73. T. J. HOGG. Repr. Journal of a Traveller.

1768   Woodstock. 173-81.

1769   Yankee Notions. No. III. (Concluded for the present.) Signed: N. 181-97. JOHN NEAL. Neal, 246.

1770   The Duties of Subjects towards their Monarch, for the Instruction, and Exercise in Reading, of the Second Class of Elementary Schools. 198-204.

1771   Matrimonial Gratitude. A Chinese Story /verse/. 205-07.

1772   Vivian Grey. 207-17. HENRY SOUTHERN. Attr. Hughes; attack on John Bull, another of Southern's recurring targets.

1773   The Ladies of Africa. 217-31. HENRY SOUTHERN. Attr. Hughes.

1774   Angeloni on Political Force. 231-42. SARAH AUSTIN. Attr. Hughes.

1775   Diary for the Month of May. 242-57. HENRY SOUTHERN. See No. 1685.

1776   Fraser's Travels and Adventures in the Persian Provinces, on the Shores of the Caspian Sea. 258-67. HENRY SOUTHERN. Attr. Hughes.

1777   Captain Maitland's Narrative of the Surrender of Buonaparte. 268-72. HENRY SOUTHERN. Attr. Hughes.

1778   Table Talk. 273-85. HENRY SOUTHERN. See No. 1693.

1779   Monthly Intelligence. 285-88. HENRY SOUTHERN, prob. See No. 1464. Signed contribution by ROBERT W. MOORE.

NEW SERIES. VOLUME V. NUMBER XIX
JULY 1826

1780 Erratum. [n.p.].

1781 Journal of a Traveller on the Continent. No. V. 289-301. T. J. HOGG. Repr. Journal of a Traveller.

1782 The Suicide, a Tale. 302-17.

1783 Mr. John Dunn Hunter: The hero of Hunter's Captivity among the Indians &c. Signed: J. N. 317-43. JOHN NEAL. Neal, 314.

1784 Mathias's Italian Translation of Spenser. 344-51. CHARLES MACFARLANE. Macfarlane, 89.

1785 Aerostatical Speculations over London. Signed: V. 351-58.

1786 Dictionaries of Quotations. 358-62.

1787 Electioneering. 362-67. HENRY SOUTHERN. Attr. Hughes.

1788 "Smiles and Tears" of Irish Faction. Signed: T. C. 367-72.

1789 Dimorphosis, or Fashionable Movements. Signed: Granby. 373-85.

1790 Dying Game [verse]. 385-88.

1791 Angel-Hunting. Signed: Oxoniensis. 388-91.

1792 Diary of the Month of June. 391-408. HENRY SOUTHERN. See No. 1685.

1793 Lives of the Forty. 408-12.

1794 The Life and Times of Frederick Reynolds. 412-21. HENRY SOUTHERN. Attr. Hughes.

1795 Table Talk. 422-30. HENRY SOUTHERN. See No. 1693.

1796 Monthly Intelligence. 431-32. HENRY SOUTHERN, prob. See No. 1464. Signed contribution by ROBERT W. MOORE.

NEW SERIES. VOLUME V. NUMBER XX
AUGUST 1826

1797 To the Editor of the London Magazine. Signed: J. N. ⟦n.p.⟧. JOHN NEAL. Signature; reference to article on John Dunn Hunter, No. 1783.

1798 Journal of a Traveller on the Continent. No. VI. 433-53. T. J. HOGG. Repr. Journal of a Traveller.

1799 Cephalostatics. Signed: Veritas. 453-62.

1800 Adventures of a Foreigner in Greece. 462-81.

1801 Paris on Diet. 481-89. HENRY SOUTHERN. Attr. Hughes.

1802 Sporting Excursion. Signed: Index. 490-500.

1803 Adventures of a French Serjeant. 500-18. HENRY SOUTHERN. Attr. Hughes.

1804 Irish Writers on Ireland. Signed: H. 519-26. HENRY SOUTHERN. Signature, as in No. 1860.

1805 An Appeal from the Shades. 527-29. CHARLES LAMB, prob. Dobell, 140-52; though Lucas in Lamb's Letters, I, 355, refutes Dobell, but earlier, both Macdonald and Hutchinson, in their respective editions of Lamb's works, reprint this. The compilers of this index are inclined to believe this by Lamb.

1806 Diary for the Month of July. 529-36. HENRY SOUTHERN. See No. 1685.

1807 Blarney and Hypocrisy. A Sketch. 536-42.

1808 A Three Day's Walk in the Highlands. 542-53.

1809 London University. 554-59. HENRY SOUTHERN. An editorial note followed by a reprinting of the Prospectus of London University which was "circulated among the subscribers."

1810 Table Talk. 559-72. HENRY SOUTHERN. See No. 1693.

1811 Monthly Intelligence. 572-74. HENRY SOUTHERN, prob. See No. 1464. Signed contribution by ROBERT W. MOORE.

NEW SERIES. VOLUME VI. NUMBER XXI
SEPTEMBER 1826

1812 Journal of a Traveller on the Continent. No. VII. 1-25. T. J. HOGG. Repr. Journal of a Traveller.

1813 Confessions of a Theorist. Signed: Ex-Theorist. 25-34.

1814 Gaston de Blondeville; with an Essay on the Life and Writings of Mrs. Radcliffe. 34-40. HENRY SOUTHERN. Attr. Hughes.

1815 Adventures of a Foreigner in Greece. No. II. 40-60.

1816 A Watering Place. Signed: Bridget Oozeley. 60-67.

1817 Scraps, from the Correspondence of a Musical Dilettante travelling in Italy. No. II. 67-70.

1818 Cupid and Death. 70-74. Signed: N. O. H. I. 70-74. JOHN PAYNE COLLIER. Signature as in No. 1174.

1819 Diary for the Month of August. 75-91. HENRY SOUTHERN. See No. 1685.

1820 Four Years in France. 91-109. HENRY SOUTHERN. Attr. Hughes; on p. 109 he states he excerpted from this book in Table Talk of the previous month, No. 1810.

1821 Private History of the Rise and Fall of a Morning Paper. By a Parliamentary Reporter. Signed: K. N. 110-18. HENRY SOUTHERN. Attr. Hughes.

1822 Mier's Travels in Chile. 119-32. HENRY SOUTHERN. Attr. Hughes.

1823 Table Talk. 133-42. HENRY SOUTHERN. See No. 1693.

1824 Monthly Intelligence. 143-44. HENRY SOUTHERN, prob. See No. 1464. Signed contribution by ROBERT W. MOORE.

NEW SERIES. VOLUME VI. NUMBER XXII
OCTOBER 1826

1825 An Apology for the "Diary of a Constant Reader."
145-46. This number was conducted by a temporary
editor who, in this note, apologizes for the
absence of Southern's feature, as "we, his
'locum tenens,' are much too modest to attempt
to supply the hiatus." Thomas Thornton may have
been the editor of this number.

1826 Journal of a Traveller on the Continent. No.
VIII. 147-59. T. J. HOGG. Repr. Journal of a
Traveller.

1827 Wrestling. Signed: Gymnast. 160-63.

1828 Lord F. L. Gower's Faust. 164-73. HENRY SOUTHERN. Attr. Hughes.

1829 Scraps from the correspondence of a Musical
Dilettante travelling in Italy. No. III. 173-76.

1830 Adventures of a Foreigner in Greece. No. III.
177-95.

1831 Newhome. Signed: Quaestor. 195-203.

1832 The Women of Italy. 204-19. UGO FOSCOLO.
Ottolini, 49. Translation of article is attributed to SARAH AUSTIN by Vincent, 203. In
Courrier Anglais, IV, Martineau mistakenly gives
this to Stendhal.

1833 Irish Politics. Signed: J. C. F. 219-24.

1834 Butleriana. From Unpublished Manuscripts. No.
IV. 225-32. HENRY SOUTHERN. See No. 1687.

1835 Head's Journies Across the Pampas. 232-42.
HENRY SOUTHERN. Attr. Hughes; many excerpts from
the book appear in this month's Table Talk, No.
1838.

1836 Much-a-do About Nothing; or the Speculations of
a Connoisseur. Signed: Sombrerus. 243-54.

1837 Memoirs of Casanova. By Himself. 254-85.
SARAH AUSTIN. Attr. Hughes; introductory note
by translator, followed by translation of a
selection from Casanova.

1838 Table Talk. 285-94. HENRY SOUTHERN. See No. 1693.

1839 Monthly Intelligence. 294-96. HENRY SOUTHERN, prob. See No. 1464. Signed contribution by ROBERT W. MOORE.

NEW SERIES. VOLUME VI. NUMBER XXIII
NOVEMBER 1826

1840 Matrimonial Tactics. Signed: Coelebs, Agt. 297-308. HENRY SOUTHERN. Attr. Hughes.

1841 The Epic and the Romantic. 309-14.

1842 Odd Chapters of Truemaine, Or the Man Without Refinement. 1820-6. Chap. X. Chap. XII. 315-33.

1843 Adventures of a Foreigner in Greece. No. IV. 333-51.

1844 Diary for the Month of October. 352-77. HENRY SOUTHERN. See No. 1685.

1845 Documents Respecting Milton, Found in the State Paper Office. 377-96. HENRY SOUTHERN. Style; largely extracts from H. I. Todd's Some Account of the Life and Writings of John Milton (1826).

1846 Butleriana. From Unpublished Manuscripts. No. V. 396-401. HENRY SOUTHERN. See No. 1687.

1847 Sketch of the History of the Museum of Natural History at Paris, Commonly Called the Jardin Des Plantes. 401-19. Untraced, perhaps Henry Southern, as the end of the article has a strong editorial tone.

1848 Memoirs of Lindley Murray. 419-30. HENRY SOUTHERN. Attr. Hughes.

1849 Elegiac Stanzas on a Watchman. 431-33.

1850 Table Talk. 433-46. HENRY SOUTHERN. See No. 1693.

1851 Monthly Intelligence. 446-48. HENRY SOUTHERN, prob. See No. 1464. Signed contribution by ROBERT W. MOORE.

NEW SERIES. VOLUME VI. NUMBER XXIV
DECEMBER 1826

1852 Appendix to the Black Book. 449-60. HENRY
SOUTHERN. Editorial statement with many extracts.

1853 A Visit to Brighton. 460-66. MARY SHELLEY.
Attr. Robinson, K-SJ, 28, and in private
correspondence, on persuasive internal evidence.

1854 American Dramatists. A Letter from Philadelphia.
Signed: S. 466-70.

1855 "The Age." 471-78.

1856 Souvenir Books, or Joint-Stock Literature. 478-
83. HENRY SOUTHERN. Attr. Hughes.

1857 Pere La Chaise. 484-96.

1858 Mr. Hood's Whims. 496-503. HENRY SOUTHERN.
Attr. Hughes; see No. 1917.

1859 War in America. 504-21. HENRY SOUTHERN.
Attr. Hughes; in No. 1879, p. 134, he refers to
this review as his.

1860 Dr. Southwood Smith's Lectures on Comparative and
Human Physiology. Signed: H. 522-30. SOUTH-
WOOD SMITH, as reported by HENRY SOUTHERN.
Hughes speculates that Smith, a frequent contri-
butor to the Westminster, of which Southern was
co-editor, lent the manuscript of the lectures to
Southern.

1861 Adventures of a Foreigner in Greece. No. V.
531-47.

1862 Diary for the Month of November. 548-57. HENRY
SOUTHERN. See No. 1685.

1863 Episodes of the Don Quixote. No. I. 557-66.

1864 The Unconscious Rivals. A Dramatic Sketch.
Signed: F. K. 566-72.

1865 Magaziniana. 572-87. HENRY SOUTHERN. This new
feature is an expansion of the Table Talk. Along
with excerpts from books as in the earlier series,
here he intends to answer correspondents, to include letters and brief pieces, parts of articles
that do not warrant full inclusion, editorial
notices, apologies, and explanations. Within two
or three months, however, this feature contained

1866 Monthly Intelligence. 588-90. HENRY SOUTHERN, prob. See No. 1464. Signed contribution by ROBERT W. MOORE.

NEW SERIES. VOLUME VII
JANUARY 1827

1867 Periodical Literature of Germany. 1-11. Untraced, perhaps Henry Southern, who ordinarily reviewed other periodicals.

1868 Episodes of the Don Quixote. No. II. Signed: G. F. 11-19.

1869 Sketches of Manners in the South of France. No. I. 19-25.

1870 Impertinent Curiosity; or Curious Impertinence. Signed: Minimum. 25-43.

1871 Dr. Southwood Smith's Lectures, on Comparative and Human Physiology. 43-51. SOUTHWOOD SMITH, as recorded by HENRY SOUTHERN. See No. 1860.

1872 Tales of the O'Hara Family.--Second Series. 51-73. HENRY SOUTHERN. Southern reviewed the first of the series, No. 1630; long excerpts; style.

1873 Adventures of a Foreigner in Greece. No. VI. 73-91.

1874 The General Trader [verse]. Signed: N. B. 92-103.

1875 Almack's, A Novel. 103-19.

1876 Diary for the Month of December. 119-26. HENRY SOUTHERN. See No. 1685.

1877 James's Naval History. 127-31. HENRY SOUTHERN, prob. Southern's interest in military history and military biography reveals itself often in his selection of books for review; ends with editorial promise to return to review in order to provide excerpts, which he does in No. 1905.

1878 Alderman Waithman v. Joint Stock Companies. 131-34.

1879   Magaziniana. 134-41. HENRY SOUTHERN. See No. 1865.

1880   Monthly Intelligence. 142-44. HENRY SOUTHERN, prob. See No. 1464. Signed contribution by ROBERT W. MOORE.

NEW SERIES. VOLUME VII
FEBRUARY 1827

1881   Sketches of Manners in the South of France. No. II. 145-51.

1882   The Troubles of a Game Proprietor. Signed: N. 152-59.

1883   Six Months in the West Indies. (Second Edition.) Signed: X. 160-67.

1884   A Trance. Signed: St. Alcohol. 167-69.

1885   Odd Chapters of Truemaine, Or the Man Without Refinement. 1820-6. Chap. XIV. Chap. XX. 170-91.

1886   Scenes and Sketches of a Soldier's Life in Ireland. 191-200. HENRY SOUTHERN, prob. See No. 1877.

1887   Thursday, Eighteenth of January. 200-04.

1888   Twelfth Night at Almack's. Signed: R--d***. 205-15.

1889   Turner's Reign of Henry the Eighth. 215-32.

1890   Birmah. 232-44.

1891   The Blue Man. Signed: L. L. 244-48.

1892   Summary of the National Lament for January 1827 /verse/. Signed: Eheu! 248-49.

1893   Newly Discovered Disinfectants. 250-61.

1894   Account of the Death of Count de Benyowsky. Signed: R. E. S. 261-68.

1895   Magaziniana. 269-85. HENRY SOUTHERN. See No. 1865.

1896 Monthly Intelligence. 285-88. HENRY SOUTHERN, prob. See No. 1464. Signed contribution by ROBERT W. MOORE.

NEW SERIES. VOLUME VII
MARCH 1827

1897 A Cockney's Journey to Ireland. Signed: Bob Trimmings. 289-309.

1898 Cranbourn Chace. Signed: Ερηυος. 309-13.

1899 Parochial and Topographical Queries. 313-24.

1900 Curious Religious Controversy Between the Chief Chaplain of the Grand Signor, and Panaiotti Nicussio, Interpreter to the Grand Vizier Kiopruli, in the Year 1662. Signed: R. E. S. 325-32.

1901 Calamities of London. Signed: L. L. 333-35.

1902 Troubadour Poems, From Original MSS. Signed: R.E.S. 335-40.

1903 Self-Introduction. 341-53.

1904 The Gondola. 354-60. HENRY SOUTHERN, prob. This review of H. S. Van Dyk's book is almost entirely excerpts, for which no editor would pay; Van Dyk was a former contributor to the London.

1905 James's Naval History. 360-77. HENRY SOUTHERN, prob. See No. 1877; Southern resumes his review of this volume in order to give excerpts.

1906 King's Australia. 377-88.

1907 Truckleborough Hall. 389-99.

1908 Munster Tales. 399-401. HENRY SOUTHERN. Style; in No. 2031, the reviewer admits to the writing of this and the admission is decidedly editorial.

1909 Discovery of the Sources of the Mississippi and Red River. 401-06.

1910 Diary for the Month of February. 406-21. HENRY SOUTHERN. See No. 1685.

1911   Dr. Lingard and the Edinburgh Review. 421-29.
       JOSEPH PARKES. Neal, 290, explains this was
       written for the Westminster, but transferred to
       the London with the author's permission.

1912   Royal Institution. 430-31.

1913   Zoological Society. 431.

1914   Magaziniana. 432-37. HENRY SOUTHERN. See No.
       1865.

1915   Monthly Intelligence. 438-40. HENRY SOUTHERN,
       prob. See No. 1464. Signed contribution by
       ROBERT W. MOORE.

NEW SERIES. VOLUME VII
APRIL 1827

1916   Alma Mater, or Seven Years at Cambridge. 441-54.
       HENRY SOUTHERN, prob. Southern was an alumnus of
       Cambridge and the writer here talks knowingly
       about his alma mater.

1917   National Tales. 454-60. HENRY SOUTHERN. Style;
       the writer admits he wrote on Hood twice before,
       in Nos. 1490 and 1858, and Hughes attributes both
       to Southern.

1918   Wallenstein. 460-66.

1919   The Living and the Dead. 466-71. HENRY SOUTHERN,
       prob. Style; the book reviewed is by a
       Cambridge-man and the reviewer indicates he is an
       alumnus, as was Southern.

1920   Vivian Grey: Second Part. 472-83. HENRY SOUTH-
       ERN, prob. Southern reviewed the first part,
       No. 1772.

1921   Fragment of a Letter from a Young Artist in Rome
       to his Friend in Venice, in 1575, Translated
       from a Foreign Original. 483-94.

1922   Daw's Reminiscences. Signed: Jack Daw. 494-504.

1923   Diary for the Month of March. 505-24. HENRY
       SOUTHERN. See No. 1685.

1924   The New Corn Law. 524-32.

1925 Sir Walter Scott and the Waverly /sic/ Novels. 533-35. HENRY SOUTHERN, prob. This strongly editorial statement declares Scott revealed himself as the author of the Waverley novels to forestall creditors from examining the books of Constable and Ballantyne, Scott's publishers.

1926 Buckingham's Mesopotamia. 536-59.

1927 Society for the Diffusion of Useful Knowledge. 559-67. Untraced, perhaps Charles Knight, who became the proprietor and editor of the London within a year and who championed the Society's aims and activities.

1928 Servian Popular Poetry. 567-83. HENRY SOUTHERN, prob. This is a highly laudatory review of a book by John Bowring, who was co-editor of the Westminster Review with Southern; in his next laudatory review of Bowring, No. 2012, he refers to this.

1929 Magaziniana. 583-89. HENRY SOUTHERN. See No. 1865.

1930 Monthly Intelligence. 590-92. HENRY SOUTHERN, prob. See No. 1464. Signed contribution by ROBERT W. MOORE.

NEW SERIES. VOLUME VIII
MAY 1827

1931 The Hamiltonian System. 1-8.

1932 Shakspeare Meeting at the Garrick's Head, Bow Street. 9-14.

1933 The Reviewers Reviewed. 15-29. Untraced correspondent and HENRY SOUTHERN. In parallel columns, Southern makes a running commentary on his correspondent's opinions.

1934 Sibyl Leaves. 29-36.

1935 DeVere. 36-50. HENRY SOUTHERN. The writer of this admits he also wrote No. 1515.

1936 Bees. 50-62.

1937 Diary for the Month of April. 63-78. HENRY SOUTHERN. See No. 1685.

1938 Mr. Canning and His Opponents. 78-84.

1939 Major Moody on Negro Labour, and the Edinburgh Review. 84-92.

1940 A Winter in Lapland. 92-108.

1941 The Military Sketch-Book. 108-15. HENRY SOUTHERN, prob. Writer notes with satisfaction the increase in military authors; see No. 1877.

1942 Flagellum Parliamentarium. 115-24.

1943 Proceedings of the Royal Institution of Great Britain. 124-25.

1944 Magaziniana. 125-33. HENRY SOUTHERN. See No. 1865.

1945 Monthly Intelligence. 134-36. HENRY SOUTHERN, prob. See No. 1464. Signed contribution by ROBERT W. MOORE.

NEW SERIES. VOLUME VIII
JUNE 1827

1946 Memoirs and Journal of Theobald Wolfe Tone. 137-51.

1947 Musical Reminiscences Respecting the Italian Opera in England. 151-60.

1948 Diary for the Month of May. 161-80. HENRY SOUTHERN. See No. 1685.

1949 French Theatre in Tottenham Street. 180-82.

1950 Hamel, the Obeah Man. 182-87.

1951 Historiettes, By the Author of "The English in Italy." 187-200.

1952 Journal of a Traveller on the Continent. 200-08. HENRY SOUTHERN, prob. Style; reference to the original publication of the book in the London as a serial.

1953 May Fair. 208-12.

1954   Alexander's Journey from India to England. 212-21. HENRY SOUTHERN, prob. Editorial statement at the end promises to resume this review.

1955   Autobiography of Thomas Dibdin. 221-40.

1956   Sir Jonah Barrington's Personal Sketches of His Own Times. 241-63.

1957   Emigration. 263-70.

1958   Proceedings of the Royal Institution of Great Britain. 270.

1959   Magaziniana. 271-82. HENRY SOUTHERN. See No. 1865.

1960   Monthly Intelligence. 282-84. HENRY SOUTHERN, prob. See No. 1464. Signed contribution by ROBERT W. MOORE.

NEW SERIES.   VOLUME VIII
JULY 1827

1961   Judson's Mission to the Burman Empire. 285-313.

1962   Political Economy. 313-20.

1963   Ben Nazir. 320-27.

1964   Banking--Small Notes. 327-38.

1965   Diary for the Month of June. 338-56. HENRY SOUTHERN. See No. 1685.

1966   Dr. Parr's Library of a Peer. 357-61. Untraced, perhaps by E. H. Barker, who was Parr's amanuensis; this "list of books, with the comments upon them, was dictated by Dr. Parr for the use of a young nobleman."

1967   Letters from a Travelling Artist to His Friend, in the Sixteenth Century. No. II. 361-74.

1968   Niebuhr's Roman History. 374-84.

1969   Philosophy in Sport. 384-400.

1970   The North American and Quarterly Reviews. 400-09. HENRY SOUTHERN, prob. Editorial policy of reviewing other periodicals.

1971   Rival Houses of York and Lancaster. 409-12.
        HENRY SOUTHERN. Style; writer of No. 2030 admits he also wrote this.

1972   History of William Pitt, Earl of Chatham. 412-18. HENRY SOUTHERN, prob. Editorial statement at the end promises to resume this review the next month.

1973   Magaziniana. 418-22. HENRY SOUTHERN. See No. 1865.

1974   Monthly Intelligence. 423-24. HENRY SOUTHERN, prob. See No. 1464. Signed contribution by ROBERT W. MOORE.

NEW SERIES.   VOLUME VIII
AUGUST 1827

1975   American Navy. 425-37. HENRY SOUTHERN, prob. See No. 1877.

1976   Madeira. 437-48. HENRY SOUTHERN. Editor admits authorship on p. 445n.

1977   High-Ways and By-Ways: Third Series. 448-53. HENRY SOUTHERN. Style; Southern reviewed first series, No. 1468.

1978   Goodhugh's Library Manual. 453-57.

1979   Diary of the Month of July. 458-77. HENRY SOUTHERN. See No. 1685.

1980   Life of Lord Eldon. 477-87. HENRY SOUTHERN. Admits to this review in No. 1994, p. 78.

1981   Thompson's Travels in Southern Africa. 487-508.

1982   The Wellesley Case. 508-17.

1983   Two Years in New South Wales. 517-31.

1984   Anecdotes of Animals. 531-41. HENRY SOUTHERN. Editorial note introduces extracts of The Animal Kingdom by BARON CUVIER translated by EDWARD GRIFFITH.

1985   Theodore Körner. 541-56.

1986 Anonymous Criticism. 556-62. HENRY SOUTHERN. Editorial defense of anonymous reviewing and criticism in periodicals.

1987 Magaziniana. 563-70. HENRY SOUTHERN. See No. 1865.

1988 Monthly Intelligence. 570-72. HENRY SOUTHERN, prob. See No. 1464. Signed contribution by ROBERT W. MOORE.

NEW SERIES. VOLUME IX
SEPTEMBER 1827

1989 The American Annual Register. 1-11.

1990 The Reign of Dr. Francia. 11-25.

1991 The Character of Lord Clarendon. 25-37.

1992 Memoirs of James Hardy Vaux. 38-55.

1993 Dr. Parr's Marginal Notes. 56-68. Untraced, perhaps E. H. Barker, who was Parr's amanuensis and who probably contributed to the London.

1994 Diary for the Month of August. 68-92. HENRY SOUTHERN. See No. 1685.

1995 The Household Book of Henry VIII. 92-102.

1996 Montgomery's Pelican Island. 102-11.

1997 The Persecution of Galileo. 112-20.

1998 Anecdotes of Animals. From Griffith's Translation of Cuvier's Animal Kingdom. 121-28. HENRY SOUTHERN, BARON CUVIER, and EDWARD GRIFFITH. See No. 1984.

1999 Two Years in Ava. 128-38.

2000 Magaziniana. 138-42. HENRY SOUTHERN. See No. 1865.

2001 Monthly Intelligence. 143-44. HENRY SOUTHERN, prob. See No. 1464. Signed contribution by ROBERT W. MOORE.

NEW SERIES. VOLUME IX
OCTOBER 1827

2002   Wadd's Mems. 145-51.

2003   Memoirs of Louis XII and Francis I. By P. L.
        Roederer. 151-61.

2004   Andrews's Journey in South America. 162-80.

2005   The Traveller's Oracle. 181-93.

2006   Diary for the Month of September. 193-206.
        HENRY SOUTHERN. See No. 1685.

2007   Notes and Reflections on a Visit to Paris. 206-
        14.

2008   Washington Papers. 215-28.

2009   Sure Methods of Improving Health and Prolonging
        Life. 228-38.

2010   Memoir of Ugo Foscolo. 238-44. ANTONIO PANIZZI.
        Attr. Hughes; repr. from the Liverpool Commercial
        Chronicle of this month.

2011   West Indies. 244-59.

2012   Bowring's Polish Poets. 259-71. HENRY SOUTHERN,
        prob. See No. 1928.

2013   Magaziniana. 271-86. HENRY SOUTHERN. See No.
        1865.

2014   Monthly Intelligence. 286-88. HENRY SOUTHERN,
        prob. See No. 1464. Signed contributions by
        ROBERT W. MOORE.

NEW SERIES. VOLUME IX
NOVEMBER 1827

2015   Club-Houses. 289-92.

2016   Kennedy's Fitful Fancies. 293-98.

2017   Nicolas's Battle of Agincourt. 299-310.

2018   A Fragment from the Memoirs of a Peasant. A
        True Story. 311-20.

2019   Diary for the Month of October. 321-341.
        HENRY SOUTHERN. See No. 1685.

2020   Chronicles of the Canongate. The Two Drovers.
        341-60. WALTER SCOTT, included by HENRY SOUTH-
        ERN. Editorial note explains that this yet
        unpublished tale of Walter Scott is part of a
        forthcoming book and is reprinted from the
        Weekly Review; see No. 2025.

2021   The Law of Blasphemy   360-62.

2022   Sketches of Persia. 363-82.

2023   Quarterly Review for October. No. LXXII. 382-
        95. HENRY SOUTHERN, prob. Editorial policy of
        reviewing other periodicals.

2024   The Annuals. 395-409. HENRY SOUTHERN, prob.
        The tone is editorial and the style is his.

2025   Sir Walter Scott's Last Novel. 409-25. HENRY
        SOUTHERN. The reviewer explains that the tale
        above, No. 2020, was set in print before the
        full work came for notice, information only the
        editor was likely to have.

2026   Magaziniana. 425-29. HENRY SOUTHERN. See No.
        1865.

2027   Monthly Intelligence. 429-32. HENRY SOUTHERN,
        prob. See No. 1464. Signed contribution by
        ROBERT W. MOORE.

           NEW SERIES.   VOLUME IX
              DECEMBER 1827

2028   The Tale of Modern Genius. 433-49.

2029   Death in a Bottle. 450-64.

2030   The Romance of History. 464-80. HENRY SOUTHERN.
        Style; writer admits to authorship of No. 1971.

2031   Tales of the Munster Festivals. 480-501. HENRY
        SOUTHERN. Style; writer admits to authorship of
        No. 1908.

2032   History of Gas-Lighting. 502-15.

2033   Diary for the Month of November. 516-37. HENRY
       SOUTHERN. See No. 1685.

2034   Hood's Whims, Second Series. 537-41. HENRY
       SOUTHERN, prob. Style; Southern reviewed three
       of Hood's earlier works, Nos. 1490, 1858, and
       1917, No. 1858 being Whims and Oddities, first
       series.

2035   Hindoo Widows. 541-52.

2036   War in Greece. 553-61.

2037   Magaziniana. 561-72. HENRY SOUTHERN. See No.
       1865.

2038   Monthly Intelligence. 573-76. HENRY SOUTHERN,
       prob. See No. 1464. Signed contribution by
       ROBERT W. MOORE.

NEW SERIES.   VOLUME X
JANUARY 1828

2039   Roberts's Voyages and Excursions in the Interior
       of Central America. 1-14.

2040   French Charity Schools. Signed: A. Y. 14-28.

2041   Lady Morgan's O'Briens and O'Flahertys. 28-45.

2042   Italian Martyrs. 45-55.

2043   The Annuals. 55-67. HENRY SOUTHERN, prob. See
       No. 2024, of which this is a continuation.

2044   Boyle Farm. 68-71.

2045   Diary for the Month of December. 71-84. HENRY
       SOUTHERN. See No. 1685.

2046   Elizabeth Evanshaw. 84-99.

2047   Sir Michael Scott. 99-101. HENRY SOUTHERN, prob.
       Style; references to an earlier review are edi-
       torial in tone.

2048   The Red Rover. 101-20.

2049   Magaziniana. 120-33. HENRY SOUTHERN. See No.
       1865.

2050 Monthly Intelligence. 134-36. HENRY SOUTHERN, prob. See No. 1464. Signed contribution by ROBERT W. MOORE.

NEW SERIES. VOLUME X
FEBRUARY 1828

2051 Character of Lord Collingwood. 137-54.

2052 Beaumont's Travels in Buenos Ayres. 154-61.

2053 Drowning the Miller. An Ulster Tale. 161-78.

2054 Musicians and Musicsellers. 178-80.

2055 The New Tragedy at Covent Garden. 180-84.

2056 Diary for the Month of January. 185-211. HENRY SOUTHERN. See No. 1685.

2057 Leigh Hunt's Lord Byron. 211-33. HENRY SOUTHERN. Style; references to his earlier discussion of Byron, No. 1364.

2058 Dr. Channing's Character of Napoleon Buonaparte. 233-38.

2059 Herbert Milton.--Herbert Lacy. 238-45.

2060 History of the Court of Chancery. 246-54.

2061 Books, Booksellers, and Bookmakers. 254-60.

2062 Crockford's: or, Life in the West. 260-69.

2063 Magaziniana. 269-78. HENRY SOUTHERN. See No. 1865.

2064 Monthly Intelligence. 278-80. HENRY SOUTHERN, prob. See No. 1464. Signed contribution by ROBERT W. MOORE.

NEW SERIES. VOLUME X
MARCH 1828

2065 Columbus. 281-325.

2066 New Brunswick Theatre, Goodman's Fields. 325-28.

2067 Sonnet, Written in the First Leaf of an Album. 328.

2068 Songs. 329.

2069 "Anticreed," or "A Code of Unbelief." 330-38.

2070 Massaniello: A Dramatic Fragment. 339-44.

2071 Sonnets. 344.

2072 Diary for the Month of February. 345-61. HENRY SOUTHERN. See No. 1685.

2073 Inundations in Holland in 1825. 362-74.

2074 Plan of an Epic Poem Designed by Pope. 374-78.

2075 The Drama. 379-81.

2076 Sayings and Doings. 381-95.

2077 On the Author of the Whole Duty of Man. 395-96.

2078 The Splügen. A Letter from a Friend. 396-402.

2079 February [verse]. 402-04.

2080 John Rose, The Gauger. 404-10.

2081 Scandal of the Court of Napoleon. 410-18.

2082 Monthly Intelligence. 419-22. HENRY SOUTHERN, prob. See No. 1464. Signed contribution by ROBERT W. MOORE.

THIRD SERIES. VOLUME I. NUMBER I
APRIL 1828

2083 Advertisement. New Series of the London Magazine. 1-2. CHARLES KNIGHT. The context makes it clear that this is by the editor. In some sets this item is bound with the March number.

2084 Education of the People. 1-13. CHARLES KNIGHT. Knight, Passages of a Working Life, II, 67.

2085 Pleasures of a Sleepless Night. 13-18.

2086 Notes on Art. 18-33.

2087 Characters of Contemporary Foreign Authors and Statesmen. No. I. Abbé Frayssinous. No. II. M. Royer Collard. 34-41. F. DEGEORGE. See No. 2166.

2088 The Roué. 41-48.

2089 Present State of Switzerland. 49-64. F. B. B. ST. LEGER. Attr. Hughes.

2090 Sonnets. 64.

2091 The Philharmonic Society. 65-66.

2092 Engravings. 66.

2093 Family Portraits. No. I. The Family Historian. 67-83. F. B. B. ST. LEGER. Clowes, 163.

2094 The Early History of Rome. 84-90.

2095 Private Correspondence, No. I. Hints from a Veteran Contributor. 90-96. CHARLES KNIGHT and F. B. B. ST. LEGER. Editors state that in this feature, which only ran another two months, they would print and answer correspondence "touching the interest and progress of this our Magazine."

2096 The Foreign Portfolio. 96-108. In July, 1828, the editor stated this "Department of the Magazine is in the hands of literary foreigners of eminence, belonging to the various countries of Europe respectively" (No. 2146, p. 578).

2097 Diary for the Month of March. 109-29. CHARLES

	KNIGHT and F. B. B. ST. LEGER. Clowes, 164.
2098	The Philosophy of Mind. 130-38.
2099	The Editor's Room. 139-60. CHARLES KNIGHT and F. B. B. ST. LEGER. This feature contains several brief book reviews and, as Hughes states, was written largely by Knight.

THIRD SERIES. VOLUME I. NUMBER II
MAY 1828

2100	Robert Burns. 161-70.
2101	The Mystic School. 170-76. CHARLES KNIGHT. Attr. Bauer, 294.
2102	The Condition of the Irish Poor: A Letter to a Member of Parliament from a Friend in Ireland. 177-83. F. B. B. ST. LEGER. Editorial admission of authorship in No. 2260, p. 312.
2103	The Eastern Story-Tellers. 183-86. F. B. B. ST. LEGER. Attr. Hughes.
2104	The Northern Frontiers of Turkey. 187-95.
2105	Stonehenge. 195-204.
2106	The Calcutta Stamp Duty. 205-08. F. B. B. ST. LEGER. Attr. Hughes.
2107	Salathiel. 209-19.
2108	Characters of Contemporary Foreign Authors and Statesmen. No. III. Baron Cuvier. No. IV. Casimir Delavigne. 220-27. F. DEGEORGE. See No. 2166.
2109	Poor-Laws--Emigration. 227-41. F. B. B. ST. LEGER. Attr. Hughes.
2110	Family Portraits. No. II. Sir Eustace the Gascon. 242-52. F. B. B. ST. LEGER. Clowes, 163.
2111	The Leading Profession. 252-57. CHARLES KNIGHT. Repr. Once Upon a Time, II.
2112	The Foreign Portfolio. 258-66. See No. 2096.
2113	Musical Chit Chat. 266-68.
2114	Diary for the Month of April. 269-81. CHARLES KNIGHT and F. B. B. ST. LEGER. Clowes, 164.

2115 Private Correspondence. No. II. Thefts of the Poets. 282-92. CHARLES KNIGHT and F. B. B. ST. LEGER. See No. 2095.

2116 The Editor's Room. No. II. 292-308. CHARLES KNIGHT and F. B. B. ST. LEGER. See No. 2099.

THIRD SERIES. VOLUME I. NUMBER III
JUNE 1828

2117 Reforms in the Law. No. I. The History of a Suit. 309-30. F. B. B. ST. LEGER. Editorial admission of authorship in headnote to No. 2131, p. 469, and again in No. 2219, p. 676. St. Leger, the co-editor, had an interest in the law and the style is his.

2118 Mr. Hunt in Paris. Signed: P. Q. 331-37. Includes a signed letter from HENRY HUNT.

2119 Our Village (Vol. III). 337-40.

2120 A Visit to an Abbey of La Trappe; with Some Account of the Rules and Regulations of the Order. 341-52.

2121 The German Gibbet. 352-59.

2122 On the State and Prospects of Portugal. 359-76.

2123 Notes on Art. 376-86.

2124 The Deserted House. 386-91.

2125 Characters of Contemporary Foreign Authors and Statesmen. No. V. Mons. Jacques Laffitte, with a Preliminary Notice of the Chamber of Deputies. 391-97. F. DEGEORGE. See No. 2166.

2126 Supply of Water in London. 398-407.

2127 Private Correspondence. No. III. House of Commons, Session 1828--Supply of Anatomical Subjects. 408-16. CHARLES KNIGHT and F. B. B. ST. LEGER. See No. 2095.

2128 The Foreign Portfolio. No. III. 417-33. See No. 2096.

2129 Diary for the Month of May. 433-49. CHARLES KNIGHT and F. B. B. ST. LEGER. Clowes, 164.

2130 The Editor's Room. No. III. 449-68. CHARLES KNIGHT and F. B. B. ST. LEGER. See No. 2099.

THIRD SERIES. VOLUME I. NUMBER IV
JULY 1828

2131 A Lecture on the Law of Descents. 469-80. This was sent by an unidentified contributor, but in the headnote on p. 469, the editor admits to the authorship of the "Reforms in the Law" series.

2132 The Two London Colleges. 480-86. CHARLES KNIGHT. Attr. Hughes; this is a plea for universal education, one of Knight's abiding concerns.

2133 On the Freemasons, Jesuits and Jews of Portugal. 487-97.

2134 Notes on Art. 497-500.

2135 The Georama. 501-04. CHARLES KNIGHT, prob. In editorial tones, the writer approves of the diffusion of knowledge.

2136 Characters of Contemporary Foreign Authors and Statesmen. No. VI. Le Vicomte de Chateaubriand. 504-10. F. DEGEORGE. See No. 2166.

2137 The Rosicrucian. 510-19.

2138 Vindiciae OEconomicae. 519-27. Untraced, perhaps F. B. B. St. Leger as indicated by the note on p. 521.

2139 The Foreign Portfolio. No. IV. 527-40. See No. 2096.

2140 The New Ministry. 540-46. F. B. B. ST. LEGER. Attr. Hughes.

2141 Lines Written at the Opera in Vienna, on seeing the Duke of Reichstadt. Signed: C. F. G. 546-47.

2142 Adventures of an Italian among the Indians of North America. 548-53. Untraced, perhaps Charles Knight as the opening sentence is clearly an editorial statement.

2143 French Plays in London. 553-63.

2144 Mornings Among the Cobwebs. No. I. 563-70. CHARLES KNIGHT, prob. Knight's interest in books and older literature is reflected by the subtitle to this series, "extracts from, and reprints of, curious and long forgotten publications, with biographical and illustrative notes."

2145 Tim Bobbin. 570-76.

2146 Diary for the Month of June. 577-90. CHARLES KNIGHT and F. B. B. ST. LEGER. Clowes, 164.

2147 Family Portraits. No. III. The Spanish Lady. 591-603. F. B. B. ST. LEGER. Clowes, 163.

2148 The Editor's Room. No. IV. 604-20. CHARLES KNIGHT and F. B. B. ST. LEGER. See No. 2099.

THIRD SERIES. VOLUME II. NUMBER V
AUGUST 1828

2149 Reforms in the Law. No. II. The Law of Real Property. 1-26. F. B. B. ST. LEGER. See No. 2117.

2150 Roads and Road-making. 26-34.

2151 Mornings Among the Cobwebs. No. II. 34-42. CHARLES KNIGHT, prob. See No. 2144.

2152 The Husband's Complaint /verse/. 42-43.

2153 Latest Intelligence of our Water Companies. Signed: AEvah. 44-46.

2154 The Religious World Displayed, In a Series of Sketches Chiefly from the Life. No. I. Rev. Edward Irving. 46-54. CHARLES KNIGHT. Editorial admission of authorship in the headnote to No. 2261, p. 327; style.

2155 Scotch Note Bill. 54-63. CHARLES KNIGHT. Editorial admission of authorship in No. 2212, p. 607; style.

2156 Historical Persons and their Portraits. 63-75.

2157 Characters of Contemporary Foreign Authors and Statesmen. No. VII. Madame de Genlis. 76-79. F. DEGEORGE. See No. 2166.

2158 Salmonia; or Days of Fly-Fishing. 79-92. CHARLES KNIGHT. Partially repr. Passages, II, 97-99.

2159 Unambitious Love /verse/. Signed: C. F. G. 92-93.

2160 Our National Architecture. 94-109. CHARLES KNIGHT, prob. Opening sentence is an editorial assertion "to devote a few papers" to this subject.

2161 Diary for the Month of June. 110-22. CHARLES KNIGHT and F. B. B. ST. LEGER. Clowes, 164.

2162 The Dreamings of an Idealist. 122-25.

2163 The Editor's Room. No. V. 126-44. CHARLES KNIGHT and F. B. B. ST. LEGER. See No. 2099.

THIRD SERIES. VOLUME II. NUMBER VI
SEPTEMBER 1828

2164 Private Bills of the Session 1828. 145-60. CHARLES KNIGHT and F. B. B. ST. LEGER. Clowes, 163.

2165 Journal of a Chaplain in the Army of the Pretender. 161-73.

2166 Characters of Contemporary Foreign Authors and Statesmen. No. VIII. De Béranger. 173-78. F. DEGEORGE. Under sentence of death for his political activities, Degeorge took refuge in London in 1824, and during his exile, he wrote for several English periodicals, including the London. In a letter to Knight of 1828 (see No. 2167 for misdating), St. Leger sent a "translation of an article on Béranger, which I have received from poor Degeorge..." (Clowes, 164). That Degeorge did this whole series is clearly indicated by Andre Fortin, who states that Degeorge's articles in the English periodicals were on literature and politics (p. 24), a description which coincides precisely with this series.

2167 Some Account of a late Trial for Murder--not Corder's. 179-87. F. B. B. ST. LEGER. Clowes, 164. Clowes quotes a letter from St. Leger to Knight which refers to an article with this title. The letter is dated 1825 by Clowes, but since Corder's trial did not take place until 1828, this is obviously incorrect. Clowes erroneously supposes the article to have been contributed to Knight's Quarterly Magazine.

2168 Historic Survey of German Poetry. 188-97.

2169 Our National Architecture. No. II. 198-202.
CHARLES KNIGHT, prob. See No. 2160.

2170 Family Portraits. No. IV. The Page. 203-17.
F. B. B. ST. LEGER. Clowes, 163.

2171 On the Secrecy of Letters in France. 218-22.

2172 The Pleasures of Ornithology. 223-28. Untraced,
perhaps Edward Stanley who, on 26 June 1828,
wrote to Knight on ornithology (see Clowes, 177).

2173 Notes on Art. 229-31.

2174 The First Time of Asking. 231-35.

2175 The Native Irish. 236-47. F. B. B. ST. LEGER.
Attr. Hughes; similar opinions were previously
expressed by the Irishman St. Leger in No. 2109.

2176 Illustrations of Virginia Water. 247-50.

2177 A Thought of Harrow [verse]. Signed: The
Harrovian. 250. R. E. A. WILLMOTT. Signature.

2178 Diary for the Month of August. 251-65. CHARLES
KNIGHT and F. B. B. ST. LEGER. Clowes, 164.

2179 Anatomy. 265-71. CHARLES KNIGHT. An abridgement of the "Report from the Select Committee on Anatomy" is preceded by an editorial paragraph which states, "we may probably reserve its consideration for a future No."

2180 Editor's Room. No. VI. 271-86. CHARLES KNIGHT
and F. B. B. ST. LEGER. See No. 2099.

THIRD SERIES. VOLUME II. NUMBER VII
OCTOBER 1828

2181 Reforms in the Law. No. III. The Magistracy.
287-98. F. B.B. ST. LEGER. See No. 2117.

2182 Dramatic Literature. 298-302. F. B. B. ST. LEGER
and CHARLES BUCKE. Editorial comment introduces
letters between Bucke and the lessee of Drury
Lane Theatre.

2183 Elementary Education. No. I. 303-17. MATHEW
D. HILL. Attr. Hughes.

2184 On the Present State of Opinion in Ireland. 318-29. F. B. B. ST. LEGER. Attr. Hughes.

2185 Mornings Among the Cobwebs. No. III. 330-42. CHARLES KNIGHT, prob. See No. 2144.

2186 A Comparative View of the State of Trade in the Years 1826, 7 & 8. 343-55.

2187 The Duke of Newcastle's Opinions upon Toleration and Liberality. 355-59.

2188 Gale of the Waters /verse/. Signed: The Harrovian. 360-61. R. E. A. WILLMOTT. Signature.

2189 An Account of the present State of Tripoli. 361-66. CHARLES KNIGHT, prob. An abstract of an article which appeared in an Italian journal, written by "the Swedish Consul at Tripoli, M. Graberg de Hemso."

2190 Biographies of Dr. Parr. 367-75.

2191 The Religious World Displayed. Sketch II. The Rev. Dr. Chalmers. 376-81. CHARLES KNIGHT. See No. 2261.

2192 Pelham: or the Adventures of a Gentleman. 371 /mispaginated/-88. CHARLES KNIGHT. Attr. Hughes.

2193 Diary for the Month of September. 389-405. CHARLES KNIGHT and F. B. B. ST. LEGER. Clowes, 164.

2194 War of Independence in South America. 406-21.

2195 Editor's Room. No. VII. 422-30. CHARLES KNIGHT and F. B. B. ST. LEGER. See No. 2099.

THIRD SERIES. VOLUME II. NUMBER VIII
NOVEMBER 1828

2196 Opening of the University of London. 431-40.

2197 Some Account of the Pauper-Colonies of Holland. 440-46. Title misplaced and mispaginated on contents page.

2198 The late Harvest. 447-54.

2199 The Last Day of the Year in Vienna. 454-56.

2200 The Narrative of a Convict. Signed: J. W. 457-59. THOMAS WILLIAMS. Editorial note gives the name of the writer, but also states that the article was sent by mail by an unknown contributor.

2201 Family Portraits. No. V. Good Sir Walter. 460-75. F. B. B. ST. LEGER. Clowes, 163.

2202 Drummond of Hawthornden; By a Lover of Old English Poetry. 476-81. CHARLES KNIGHT. Attr. Hughes.

2203 Arrest of Mr. Lawless. 481-90. F. B. B. ST. LEGER. Attr. Hughes; opening sentence refers to No. 2184.

2204 Quarter Sessions. Signed: A Barrister. 490-92.

2205 A Woman's History. 493-503.

2206 Elementary Education. No. II. 504-06. MATHEW D. HILL. Attr. Hughes.

2207 Mr. Haydon's Picture of Chairing the Members. 507-16.

2208 Diary for the Month of October. 517-42. CHARLES KNIGHT and F. B. B. ST. LEGER. Clowes, 164.

2209 The Editor's Room. No. VIII. 543-74. CHARLES KNIGHT and F. B. B. ST. LEGER. See No. 2099.

THIRD SERIES. VOLUME II. NUMBER IX
DECEMBER 1828

2210 Comparative Statistics of France and Great Britain. 575-90.

2211 The English Almanacs. 591-606. CHARLES KNIGHT. Attr. Hughes.

2212 The Money Market. 607-15. CHARLES KNIGHT. On p. 607 editor admits to authorship of earlier article, No. 2155.

2213 Traps for Human Beings. 615-19. CHARLES KNIGHT or F. B. B. ST. LEGER. See No. 2219.

2214 Monti. 619-29.

2215   On Sympathetic Numbers. 629-33.

2216   Fagging. 633-44.

2217   Copyright. 645-60.

2218   The Minister of Inverdonhuil. 661-74.

2219   Diary for the Month of November. 675-89. CHARLES KNIGHT and F. B. B. ST. LEGER. See No. 2097. On p. 676 is an editorial admission of authorship of the series, "Reforms in the Law." On p. 683, one of the editors states, "we have, in another part of our present Number, commented with some severity upon the conduct of this person who set the pit-fall trap," an allusion to No. 2213 above.

2220   Sonnet. Written in a Theatre. 689.

2221   The Editor's Room. No. IX. 690-800 /misnumbered for 710/. CHARLES KNIGHT and F. B. B. ST. LEGER. See No. 2099.

THIRD SERIES. VOLUME III. NUMBER X
JANUARY 1829

2222   The Silk Question. 1-9. F. B. B. ST. LEGER. Attr. Hughes.

2223   The Theatre. 10-14.

2224   Arrivals at a Watering Place /verse/. Signed: Ξ. 14-16. W. M. PRAED. Young, xxx.

2225   A Visit to the Court of Madagascar. Signed: H. M. 17-27.

2226   The Disowned. 28-44. CHARLES KNIGHT. Attr. Hughes.

2227   A Looking-Glass for London. No. I. The Tower. 45-65. CHARLES KNIGHT. Attr. Hughes; in the next number, Knight shifts focus and directs his looking-glass to the country, "Windsor as it was"; see Nos. 2236 and 2241.

2228   Diary for the Month of December. 66-78. CHARLES KNIGHT and F. B. B. ST. LEGER. Clowes, 164.

2229   Hungarian Tales. 78-86. CHARLES KNIGHT. Attr. Hughes.

2230 The Separation /verse/. Signed: ξ. 87-88. E. M. FITZGERALD. Young, xxx.

2231 The Editor's Room. No. X. 89-96. CHARLES KNIGHT and F. B. B. ST. LEGER. See No. 2099.

THIRD SERIES. VOLUME III. NUMBER XI
FEBRUARY 1829

2232 On the Approaching Session of Parliament. 97-103. F. B. B. ST. LEGER. Attr. Hughes.

2233 The Colosseum. 104-08. CHARLES KNIGHT. Attr. Hughes; similar to Passages, II, 107-08.

2234 Imprisonment for Debt. 109-12.

2235 The Best Bat in the School. Signed: P. C. 113-17. W. M. PRAED. Repr. Essays.

2236 On the Armour in the Tower. 117-20. CHARLES KNIGHT and SAMUEL R. MEYRICK. Editorial comments with a signed letter by Meyrick discussing No. 2227.

2237 Supply of Anatomical Subjects. 121-32.

2238 You'll Come to Our Ball /verse/. Signed: Ξ. 133-34. W. M. PRAED. Young, xxx.

2239 Paris in 1828. 135-42.

2240 Moral Tendencies of Knowledge. 143-55. CHARLES KNIGHT. Attr. Hughes; discusses the Society for the Diffusion of Useful Knowledge, one of Knight's abiding concerns.

2241 A Looking-Glass for the Country. No. I. Windsor as it was. 155-63. CHARLES KNIGHT. Repr. Once Upon a Time, II.

2242 Stanzas. To---. Signed: ξ. 164-65. E. M. FITZGERALD. Young, xxx.

2243 Diary for the Month of January. 166-79. CHARLES KNIGHT and F. B. B. ST. LEGER. Clowes, 164.

2244 Hobbledehoys /verse/. Signed: ξ. 180-81. E. M. FITZGERALD. Young, xxx.

2245 The Editor's Room. No. XI. 181-96. CHARLES KNIGHT and F. B. B. ST. LEGER. See No. 2099.

THIRD SERIES. VOLUME III. NUMBER XII
MARCH 1829

2246 Currency.--Mr. Tooke's Letter to Lord Grenville. 197-207. CHARLES KNIGHT, prob. Knight wrote on this subject in Nos. 2155 and 2212.

2247 Universal Biographies. 207-23. CHARLES KNIGHT. Attr. Hughes; this is a defense of the "Library of Entertaining Knowledge" which Knight later published.

2248 The Inconvenience of having an Elder Brother. Signed: P. C. 224-27. W. M. PRAED. Repr. Essays.

2249 School and Schoolfellows /verse/. Signed: ııı . 227-28. W. M. PRAED. Young, xxx.

2250 The Life and Writings of Dr. Thomas Brown. 229-39.

2251 Stanzas. To--. Signed: ξ. 239-40. E. M. FITZ-GERALD. Young, xxx.

2252 Modern French Poetry. "Les Orientales." Par Victor Hugo. 240-46.

2253 Crime and its Prevention. No. I. 246-60. F. B. B. ST. LEGER. Attr. Hughes.

2254 The Philosophy of Statistics. 261-66.

2255 The Catholic Question. 267-71. F. B. B. ST. LEGER. Attr. Hughes; the opening sentence refers to No. 2232.

2256 Pope Leo XII. 272-75.

2257 Diary for the Month of February. 275-90. CHARLES KNIGHT and F. B. B. ST. LEGER. Clowes, 164.

2258 Notes on Art. The British Institution. 290-94.

2259 The Editor's Room. No. XII. 294-304. CHARLES KNIGHT and F. B. B. ST. LEGER. See No. 2099.

THIRD SERIES. VOLUME III. NUMBER XIII
APRIL 1829

2260 The One Subject. 305-27. F. B. B. ST. LEGER. Attr. Hughes; on p. 312 the writer admits to authorship of No. 2102.

2261 The Rev. Thomas Chalmers, D. D. Professor of Divinity in the University of Edinburgh. 327-33. In the headnote on p. 327, referring to the second article in the series, "The Religious World Displayed," No. 2191, the editor indicates that he is the author of the series.

2262 Toujours Perdrix. Signed: P. C. 333-36. W. M. PRAED. Repr. Essays.

2263 Barba Yorghi, the Greek Pilot. 337-46.

2264 Every Man's Master. L'Hygiene.--French and English Dietetics. 346-58. CHARLES KNIGHT. Editorial admission of authorship, for which see No. 2288.

2265 American Criticism. 358-66.

2266 A Visit to Hazelwood School. Signed: A Friend of Education. 367-86. Untraced, perhaps Mathew D. Hill who wrote two articles, Nos. 2183 and 2206, on education for Knight.

2267 Breaking the Spell. 386-89.

2268 The Death of the Catholic Question. 389-95.

2269 April Fools /verse/. Signed: Ξ. 396-97. W. M. PRAED. Young, xxx.

2270 Carsten Niebuhr. A Biography by His Son, The Author of the Roman History. 398-406.

2271 Dreams /verse/. Signed: ξ. 406-07. E. M. FITZGERALD. Young, xxx.

2272 Diary for the Month of March. 407-16. CHARLES KNIGHT and F. B. B. ST. LEGER. Clowes, 164.

THIRD SERIES. VOLUME III. NUMBER XIV
MAY 1829

2273 Reforms in the Law. No. IV. The Magistracy Bill. 417-28. F. B. B. ST. LEGER. See No. 2117.

2274   The Present Proceedings of the Theatres. 429-32.
        F. B. B. ST. LEGER. Attr. Hughes.

2275   Every Man's Master (concluded from p. 358). 433-
        37. CHARLES KNIGHT. Editorial admission of
        authorship, for which see No. 2288.

2276   Family Portraits. No. VI. The Second Best. 437-
        47. F. B. B. ST. LEGER. Clowes, 163.

2277   Popular Education. 447-63. CHARLES KNIGHT. On
        p. 451 the reference to No. 2084 reveals common
        authorship; contains many comments on the Society
        for the Diffusion of Useful Knowledge.

2278   A Short Story. 464-69.

2279   The Dramas of Euripides: The Hecuba. Signed: The
        Harrovian. 469-75. R. E. A. WILLMOTT. Signature.

2280   Professor Leslie. 475-81.

2281   A Journey from Athens to Missolonghi, In the
        Autumn of 1822. 481-95.

2282   The Journal of a Naturalist. 495-504.

2283   Diary for the Month of April. 505-14. CHARLES
        KNIGHT and F. B. B. ST. LEGER. Clowes, 164.

2284   Good Night /verse/. Signed: ξ. 514-15. E. M.
        FITZGERALD. Young, xxx.

2285   The Editor's Room. No. XIII. 515-28. CHARLES
        KNIGHT and F. B. B. ST. LEGER. See No. 2099.
        A poem, "Beauty," signed Y, appears on pp. 527-28.

THIRD SERIES. VOLUME III. NUMBER XV
JUNE 1829

2286   Washington Irving's Conquest of Granada. 529-56.
        CHARLES KNIGHT. Attr. Hughes.

2287   Tam O'Shanter.--Burns. 557-60.

2288   Philosophy of Dress, Exercise, and Sleep. 561-
        68. CHARLES KNIGHT. He begins the article by
        stating, "Having discussed the subject of diet
        pretty fully in some of our late numbers, we are
        induced to add a few remarks on the kindred
        Hygienique consideration of clothing..."; the
        reference is to Nos. 2264 and 2275.

2289   Population--Senior versus Malthus. 568-75.
       CHARLES KNIGHT. In the opening sentence the editor states, "we have pledged ourselves, in our monthly labours, to mingle the useful with the pleasant."

2290   The Chosen One /verse_7. 576.

2291   The Reviews of the Quarter. 577-92. CHARLES KNIGHT. Attr. Hughes; the editor speaks here also as proprietor.

2292   Case of East Retford.--State of Parties. 593-604.

2293   The Exhibition of the Royal Academy. 604-09.

2294   To a Friend on his Birthday /verse_7. Signed: The Harrovian. 609-10. R. E. A. WILLMOTT. Signature.

2295   New Edition of the Waverley Novels. 610-17.

2296   Diary for the Month of May. 618-24. CHARLES KNIGHT and F. B. B. ST. LEGER. Clowes, 164.

2297   The Editor's Room. No. XIV. 624-33. CHARLES KNIGHT and F. B. B. ST. LEGER. See No. 2099.

2298   The Journal of Facts. 1-216. CHARLES KNIGHT and F. B. B. ST. LEGER. This feature of the London was introduced in January 1829 and ran monthly until the magazine was discontinued in June. Each installment was paginated continuously, and separate from the number in which it appeared. In all of the copies of the London we have seen, the installments of the Journal are gathered together at the end of the number for June 1829. The Journal consisted of useful information extracted from newspapers, periodicals and books. Knight was clearly responsible for this feature, but St. Leger no doubt provided some items.

PART TWO:

INDEX OF AUTHORS AND CONTRIBUTORS

AINSWORTH, WILLIAM HARRISON, 1805-82, editor and novelist. DNB; Ellis.

The Falls of Ohiopyle, 722.

ARTIS, EDMUND TYRELL, archaeologist and artist. Clare, Letters.

John Taylor wrote to Clare in February 1822 (BM. MSS. Eg. 2245) asking if Artis would do an account of his excavations and discoveries on the Roman site of Caistor for The London Magazine's "Literary Intelligence" section, but it has not been traced there and may have been published in The New Monthly Magazine in October 1826.

ATKINSON, SOLOMON, 1797-1865, writer on legal subjects. Allibone; Venn.

Struggles of a poor student through Cambridge, 1511, 1553.

Regrets of a Cantab, 1660.

AUSTIN, SARAH, 1793-1867, translator and miscellaneous writer. DNB.

Memoirs of Madame du Hausset, 1504.

The Plays of Clara Gazul, trans., 1588.

Journal Descriptive of the Route from New York to Real del Monte, 1696.

Memoirs of the Margravine of Anspach, 1705.

The Count de St. Germain's Tale, 1717.

Angeloni on Political Force, 1774.

The Women of Italy, trans., 1832.

Memoirs of Casanova, 1837.

AYTON, RICHARD, 1786-1823, essayist. DNB.

    On the Spirit of Youth, 741.

    On the Diversity of Opinions, 791.

    On the Moral Influence of Etiquette, 822.

    Of cruelty to animals and "Mr. Martin's Act," 841.

    Of exaggeration and matter-of-fact people, 856.

    On Honesty, 884.

    On Hunting, 907.

    A Shipwreck, 931.

    On Beauty, 961.

    Signs of the Times, 973.

    A Sailor's Receipt for tying his Pig-tail, 973.

    The Ruling Passion, 973.

    On Fame and Monuments, 1018.

    Sea-Roamers, 1053.

    See also No. 873.

BACON, RICHARD MACKENZIE, 1775-1844, journalist and writer on music. DNB.

    Sketch of the Progress of Vocal Science, 211, 282, 459.

    See also Report of Music, from No. 26 (Jan. 1820) monthly to No. 1431 (Dec. 1824).

BALDWIN, ROBERT, publisher. Prance, Peppercorn Papers, 118.

    Preface and Prospectus, 1.

    Monthly Register, 364, 389, 418.

    See also Nos. 85, 419.

BARKER, CHARLES, b. 1797, critic and journalist, Allibone; Venn.

    Chit Chat of the Times of Charles II, 1669.

    Manners of the Court of Charles II, 1690.

BARKER, EDMUND HENRY, 1788-1839, classical scholar. DNB.

    See Nos. 1516, 1966, 1993.

BARTON, BERNARD, 1784-1849, Quaker poet. DNB; Lucas.

    The Ivy, 18.

    Stanzas, 207.

    Drab Bonnets, 210.

    Stoke Hills, 261.

    Verses to Longman, Hurst, Rees, Orme and Brown, 324.

    Lines, 342.

    Verses to the Memory of a Young Friend, 395.

    To Mary, 396.

    To the Memory of Emma Fuller, 428.

    To the Sun, 481.

    The Maniac, 870.

    Sonnet to Elia, 893.

    A Poet's Thanks, 937.

    Stanzas to a Young Friend, 973.

    Verses on the Death of Bloomfield, 1073.

    Stanzas from the Italian of Lorenzo de Medici, 1153.

    See also No. 632.

BEAUFOY, MARK, 1764-1827, astronomer and physicist. DNB.

Meteorological Table (included under Monthly Register), from No. 84 (March 1820) monthly to No. 335 (Feb. 1821).

BERCHET, GIOVANNI, 1783-1851, Italian poet. EI.

On Italian Tragedy, 209, 252.

Goethe, on Manzoni's Tragedy of Il Conte di Carmagnola, 383.

BERNAYS, ADOLPHUS, d. 1864, Professor of German. Boase.

N.L. of S.MS. 1706-11 has a letter from Bernays to John Scott dated 19 December 1820 asking about items sent, but not yet printed, and for payment of "the trifle which is due to me." Nothing has been traced to him in the magazine.

BEST, CHARLES, fl. 1602, poet. DNB.

A Sonnet of the Moon, 1086.

BEYLE, MARIE HENRI. See STENDHAL.

BLISS, PHILIP, 1787-1857, antiquarian and bibliographer. DNB.

Additions to Lord Orford's Royal and Noble Authors, 623, 660, 667, 748, 766, 846, 1127.

Dr. Routh's new edition of Bishop Burnet's History, 914.

Facetiae Bibliographicae, 958, 984, 1121, 1188, 1225, 1252, 1298, 1351, 1374.

Excerpta Antiquaria, 1268, 1311, 1392.

See also No. 1273.

BORROW, GEORGE HENRY, 1803-81, traveller and linguist. DNB.

The Old Oak, 1416.

BOUNDEN, JOSEPH, poet.

    Sonnet, 1337.

BOWLES, WILLIAM LISLE, 1762-1850, poet and antiquary.
DNB.

    The Character of Pope, 202.

BOWRING, SIR JOHN, 1792-1872, linguist and translator.
DNB.

    A Promenade on the Prado at Madrid, 258.

    Spanish Romances, 935, 957, 981, 1022, 1042, 1101, 1122, 1157.

    Ode on the Death of Marco Bozzari, 1118.

    Specimen of popular Poetry from the Old Sclavonico-Polish Dialect, 1166.

    From the Polish of Zimorowicz, 1175.

    German Epigrams, 1187, 1217, 1264.

    See also Nos. 118, 161, 321, 349, 455, 520, 752, 777, 1400.

BROUGHTON, JAMES, fl. 1830, editor. Reiman, VI, 682.

    On Clenches, 1331.

BRYDGES, SIR SAMUEL EGERTON, 1762-1837, bibliographer and genealogist. DNB.

    Sir Egerton Brydges and the New Monthly Magazine, 1720.

BUCKE, CHARLES, 1781-1846, dramatist and miscellaneous writer. DNB.

    Dramatic Literature, 2182.

BULL, JOHN. This name appears in the Taylor Commonplace Book, but may be a pseudonym.

The Elgin Gallery, 1015.

Sonnet, 1320, 1356.

BUSK, MARY.

See Nos. 232, 283, 397, 407. Though attributed to Mary Russell Mitford by Hughes, these may be by either Mary Margaret Busk, 1779-1863, wife of William Busk, who contributed to Blackwood's Magazine over the initials M.M., or Mary Busk, daughter of Hans Busk, who married James Milnes, an ancestor of Lord Houghton. See Bryne, I, 251.

BYRON, GEORGE GORDON, 6th LORD, 1788-1824, poet. DNB.

Extract from Lord Byron's Journal, 71.

Swimming across the Hellespont, 367.

CAMPBELL, NEIL, 1776-1827, general. DNB.

Letter to the editor, 1695.

CAMPBELL, THOMAS, 1777-1844, poet. DNB.

Mr. Campbell's Last Man, 1521.

Two Songs, 1753.

CANOVA, ANTONIO, 1757-1822, Italian sculptor. EI.

Conversations of Napoleon with Canova, 1507.

CARLYLE, THOMAS, 1795-1881, historian and essayist. DNB.

Schiller's Life and Writings, 1081, 1152, 1285, 1318, 1346.

CARY, HENRY FRANCIS, 1772-1844, translator and poet. DNB; King.

On Gray's Opinion of Collins, 447.

Continuation of Dr. Johnson's Lives of the Poets, 470, 561, 576, 597, 630, 649, 674, 703, 715, 771, 793, 815, 839, 1023, 1043, 1272, 1399, 1425.

Zariadres and Odatis, 471.

Travels of Cosmo the Third, 478.

On Sadoleti's Dialogue on Education, 484.

Méditations Poétiques, 500.

Estephania de Gantelmes, 513.

Song, 519.

The Early French Poets, 533, 554, 579, 608, 626, 651, 679, 691, 725, 762, 802, 814, 863, 886, 969, 1065, 1090, 1148, 1191, 1226.

Specimen of a translation of Valerius Flaccus, 599.

Hymn to the Morning ... of Flaminio, 728.

The Funeral of Eleanor, 753.

Eustace de Rimbaumont, 792.

Les Machabées ou le Martyre, 797.

A Comment on the Divine Comedy of Dante, 918, 933.

M. Tullii Ciceronis de Re Publica quae supersunt, 941.

Essays on Petrarch by Foscolo, 972.

The Clouds, 1100.

Early Italian Poets, 1104, 1136.

Rose's Orlando Furioso, 1270.

The Land of Logres, 1419.

The Tenth Nemean Ode of Pindar, 1448.

See also Nos. 673, 1150, 1405.

CHATEAUBRIAND, FRANÇOIS RENÉ DE, 1768-1848, French author, DBF.

Chateaubriant's Sketch of Roman History, 1723.

CLARE, JOHN, 1793-1864, poet. DNB; Tibble.
    Address to a copy of Clare's Poems, 81.
    The Request, 419.
    Ballad, 461.
    Sonnet. To a twin sister, 472.
    Farewell to Mary, 498.
    Sonnet. A Reflection on Summer, 517.
    Sonnet, 536, 772, 778, 849, 1006, 1021, 1295.
    Hymn to Spring, 580.
    To ****, 601.
    Superstition's Dream, 611.
    The Approach of Spring, 622.
    To the Cowslip, 676.
    Sonnet. To Nature, 681.
    Life, Death and Eternity, 696.
    Song, 701.
    Wanderings in June, 713.
    Sonnet, to the Nightingale, 723.
    To Elia, 749.
    A Sketch from Nature, 765.
    Forest Flowers, 774.
    The Ass, 782.
    Sonnet: Sun-Rise, 794.
    Sonnet: Sun-Set, 796.
    The Last of Autumn, 811.

Poesy, 898.

Antiquity, 930.

A Valentine to ----, 973.

Two Sonnets to Mary, 1039.

See also No. 1395.

CLARKE, WILLIAM BRANWHITE, 1798-1878, poet and geologist. DNB.

To Allan Cunningham, 928.

COLERIDGE, DAVID HARTLEY, 1796-1849, poet and essayist. DNB.

A Selection of Irish Melodies, 438.

On Parties in Poetry, 534.

On the Poetical Use of the Heathen Mythology, 598.

On Black Cats, 638.

Brief Observations upon Brevity, 655.

Parting, 716.

Atrabilious Reflections upon Melancholy, 781.

Sonnets addressed to R. S. Jameson, 889.

Stanzas, 956, 993, 1014.

COLERIDGE, SAMUEL TAYLOR, 1772-1834, poet, philosopher and critic. DNB.

See Nos. 544, 571, 621, 659, 684. Although Brooks suggested Coleridge as the author of these contributions, it seems unlikely that Taylor and Hessey would have neglected to advertise as a contributor such a well known author, or to mention him in their letters, unless they were ignorant of the authorship.

COLLIER, JOHN PAYNE, 1789-1883, critic and scholar. DNB.

On the Character and Writings of James Shirley, 121, 163, 234.

To his Mistress's Lips, 1133.

Note to Elia, 1134.

Cupid's Revenge, 1144.

The Dedication prefixed by Goethe to his Poems, 1174.

The Partition of the Earth by Schiller, 1221.

Cupid and Death, 1818.

See also No. 295.

COMBE, GEORGE, 1788-1858, phrenologist. DNB.

Observations on Phrenology, 761.

CONDER, JOSIAH, 1789-1855, bookseller and poet. DNB.

Song, 1125.

Sonnet, 1126.

CONRATH, JOHN.

The Apotheosis of Homer, 307.

COSTELLO, LOUISA STUART, 1799-1870, miniature painter and poet. DNB.

Mr. Bowles--as Editor of Pope, 160.

CROLY, GEORGE, 1780-1860, poet and novelist. DNB.

On the Oracles of the Ancients, 40.

Ancient State of the Jews in England, 116.

Goethe and his Faustus, 177.

Christian VII of Denmark and his Queen, 186.

With a Lampe for Mie Ladie Faire, 291.

Major Schill, 400.

Count Julius, 425.

The Hermit, 523.

See also Nos. 58, 91, 96, 143, 254, 321, 352, 372, 455, 516, 520.

CROWE, WILLIAM, 1745-1829, poet. DNB.

On English Versification. 860, 888, 912, 940, 995, 1287.

Ode. Addressed to His Majesty the King of France, 934.

St. Paul's Character of the Ancient Cretans, 988.

CUNNINGHAM, ALLAN, 1784-1842, poet and man of letters. DNB; Hogg.

Traditional Literature, 276, 293, 325, 339, 377, 424, 450, 473, 491, 518, 540, 555.

Epitaphs, 499.

The Twelve Tales of Lyddalcross, 574, 596, 604, 628, 650, 680, 699, 726.

The Seven Foresters of Chatsworth, 602.

As I came down through Cannobie, 668.

Lovely Woman, 694.

The Downfall of Dalzell, 718.

The Mariner's Song, 743.

Narrative of Nathan Adamson, 750.

It's Hame and it's Hame, 767.

King Bruce's Bowl, 770.

Luke Lorance, the Cameronian, 790.

Charlie Stuart, 799.

The Tale of Allan Lorburne, 816, 843.

Song: Awake, my Love, 821.
A Wish, 849.
I'll Daut Nae Mair a Posie, 865.
Christina Swayne, 869.
Corporal Colville, 881.
Riley Grave-Stones, 913.
Kate of Windiewa's, 936.
Lord William, 965.
The Land's End of Cornwall, 968.
Bannocks of Barley, 990.
The Fairy Miller of Croga, 1000.
The Yorkshire Alehouse, 1024.
Andrew Laurie's Return, 1045.
The Nuns and Ale of Caverswell, 1057.
Sir Hugh Heron, 1063.
Lord Roland Cheyne, 1085.
Old Corehead's Fireside, 1107.
The Curse of Coldengame, 1132.
Another Bode for Bodenton, 1156.
Song of the Maidens, 1170.
A Sabbath among the Mountains, 1200.
Gordon of Brackley, 1215.
The Two Ravens, 1243.
The Pirate's Song, 1263.
The Cuckoo, 1289.
Robert Burns and Lord Byron, 1310.
Montgomery's Mistress, 1378.

Fair Annie of Lochroyan, 1424.

See also Nos. 531, 900, 1130, 1246, 1271.

CUNNINGHAM, THOMAS MOUNSEY, 1776-1834, poet. DNB.

Fugitive Literature, 457.

CUVIER, GEORGES, Baron, 1769-1832, zoologist. OCFL.

Anecdotes of Animals, 1984, 1998.

DARLEY, GEORGE, 1795-1846, poet and critic. DNB; Abbott.

To Helene, 341.

Song to Twilight, 480.

The Voyage, 847.

Friar Bacon, 849.

The Ruelle, 890.

Olympian Revels, 915.

Lines from the Port-folio of H----, 980.

The Exhibition of the Royal Academy, 1003.

The Chase, 1011.

Letters to the Dramatists of the Day, 1026, 1036, 1060, 1083, 1109, 1137, 1154.

The Drama, 1089, 1113, 1357, 1380, 1407, 1432.

The Rhapsodist, 1201, 1240.

The Characteristic of the Present Age of Poetry, 1230.

John Lacy's Reply to the letter of Terentius Secundus, 1241.

Advice to a young Essayist, 1249.

The Nightingale and the Thorn, 1251.

Mexican Wonders, 1253.

Lilian of the Vale, 1284.

Old English Drama: The Second Maiden's Tragedy, 1314.

Le Cuisinier Francais versus Dr. Kitchiner, 1325.

Female Genius, 1327.

The Portrait Painter, 1345, 1396.

Nugae Philosophicae, 1347, 1391.

The Oramas, 1348.

Macadamization, 1366.

Memento Mori, 1370.

Raising the Dead, 1372.

On the Death of a young girl, 1377.

In my Bower so bright, 1422.

Theatricals of the Day, 1430, 1441.

The Fallen Star, 1440.

Juaniana, 1454.

Sonnet, 1472, 1498.

A Word with Blackwood, 1502.

Niaseries of the Newspapers, 1513.

Letter from an Absent Contributor on Hazlitt's Spirit of the Age, 1554.

Broster's System for the Cure of Impediments of Speech, 1601.

See also Nos. 804, 990, 1462, 1485.

DARLING, GEORGE, 1782?-1862, physician. DNB.

See Nos. 28, 48, 77, 105, 1305.

DEGEORGE, FREDERIC, 1797-1854, French author. DBF.

    Characters of Contemporary Foreign Authors and Statesmen, 2087, 2108, 2125, 2136, 2157, 2166.

DE QUINCEY, THOMAS, 1785-1859, essayist. DNB; Eaton; Sackville-West.

    Confessions of an English Opium-Eater, 503, 511, 512, 553, 837.

    John Paul Frederick Richter, 557.

    The Happy Life of a Parish Priest, 558.

    Last Will and Testament, 559.

    Letters to a Young man whose education has been Neglected, 871, 892, 919, 970, 1027.

    Anecdotage, 910.

    Letter from De Quincey, 928, 1117.

    Death of a German Great Man, 929.

    Anglo-German Dictionaries, 942.

    Prefiguration of Remote Events, 946.

    Mr. Schnackenberger, 954, 992.

    Moral Effects of Revolutions, 973.

    The Dice, 1034.

    Notes from the Pocket-Book of a late Opium-Eater, 1056, 1074, 1103, 1274, 1286, 1428.

    The King of Hayti, 1108.

    Measure of Value, 1120.

    Historico-Critical Inquiry into the origin of the Rosicrucians and the Free-Masons, 1145, 1169, 1193, 1276.

    Analects from John Paul Richter, 1164.

    Dream upon the Universe, 1189.

The Services of Mr. Ricardo, 1206.

Dialogues of Three Templars, 1214, 1231, 1257.

Kant on National Character, 1222.

Education. Plans for the Instruction of Boys in large numbers, 1228, 1250.

Abstract of Swedenborgianism by Kant, 1245.

Goethe, 1329, 1353.

Walladmor, 1367.

Idea of a Universal History by Kant, 1369.

The Street Companion, 1451.

See also Nos. 625, 652, 752, 1084.

DILKE, CHARLES WENTWORTH, 1789-1864, antiquary and critic. DNB; Dilke.

The Antiquary, 494.

Westminster Abbey, 565.

Pleasant and Unpleasant People, 600.

Bauer, p. 135, suggests that Dilke may have written the political columns from sometime in 1823. Dilke, I, 16, states that about 1825 C. W. Dilke was for a time editor of The London Magazine. Nothing further has been traced to substantiate either claim.

DONE, JOSHUA.

Narrative of the Imprisonment and Adventures of Joshua Done, 1679.

DUBOIS, EDWARD, 1774-1850, barrister and editor. DNB.

The Lawyer, 1341.

EAGLES, JOHN, 1783-1855, artist and author. DNB.

Account of a New Process in painting, 955.

EASTLAKE, SIR CHARLES LOCK, 1793-1865, artist. DNB.

    The Advantages and Disadvantages of Rome as a school of art, 11.

    The Searching of the River Tyber, 13.

    News from Rome, 57.

    Postscript to the News from Rome, 69.

    Vindication of Eustace, 123.

    On Musical Style, 140.

    See also No. 38.

ELTON, CHARLES ABRAHAM, 1778-1853, poet and scholar. DNB.

    Horace's Ode to the Bandusian Fountain, 429.

    Epistle to Elia, 474.

    Leisure Hours, 497, 515, 535, 562, 581, 610, 653, 698, 763.

    Verses written in an album, 541.

    Ode of Casimir to his Lyre, 588.

    Defence of the claims of Propertius, 742.

    On the poetry of Nonnus, 795, 818.

    On the Supplemental Iliad of Quintus Calaber, 836, 867, 895.

    On the Tragic Drama of Greece, 985, 1058, 1080, 1105.

    The Negro's Euthanasia, 1075.

    On modern French poetry, 1119, 1171, 1421.

    The Idler's Epistle to John Clare, 1316.

    A Dream of Orpheus, 1342.

    Elegy, 1344.

    Excerptions from an Idler's Scrap-book, 1493.

The Lay of Arion, 1514.

See also Nos. 636, 1015, 1128, 1204, 1265.

EVELYN, JOHN, 1620-1706, diarist. DNB.

Original letter of Evelyn's, 1420.

FARREN, WILLIAM, 1786-1861, actor. DNB.

On the Madness of Hamlet, 1220.

On the Madness of Ophelia, 1244.

On Hamlet's Soliloquy, 1275.

On the Madness of Lear, 1302.

FEATHERSTONHAUGH, CHARLES FORSTER.

Memoir and Remains of Charles Forster Featherstonhaugh, 1167.

FIELD, BARRON, 1786-1846, judge and miscellaneous writer. DNB.

Narrative of a Voyage to New South Wales, 624.

Journal of an Excursion across the Blue Mountains, 1096.

Journal of an Excursion to the Five Islands...New South Wales, 1326.

Important Intelligence from New South Wales, 1333.

Narrative of a Voyage from New South Wales, 1343.

See also Nos. 192, 1541.

FITZGERALD, EDWARD MARLBOROUGH, b. 1802, Irish journalist. Young; Venn.

The Separation, 2230.

Stanzas to ----, 2242, 2251.

Hobbledehoys, 2244.

Dreams, 2271.

Good Night, 2284.

FONBLANQUE, ALBANY, 1793-1872, journalist and editor. DNB.

A letter to Thomas Carlyle from John Stuart Mill of 22 October 1832 states Fonblanque used to write in The London Magazine (Collected Works of John Stuart Mill (Toronto: Un. of Toronto Pr., 1963), XII, 126). Nothing has been traced.

FOSCOLO, UGO, 1778-1827, Italian poet. Vincent.

Ancient Encaustic Paintings of Cleopatra, 1755.

Boccaccio, 1766.

The Women of Italy, 1832.

FOSS, EDWARD, 1787-1870, biographer. DNB.

In the Memoir by J. C. Robertson prefixed to Foss's Biographia Juridica, 1870, it is stated that Foss was a contributor to The London Magazine. No items have been traced, but see No. 1068.

FRANCIS, SIR PHILIP, 1740-1818, politician. DNB.

Original letter from Sir Philip Francis to Mr. George Thicknesse, 943.

FRANKLIN, BENJAMIN, 1706-90, printer, author and statesman. DAB.

Original letters of Dr. Franklin, 1615, 1657, 1663.

FYFE, ANDREW, 1792-1861, surgeon. DNB.

Report on the progress of science, from No. 901 (Feb. 1823) monthly to No. 1140 (Dec. 1823), except for June 1823.

GALIFFE, JACQUES AUGUSTIN, poet.

Song of the Parguinotes, 432.

The Dying Soldier, 433.

GANDY, EDWARD, poet.

On 13 October 1819 John Scott wrote to Gandy inviting him to contribute to the forthcoming London Magazine and suggesting he write on the theatre or other subjects congenial to him. Nothing has been traced. See Prance, Peppercorn Papers, pp. 120-21.

GILCHRIST, OCTAVIUS GRAHAM, 1779-1823, antiquary. DNB; Clare, Letters.

Some account of John Clare, 4.

Spence's Anecdotes, 51.

Memoirs of the Life and Writings of Sir John Suckling, 86.

Memory, 146.

A Recollection, 148.

A new bibliographical work, 164.

Mr. Ebert and Mr. Dibdin, 183.

Bibliographia Curiosa, 185.

The Character of Pope, 189.

On Epitaphs and Monuments, 849.

Letter to the Editor, 1009.

See also No. 777.

GOETHE, JOHANN WOLFGANG VON, 1749-1832, German poet. Encyc. Britannica.

Goethe on Art and Antiquity, 120.

GRAY, THOMAS, 1787-1848, railway pioneer. DNB.

Rail-ways, 1443.

GRIFFITH, EDWARD, 1790-1858, naturalist. DNB.

Cuvier's Anecdotes of Animals, trans., 1984, 1998.

HARE, JULIUS CHARLES, 1795-1855, essayist. DNB.

On Walter Savage Landor's Imaginary Conversations, 1254.

See also Nos. 625, 652.

HARLEY, JAMES, poet. BMCat.

Letter from John O'Groats, 302.

Stanzas, 343.

HATCHER, HENRY, 1777-1846, schoolmaster and antiquary. DNB.

N.L. of S. MS. 1706-53 has a letter from Hatcher to Taylor and Hessey dated 3 April 1825 indicating that they owe him money. He adds, "I shall be happy at all times to contribute my mite towards your magazine in the way of reviewing particularly anything connected with geography, which has been my hobby horse." Possibly he was responsible for some of the many reviews of travel books in the magazine, but none has been identified.

HAY, ROBERT, 1799-1863, traveller and archaeologist. DNB.

On the cookery of the French, 1324.

HAYDON, BENJAMIN ROBERT, 1786-1846, artist. DNB.

Notices of the Fine Arts, 103, 195.

HAZLITT, WILLIAM, 1778-1830, essayist and critic. DNB; Howe; Baker.

The Drama, 21, 44, 73, 101, 131, 152, 171, 193, 217, 285.

Notices of the Fine Arts, 46, 75, 103, 671.

Table Talk, 145, 159, 203, 226, 269, 296, 318, 351, 370, 405, 483, 537, 560.

On Population, 281.

The Lion's Head, 365, 390.

Living Authors. Crabbe, 392.

On the writings of Mr. Maturin, 401.

Mr. Haydon's picture of Christ's Agony, 409.

Lord Byron's Marino Faliero, 412.

Pope, Lord Byron and Mr. Bowles, 420.

The Pirate, 590.

On the Elgin Marbles, 606, 677.

Fonthill Abbey, 812.

Sir Marmaduke Maxwell, 823.

Mr. Angerstein's collection of pictures, 831.

The Dulwich Gallery, 857.

The Marquis of Stafford's pictures, 883.

Peveril of the Peak, 897.

The Pictures at Windsor Castle, 916.

The Pictures at Hampton-Court, 982.

Lord Grosvenor's collection of pictures, 1016.

Pictures at Wilton, Stourhead, 1076.

Letter from William Hazlitt on De Quincey, 1095.

Pictures at Oxford and Blenheim, 1106.

See also Nos. 25, 85, 336, 384.

HEBER, REGINALD, 1783-1826, poet. DNB.

Sonnet, 19.

Southey's Life of Wesley, 192.

On the connexion between the Character and the Poetry of Nations, 236.

HESSEY, JAMES AUGUSTUS, 1785-1870, publisher. Rollins; Chilcott.

From time to time Hessey helped Taylor and Thomas Hood in compiling the Lion's Head and with various other editorial duties. See No. 1213.

HILL, E., Professor of physic.

Letter on the author of "Connubia Florum," 873.

HILL, MATHEW DAVENPORT, 1792-1872, writer on education. DNB.

Elementary Education, 2183, 2206.

See also No. 2266.

HILTON, WILLIAM, 1786-1839, artist. DNB.

Hilton's picture "Nature Blowing Bubbles for her Children" was reproduced in the magazine in August 1821. He was an old friend of both Taylor and Hessey and may well have contributed other items.

HOGG, THOMAS JEFFERSON, 1792-1862, biographer, friend of Shelley. DNB.

Letters from the Continent, 1636, 1736, 1752, 1767, 1781, 1798, 1812, 1826.

HOOD, THOMAS, 1799-1845, poet and sub-editor of The London Magazine. DNB; Reid; Jerrold.

The Lion's Head, from No. 445 (July 1821) monthly to No. 1185 (March 1824), except for October 1823.

The Heroes of Naples, 449.

To Hope, 464.

Ode to Dr. Kitchener, 531.

The Departure of Summer, 538.

A Sentimental Journey, 542.

Please to ring the Belle, 573.

On Imitation, 583.

To a Critick, 596.

Faithless Sally Brown, 620.

The Sea of Death, 631.

To Celia, 648.

To an Absentee, 658.

Moral Reflections on the Cross of St. Paul's, 665.

The Stag-eyed Lady, 670.

Mr. Martin's pictures and the Bonassus, 672.

Lycus the Centaur, 746.

Fare Thee Well, 759.

Hymn to the Sun, 780.

The Two Peacocks of Bedfont, 789.

Now the loud cry, 809.

Sonnet: Midnight, 832.

On a sleeping child, 834.

Presentiment, 838.

Sonnet: To Fancy, 842.

The Old Seaman, 848.

Fair Innes, 873.

Presence of Mind in a Ghost, 873.

Ode. Autumn, 891.

Sonnet--Silence, 900.

Thoughts on Sculpture, 900.

Sonnet written in Keats's Endymion, 967.

Sonnet to an Enthusiast, 973.

Sonnet: Death, 987.

To a cold Beauty, 994.

Epigram, 1004.

Sonnet, 1009.

Observations on "The Ghost-Player's Guide," 1239.

The Art of Advertising made easy, 1477.

An Epistle to a Country Cousin, 1558.

See also Nos. 444, 476, 504, 549, 563, 569, 683, 695, 756, 783, 953, 1040, 1304, 1309, 1458, 1467, 1473, 1520, 1581, 1610, 1620, 1625, 1639, 1651.

HOWARD, R., meteorologist.

Meteorological Table and Observations, 364, 389, 418, 444, 468.

HUNT, HENRY, 1773-1835, politician. DNB.

Letter from Henry Hunt, 2118.

HUNT, JAMES HENRY LEIGH, 1784-1859, poet and essayist. DNB.

Euphrosyne and Melidore, 115.

Fiametta and Boccaccio, 141.

IRVING, WASHINGTON, 1783-1859, essayist. DAB.

See No. 625.

JACKSON, JAMES GREY, Professor of Arabic.

On the Nile and the Niger, 125.

JAMESON, ANNA BROWNELL, 1794-1860, critic. DNB.

Farewell to Italy, 809.

JEFFERSON, THOMAS, 1743-1826, President of the U.S.A. DAB.

Anecdote of Dr. Franklin, 896.

KEATS, JOHN, 1795-1821, poet. DNB.

Sonnet--A Dream, 545.

KENT, ELIZABETH, 1790-1860, sister-in-law of Leigh Hunt, botanist. Tatchell.

The Daisy, 1038.

KNIGHT, CHARLES, 1791-1873, author, publisher, and editor of The London Magazine. DNB; Clowes.

Advertisement. New Series of The London Magazine, 2083.

Education of the People, 2084.

Private Correspondence, 2095, 2115, 2127.

Diary for the month, from No. 2097 (April 1828) monthly to No. 2296 (June 1829).

The Editor's Room, from No. 2099 (April 1828) monthly to No. 2297 (June 1829) except for April 1829.

The Mystic School, 2101.

The Leading Profession, 2111.

The Two London Colleges, 2132.

The Georama, 2135.

Mornings among the Cobwebs, 2144, 2151, 2185.

The Religious World Displayed, 2154, 2191.

Scotch Note Bill, 2155.

Salmonia, 2158.

Our National Architecture, 2160, 2169.

Private Bills of the Session 1828, 2164.

Anatomy, 2179.

An Account of the present State of Tripoli, 2189.

Pelham, 2192.

Drummond of Hawthornden, 2202.

The English Almanacs, 2211.

The Money Market, 2212.

Traps for Human Beings, 2213.

The Disowned, 2226.

A Looking-Glass for London, 2227.

Hungarian Tales, 2229.

The Colosseum, 2233.

On the Armour in the Tower, 2236.

Moral Tendencies of Knowledge, 2240.

A Looking Glass for the Country, 2241.

Currency--Mr. Tooke's Letter to Lord Grenville, 2246.

Universal Biography, 2247.

Every Man's Master, 2246, 2275.

Popular Education, 2277.

Washington Irving's Conquest of Granada, 2286.

Philosophy of Dress, Exercise and Sleep, 2288.

Population, 2289.

The Reviews of the Quarter, 2291.

The Journal of Facts, 2298.

See also Nos. 1927, 2142.

KNOWLES, JAMES SHERIDAN, 1784-1862, dramatist. DNB.

    See No. 1131.

LAMB, CHARLES, 1775-1834, essayist. DNB; Lucas; Barnett.

    Recollections of the South Sea House, 178.

    Sonnet to...Barry Cornwall, 213.

    To R. S. Knowles, 214.

    Oxford in the Vacation, 224.

    The Ape, 230.

    Christ's Hospital Five and Thirty Years Ago, 247.

    Letter from Charles Lamb, 268.

    The Two Races of Men, 273.

    New Year's Eve, 290.

    Mrs. Battle's Opinions on Whist, 323.

    A Chapter on Ears, 340.

    All Fools' Day, 366.

    Sonnet, 369.

    The Confessions of F. H. V. H. Delamore Esq.', 373.

    A Quaker's Meeting, 374.

    Letter from Charles Lamb, 390.

    The Old and the New Schoolmaster, 394.

    My Relations, 422.

    Mackery End in Hertfordshire, 451.

    The Lawyer, 476.

    Jews, Quakers, Scotchmen and other Imperfect Sympathies, 477.

    The Old Benchers of the Inner Temple, 501.

Witches and other Night Fears, 514.

Elia to his Correspondents, 531.

Grace before Meat, 532.

My First Play, 556.

Dream-Children, 575.

Dramatic Fragment, 584.

On Some of the Old Actors, 613, 647, 800.

Distant Correspondents, 637.

The Praise of Chimney-Sweepers, 666.

A Complaint of the Decay of Beggars, 697.

Detached Thoughts on Books and Reading, 720.

Reprints of Elia, 735.

Confessions of a Drunkard, 740.

A Dissertation upon Roast Pig, 773.

A Bachelor's Complaint of the Behaviour of Married People, 776.

Modern Gallantry, 820.

The Gentle Giantess, 840.

Scraps of Criticism, 849.

Rejoicings upon the New Year's Coming of Age, 855.

A Character of the late Elia, 858.

The Choice of a Grave, 873.

Wilks, 873.

Milton, 900.

A Check on Human Pride, 900.

Letter from Charles Lamb, 906.

Old China, 911.

Ritson versus John Scott the Quaker, 944.

Poor Relations, 963.

The Child Angel, 999.

The Old Margate Hoy, 1013.

Nugae Criticae, 1054, 1102.

Letter of Elia to Robert Southey, 1082.

Cockney Latin, 1097.

Guy Faux, 1099.

Amicus Redivivus, 1129.

Blakesmoor in H----shire, 1338.

Original Letter of James Thomson, 1389.

Captain Jackson, 1393.

Biographical Memoir of Mr. Liston, 1439.

A Vision of Horns, 1442.

Letter to the Editor of The London Magazine, 1455.

Letter to an old Gentleman whose education has been neglected, 1456.

Unitarian Protests, 1466.

Autobiography of Mr. Munden, 1474.

Reflections in the Pillory, 1494.

Barbara S---, 1512.

The Last Peach, 1523.

Quatrains to the Editor of the Every Day-Book, 1535.

The Three Graves, 1538.

The Superannuated Man, 1542.

The Wedding, 1560.

The Convalescent, 1585.

Imperfect Dramatic Illusion, 1613.

An Appeal from the Shades, 1805.

See also Nos. 384, 1117, 1304, 1625, 1681, 1689.

LAMB, MARY ANNE, 1764-1847, writer for children, sister of Charles Lamb. DNB; Gilchrist.

The Two Boys, 720.

Helen, 1338.

LANDOR, WALTER SAVAGE, 1775-1864, poet and prose writer. DNB.

Imaginary Conversation between Mr. Southey and Professor Porson, 1010.

LANDSEER, JOHN, 1769-1852, artist. DNB.

In his Memoir of William Hazlitt (II, 10), W. C. Hazlitt quotes an undated letter from Landseer to William Hazlitt, in which he asks if his letters are to appear in The London Magazine, for if Baldwin does not want them he will submit them elsewhere. They have not been traced, but he may have sent other items.

LEEDS, WILLIAM HENRY, 1786-1866, miscellaneous writer. Boase.

Gleanings from Foreign Journals: from No. 23 (Jan. 1820) to No. 264 (Nov. 1820) Leeds was probably sharing this item with John Scott; after Scott's death he wrote the series alone, Nos. 361, 381, 436, 505, 528.

Lichtenberg's Descriptions of Hogarth's Works, 208, 229.

Ochlenschager's Corregio, 231.

Lodoiska and her daughter, 233.

Literary and Scientific Intelligence, from No. 362 (March 1821) monthly to No. 828 (Nov. 1822), except for Dec. 1821 and April-July 1822.

Retrospective View of the Commerce of Great Britain, 1007, 1142, 1281, 1434.

See also Nos. 227, 251, 321, 344, 358, 455, 520, 752. See also Sketch of Foreign Literature, from No. 877 (Jan. 1823) monthly to No. 1408 (Nov. 1824).

LICHTENBERG, GEORG CHRISTOLF, 1742-99, German physicist and satirist. Encyc. Britannica.

German Descriptions of Hogarth's Works, 208, 229.

LOCKHART, JOHN GIBSON, 1794-1854, editor, novelist and biographer. DNB.

Letter to John Scott, 316.

MACFARLANE, CHARLES, 1799-1858, miscellaneous writer. DNB.

The Fisherman's Rebellion, 259.

A New Opera by Rossini, 347.

Sketches on the Road, 378, 452, 475, 539, 564, 586, 633.

Sketch of the City of Naples, 693, 729, 769.

A Visit to the Franciscan Monastery of Sorrento, 866, 922.

Visit to the City of Sorrento, 1012, 1041.

A Walk to Paestum, 1165, 1376, 1402.

Re-establishment of the Jesuits in Naples, 1186.

Mathias's Italian translation of Spenser, 1784.

See also Nos. 180, 215, 582, 1176.

MACREADY, WILLIAM CHARLES, 1793-1873, actor. DNB.

Letter from W. C. Macready, 953.

MAISTRE, COMTE XAVIER DE, 1763-1852, writer and Royalist sympathizer. DBF.

The Leper of the City of Aosta, 97.

MELLISH.

A Convict's Recollections of New South Wales, 1541.

MEYRICK, SIR SAMUEL RUSH, 1783-1848, antiquary. DNB.

On the Armour in the Tower, 2236.

MITFORD, JOHN, 1781-1859, scholar and editor. DNB.

Sonnet addressed to Bernard Barton, 983.

MITFORD, MARY RUSSELL, 1787-1855, novelist and dramatist. DNB; Watson.

Emily, 398.

Theodore and Bertha, 495.

See also Nos. 232, 283, 397, 407.

MONTGOMERY, JAMES, 1771-1854, poet. DNB.

Thoughts and Images, 454.

Imitations of Psalm XLII and XLIII, 567.

A Hermitage, 605.

War Song, 678.

The Falling Leaf, 826.

The Daisy in India, 998.

A Sea-Piece, 1453.

MOORE, ROBERT W., stockbroker.

Periodical Stock Prices (included under Monthly Register), from No. 1464 (Jan. 1825) monthly to No. 2082 (March 1828).

MURRAY, JAMES.

> The Brooke-Taylor MSS mention a James Murray who wrote to Taylor in January 1826 for payment for articles which had appeared in the magazine in July and August 1825, but they have not been identified. Perhaps this was the James Murray thought to be connected with The Times and who died in 1835.

NEAL, JOHN, 1793-1876, American novelist and critic. DAB.

> The Chamber of Psyche, 1469.
>
> Yankee Notions, 1731, 1756, 1769.
>
> Mr. John Dunn Hunter, 1783.
>
> Letter to the Editor, 1797.

NIEMEYER, AUGUST HERMANN, 1754-1828, poet and theologian. EI.

> The English Universities, 752.

O'DRISCOLL, JOHN, Irish writer. Allibone; LCCat.

> The Early Life and Education of Counsellor O'D---, 1713.

OTTLEY, WILLIAM YOUNG, 1771-1836, artist and writer on art. DNB.

> See No. 1426.

PANIZZI, SIR ANTONIO, 1797-1879, librarian. DNB; Miller.

> Italian Literature, 1721.
>
> Memoir of Ugo Foscolo, 2010.

PARKES, JOSEPH, 1796-1865, lawyer and politician. DNB.

> Dr. Lingard and the Edinburgh Review, 1911.

PARLBY, BROOK BRIDGES, 1783-1873, writer. LCCat.

    Epithalamium, 390.

PATMORE, PETER GEORGE, 1786-1855, poet and prose writer. DNB; Champneys.

    Endymion, 87.

    Sonnets, 94, 128.

    The Grave, 95.

    Mr. Hunt's Hero and Leander, 167.

    Star-Gazing, 235.

    Croly's Angel of the World, 260.

    On Riding on Horse-back, 294, 345.

    The Drama, 308, 332, 360.

    Letter from P. G. Patmore, 316.

    On Magazine Writers, 717.

    See also Nos. 127, 430.

PEACOCK, THOMAS LOVE, 1785-1866, novelist and poet. DNB; Felton.

    Le Mois Bubblose, 1476.

PERCIVAL, JOHN, 1788-1837?, clergyman and Fellow of Wadham College, Oxford. Blunden, *Keats's Publisher*.

    Thomas Bennion's letter to Clare in March 1824 (BM. MSS. Eg. 2246) lists those contributors who attended a recent magazine dinner and includes "Revd. Mr. Percival." Percival was an old friend of John Taylor, and in *Keats's Publisher*, p. 149, Blunden refers to his offering Taylor his "paper on Virgil's imitation of Homer" for *The London Magazine*. Nothing of his has been traced.

PHILLIPS, CHARLES, 1787-1859, Irish barrister and political writer. DNB.

Life of Hölty, 544.

Authentic Anecdotes of the late Rev. Dr. Barrett, 585.

Abstract of Foreign and Domestic Occurrences, from No. 468 (July 1821) monthly to No. 876 (Jan. 1823); the first six months of this feature, No. 468 to No. 572 (Dec. 1821), are included under Monthly Register in this Index.

View of Public Affairs, from No. 903 (Feb. 1823) monthly to No. 1574 (June 1825), though the ascription is less firm after No. 1433 (Dec. 1824).

A Visit Incog., 1238.

Memoirs of Captain Rock, 1262.

See also Nos. 444, 468.

POOLE, JOHN, 1786-1872, dramatist. DNB.

Beauties of the Living Dramatists, 577, 603, 629, 656, 721.

A Cockney's Rural Sports, 835.

New Year's Day in Paris, 859.

Sterne at Calais and Montreuil, 1445.

Sterne at Paris and Versailles, 1497.

POOLE, THOMAS, 1765-1837, tanner, friend of S. T. Coleridge. DNB.

The Doomed Man, 1066.

The Pirate's Treasure, 1194.

PRAED, WINTHROP MACKWORTH, 1802-39, poet. DNB.

Arrivals at a Watering Place, 2224.

The Best Bat in the School, 2235.

You'll Come to our Ball, 2238.

The Inconvenience of Having an Elder Brother, 2248.

School and Schoolfellows, 2249.

Toujours Perdrix, 2262.

April Fools, 2269.

PRICE, THOMAS, d.c. 1840, Rector of Enville, friend of H. F. Cary. King.

See No. 1117.

PROCTER, BRYAN WALLER, 1787-1874, poet.   DNB; Armour.

Tomb-Stone Warehouse, 8.

Hereafter, 41.

The Last Song, 63.

Charles the Fifth and a Monk, 65.

Song, 89, 692, 946.

Melancholy, 90.

On May Day, 112.

On Fighting, 119, 144.

On the Panorama of Venice, 147.

The Lady and the Devil (in The Drama), 152.

To --- On a Dispute, 162.

The Fancy by J. H. Reynolds, 170.

Stanzas written in a Forest, 190.

Excursion to the top of Skiddaw, 191.

The Cider Cellar, 228.

Sonnet, 249, 279, 299, 300, 448, 739, 862, 939.

Helvellyn, 250.

Letters of Foote, Garrick, 277, 330.

Derwent-Water and Skiddaw, 354.

Stanzas, 355, 1301.

Death of Mr. John Keats, 384.

A May Dream, 391.

The Memoir of a Hypochondriac, 775, 801.

A Few Words on "Christmas," 833.

Philosophy, 845.

To an Unknown, 849.

The Miscellany, 849, 873, 900, 946, 973.

Twelfth Night, 861.

On Dedications, 873.

Obituary, 873.

Valentine's Day, 882.

The Brides' Tragedy, 887.

Cooke's Exhibition of Drawings, 900.

On Signs, 989.

The Fate of Hylas, 1087.

A Letter from one of the "Dramatists of the Day," 1197.

Death, 1269.

Time, 1288.

The Last Day of Summer, 1293.

A Storm, 1313.

On a Picture, 1319.

The Errors of Ecstasie, 1415.

To the Nightingale, 1438.

To Charles Lamb, 1578.

On the Domestication of Wild Animals, 1626.

See also Nos. 61, 504, 900, 973, 1581.

QUIN, W.

English Eating, 492.

READ, WILLIAM, 1795?-1866, Irish poet. DNB.

Withered Violets, 297.

See also Nos. 393, 634.

REDDING, CYRUS, 1785-1870, journalist and editor. DNB; Boase.

The Tea-Garden, 745.

The Malvern Hills, 764.

My Father's House, 844.

See also Nos. 719, 1605, 1623, 1638.

REYNOLDS, JOHN HAMILTON, 1794-1852, poet, essayist and critic. DNB; Marsh, John Hamilton Reynolds.

Winter, 20.

A Literary Gem, 59.

The Jewels of the Book, 182, 205.

Address Spoken ... by Miss Kelly, 218.

Exmouth Wrestling, 270.

The Drama, 414, 440, 463, 486, 507, 524, 549, 569, 591, 614, 641, 662, 685, 707, 731, 824, 850, 874, 894, 925, 950, 971, 1005, 1030, 1048, 1068, 1135, 1158, 1178, 1207, 1232, 1258, 1278, 1304, 1330.

Legal Lyrics, 427.

Warwick Castle, 446.

Lamb's translation of Catullus, 465.

The Coronation, 485.

Letter from Edward Herbert, 490.

The Champion's Farewell, 490.

A new Hymn-Book, 508.

The Cook's Oracle, 526.

Warner's Church of England Theology, 543.

Greenwich Hospital, 546.

Letter to Cornelius Van Vinkbooms, 547.

Bradgate Park, 612.

The Green Room, 627.

A Bachelor's Soliloquy, 642.

Don Giovanni the XVIII, 675.

Some Passages in the Life of Mr. Adam Blair, 686.

The Princess of Moonland, 695.

Ode to a Sparrow, 747.

The Inside of a Stage Coach, 751.

The Cockpit Royal, 810.

Walking Stewart, 813.

Grimm's German Popular Stories, 872.

The Literary Police Office, 885.

The Loves of the Angels, 899.

Mrs. Siddons's Abridgement of Paradise Lost, 900.

Mr. Kemble, 945.

The Flood of Thessaly, 946, 996.

A Parthian Peep at Life, 960.

Spring Song, 962.

Angling and Izaak Walton, 986.

Ode to the Printer's Devil, 991.

Table Talk by Hazlitt, 1001.

A Chit Chat Letter, 1077.

Stanzas to the Memory of Richard Allen, 1151.

A Pen and Ink Sketch of a late Trial for Murder, 1173.

Fleet-Street Biography, 1229.

Vauxhall Meminiscences, 1352.

The Vagrant Act, 1437.

Remonstratory Ode, 1555.

Four Sonnets composed during Ascot Race Week, 1590.

See also Nos. 127, 239, 359, 419, 426, 476, 620, 621, 659, 684, 804, 953, 1458, 1467, 1473, 1520, 1581, 1610, 1620, 1639.

RICE, JAMES, d. 1833, lawyer. Rollins.

Sonnet, 609.

See also Nos. 493, 571, 621, 634, 659, 684.

RICHARDSON, DAVID LESTER, 1801-65, poet and miscellaneous writer. DNB.

An Address to Sleep, 1283.

RICHARDSON, J. M., stockbroker.

Daily prices of stocks (included under Monthly Register), from No. 31 (Jan. 1820) monthly to No. 853 (Dec. 1822).

RIPPINGILLE, EDWARD VILLIERS, 1798?-1859, artist. DNB; Clare, Letters.

An Address to the Echo, 1309.

RITCHIE, JOSEPH, 1788?-1819, African explorer. DNB.

Lines on the Death of Princess Charlotte, 368.

Consolation, 375.

Albion, 376.

ROBINSON, HENRY CRABB, 1775-1867, barrister and diarist. DNB.

See No. 657.

ROCHE, EUGENIUS, 1786-1829, journalist. DNB.

See Nos. 403, 493, 571, 634.

ROSE, WILLIAM STEWART, 1775-1843, poet and translator. DNB.

See No. 1328.

ST. LEGER, FRANCIS BARRY BOYLE, 1799-1829, novelist, sub-editor of The London Magazine. DNB.

Present State of Switzerland, 2089.

Family Portraits, 2093, 2110, 2147, 2170, 2201, 2276.

Private Correspondence, 2095, 2115, 2127.

Diary for the month, from No. 2097 (April 1828) monthly to No. 2296 (June 1829).

The Editor's Room, from No. 2099 (April 1828) monthly to No. 2297 (June 1829), except for April 1829.

The Conditions of the Irish Poor, 2102.

The Eastern Story-Tellers, 2103.

The Calcutta Stamp Duty, 2106.

Poor-Laws--Emigration, 2109.

Reforms in the Law, 2117, 2149, 2181, 2273.

The New Ministry, 2140.

Private Bills of the Session, 2164.

Some Account of a late trial for murder--not Corder's, 2167.

The Native Irish, 2175.

Dramatic Literature, 2182.

On the present state of opinion in Ireland, 2184.

Arrest of Mr. Lawless, 2203.

Traps for Human Beings, 2213.

The Silk Question, 2222.

On the approaching session of Parliament, 2232.

Crime and its Prevention, 2253.

The Catholic Question, 2255.

The One Subject, 2260.

The Present Proceedings of the Theatres, 2274.

The Journal of Facts, 2298.

See also No. 2138.

SCOTT, JOHN, 1783-1821, poet, essayist and editor of The London Magazine. DNB; Bauer; Prance, Peppercorn Papers.

Preface and Prospectus of The London Magazine, 1.

Editorial Notes, 2, 32, 55, 111, 138.

General Reflections suggested by Italy, 3.

Living Authors, 5, 66, 184, 303.

The Memoirs of Mr. Hardy Vaux, 7.

The Influence of Religious and Patriotic Feeling, 9.

The Traveller, 10, 43, 64, 179.

French Criticism (on Goethe's Werther), 12.

The Collector, 17, 42, 70, 129, 150, 169, 238.

Notices of the Fine Arts, 22, 133, 153, 195.

Gleanings from Foreign Journals, 23, 47, 76, 104, 134, 154, 196, 241, 264.

Critical Notices of new Books, 24, 51, 80, 108, 130, 151, 170, 192, 216.

Literary and Scientific Intelligence, from No. 25 (Jan. 1820) monthly to No. 334 (Feb. 1821).

Commercial Report, 29, 50, 79, 107.

Historical and Critical Summary of Public Events, 30, 53, 83, 136, 174, 198, 221, 243, 266, 287.

Monthly Register, from No. 31 (Jan. 1820) monthly to No. 335 (Feb. 1821).

Poetry and Prose, 33.

The Spirit of French Criticism, 34.

Notices of some of the Early French Poets, 56.

On the Comparative Refinement of the Age, 60.

On Human Perfectability, 62.

Postscript to the News from Rome, 69.

Extract from Lord Byron's Journal, 71.

The Leper of the City of Aosta, 97.

Lord Byron, 113.

The Chronicle of Don Pierre Nino, 114.

Extracts from Dr. S. H. Spiker's Tour, 117.

Goethe on Art and Antiquity, 120.

Nero--Elliston, 139.

The Lion's Head, 157, 176, 200, 223, 245, 268, 289, 315.

The History of Madame Krudener, 158.

To ----, 165.

Supposed to be spoken by a dying son, 187.

Sbogar the Dalmatian Brigand, 204.

German Descriptions of Hogarth's Works, 208.

The Abbot by W. Scott, 237.

The Literature of the Nursery, 246.

Blackwood's Magazine, 253.

Lines...at the Tomb of Alfieri, 256.

The Society...of Sicily, 262.

Our Arrears, 274.

The Mohock Magazine, 284.

The Travels and Opinions of Edgeworth Benson, 292, 326.

Lines written for a young lady's pocket book, 301.

The Literary Pocket Book, 304.

Town Conversation, 305, 331, 357.

The Apotheosis of Homer, 307.

Belzoni's Narrative, 309.

The Earthquake, 310.

Melmoth the Wanderer, 311.

Statement by John Scott, 316.

The Signs of the Times, 322.

Kenilworth, 328.

See also Nos. 16, 37, 38, 68, 75, 126, 152, 181, 320.

SCOTT, SIR WALTER, 1771-1832, poet and novelist. DNB.

Chronicles of the Canongate: The Two Drovers, 2020.

SESTINI, BARTOLOMEO, 1792-1822, Italian poet. EI.

Sonetti, 909.

SHELLEY, MARY WOLLSTONECRAFT, 1797-1851, novelist, wife of P. B. Shelley. DNB; Nitchie.

Recollections of Italy, 1147.

On Ghosts, 1192.

The Bride of Modern Italy, 1216.

A Visit to Brighton, 1853.

SKOTTOWE, AUGUSTINE, poet and biographer.

See No. 730.

SMITH, HORACE, 1779-1849, poet and novelist. DNB; Beavan.

Farewell to England, 15.

The Contrast, 72.

Miller Redivivus, 306, 329, 348, 435.

Letter from Horace Smith, 316.

Memnon's Head, 317.

The Statue of Theseus, 337.

Death--Posthumous Memorials--Children, 338.

Auto-biography of John Huggins, 371.

The Shriek of Prometheus, 421.

The Dying Poet's Farewell, 635.

The Old White Hat, 654.

Marshal Soult and his Murillos, 738.

An Inquiry why candles invariably burn blue in the presence of a ghost, 744.

Ferdinand Mendez Pinto, 798.

See also No. 788.

SMITH, JAMES, 1775-1839, miscellaneous writer. DNB; Beavan.

Halidon Hill, 754.

Bracebridge-Hall, 817.

SMITH, JOHN GORDON, 1792-1833, Professor of medical jurisprudence. DNB.

See No. 35.

SMITH, SYDNEY, 1771-1845, clergyman and author. DNB.

Rev. Sydney Smith's Speech on the Catholic Claims, 1572.

SMITH, THOMAS SOUTHWOOD, 1788-1861, doctor and medical reformer. DNB.

Dr. Southwood Smith's Lectures on Comparative Human Physiology, 1860, 1871.

SOANE, GEORGE, 1790-1860, dramatist and novelist. DNB.

From an unpublished play, 607.

English Smugglers, 736.

The Siege of Vienna, 803.

SOUTHERN, HENRY, 1799-1853, editor of The London Magazine. DNB.

Personal Character of Lord Byron, 1364.

Conversations of Lord Byron, 1387.

Address on the new series, 1412.

The Fanariotes of Constantinople, 1414.

The Thames Quay, 1436.

Madame Campan's Journal, 1452.

Letter to a Friend in Natchitoches, 1457.

Monthly Intelligence, from No. 1464 (Jan. 1825) monthly to No. 2082 (March 1828).

High-ways and By-ways, 1468, 1977.

The British Code of Duel, 1470.

Letter from Abraham Twaddler, 1475, 1491.

Colburniana, 1481, 1751.

Odes and Addresses to Great People, 1490.

The Last Days of Napoleon, 1503.

Surrey Quay, 1506.

Conversations of Napoleon with Canova, 1507.

Tremaine, or the Man of Refinement, 1515, 1549.

Voyage en Angleterre et en Écosse (A. Blanqui), 1518.

Theatrical Register, 1530.

Proverbes Dramatiques, trans., 1536.

Mr. Campbell's University, 1537.

Gaieties and Gravities, 1545.

Don Esteban, 1561.

Loss of the Kent East Indiaman, 1579, 1666.

The Highlands and Western Isles of Scotland, 1582.

To-Day in Ireland, 1586.

The Quarterly Review, 1589.

The late Editor of the Quarterly Review, 1598.

Voyage en Angleterre et en Écosse (A. Pichot), 1607.

Tales by the O'Hara Family, 1630, 1872.

Butleriana, 1631, 1656, 1687, 1724, 1834, 1846.

On Fashions in Physic, 1635.

A Tale of Paraguay, 1640.

The Eventful Life of a Soldier, 1650.

Notice to Correspondents, 1659.

Flowers of Speech, 1672.

Annual Souvenir Books, 1673.

Editorial Note, 1676.

Greece in 1825, 1677.

The Progress of Cant, 1681.

Lord Normanby's Matilda, 1682.

Miss Edgeworth's Harry and Lucy, 1683.

Diary of "A Constant Reader" (later, Diary for the month of ...), from No. 1685 (Jan. 1826) monthly to No. 2072 (March 1828), with the exception of Oct. 1826 and Feb. 1827.

On Dilettante Physic, 1686.

Monthly Advice to Purchasers of Books, 1692, 1707, 1728, 1745.

Table Talk, 1693, 1708, 1729, 1746, 1764, 1778, 1795, 1810, 1823, 1838, 1850.

The Naval Sketch-Book, 1698.

The Duties of a Lady's Maid, 1699.

North American Review of Lord Byron's Works and Pinkney's Poetry, 1703.

The Cambridge University, 1704.

Adventures of a Young Rifleman, 1706.

The Cambridge University. Senate-House Examinations for degrees, 1710.

Brambletye House, 1712.

Waterton's Wanderings in South America, 1716.

Chateaubriant's Sketch of Roman History, trans., 1723.

Sir Thomas Lethbridge and the Edinburgh Review, 1727.

Kalproth's Asiatic Magazine, 1733.

Williams's Tours in Jamaica, 1742.

Mathews at Home, 1744.

Six Months in the West Indies, 1749.

Two Songs, 1753.

The Three Magazines, 1757.

Execution of Mr. Berney at Norwich, 1758.

Sheridaniana, 1759.

The Diary of Luc'Antonio Viterbi, 1761.

The last number of the Quarterly Review, 1762.

Vivian Grey, 1772, 1920.

The Ladies of Africa, 1773.

Fraser's Travels and Adventures in the Persian Provinces, 1776.

Captain Maitland's Narrative of the Surrender of Buonaparte, 1777.

Electioneering, 1787.

The Life and Times of Frederick Reynolds, 1794.

Paris on diet, 1801.

Adventures of a French Serjeant, 1803.

Irish Writers on Ireland, 1804.

London University, 1809.

Gaston de Blondville, 1814.

Four Years in France, 1820.

Private History...of a morning paper, 1821.

Mier's Travels in Chili, 1822.

Lord F. L. Gower's Faust, 1828.

Head's Journies across the Pampas, 1835.

Matrimonial Tactics, 1840.

Documents respecting Milton, 1845.

Memoirs of Lindley Murray, 1848.

Appendix to the Black Book, 1852.

Souvenir Books, 1856.

Mr. Hood's Whims, 1858, 2034.

War in America, 1859.

Dr. Southwood Smith's Lectures, 1860, 1871.

Magaziniana, from No. 1865 (Dec. 1826) monthly to No. 2063 (Feb. 1828).

James's Naval History, 1877, 1905.

Scenes and Sketches of a Soldier's Life in Ireland, 1886.

The Gondola, 1904.

Munster Tales, 1908.

Alma Mater, or Seven Years at Cambridge, 1916.

National Tales, 1917.

The Living and the Dead, 1919.

Sir Walter Scott and the Waverley novels, 1925.

Servian Popular Poetry, 1928.

The Reviewers Reviewed, 1933.

De Vere, 1935.

The Military Sketch-Book, 1941.

Journal of a Traveller on the Continent, 1952.

Alexander's Journey from India to England, 1954.

The North American and Quarterly Reviews, 1970.

Rival Houses of York and Lancaster, 1971.

History of William Pitt, Earl of Chatham, 1972.

American Navy, 1975.

Madeira, 1976.

Life of Lord Eldon, 1980.

Anecdotes of Animals, 1984, 1998.

Anonymous Criticism, 1986.

Bowring's Polish Poets, 2012.

Chronicles of the Canongate, 2020, 2025.

Quarterly Review for October, 2023.

The Annuals, 2024, 2043.

Sir Walter Scott's last novel, 2025.

The Romance of History, 2030.

Tales of the Munster Festivals, 2031.

Hood's Whims. Second Series, 2034.

Sir Michael Scott, 2047.

Leigh Hunt's Lord Byron, 2057.

See also Nos. 1420, 1521, 1548, 1567, 1624, 1660, 1847, 1867.

STANLEY, EDWARD SMITH, 13th Earl of Derby, 1775-1851, zoologist. DNB.

See No. 2172.

STENDHAL (Henri Marie Beyle), 1783-1842, French essayist and novelist. DBF; Gunnell.

M. Benjamin Constant, 1394.

The Parisian Aristocracy, 1429.

Letters from Paris, 1447, 1483, 1489, 1525, 1550, 1570, 1592, 1609, 1628, 1643, 1654, 1670.

Men, Measures and Manners in France, 1465.

History of Napoleon and the Grand Army, 1471.

The Stranger, 1500.

Proverbes Dramatiques, 1536.

Italy. Secret History of the last Conclave, 1577.

The Plays of Clara Gazul, 1588.

Letter from Rome on the Present State of Italian Literature, 1619, 1678.

The Life and Adventures of an Italian Gentleman, 1633, 1646, 1684, 1735.

See also Nos. 1504, 1832.

STODDART, ISABELLA, d. 1846, writer of children's books.

She was the wife of William Hazlitt's brother-in-law, Sir John Stoddart, and she is said to have contributed to The London Magazine under the name of "Martha Blackford" (Lamb, Letters, II, 115). E. C. Ross in The Ordeal of Bridget Elia, p. 178, also states she was a contributor. Nothing by her has been traced in the magazine.

STOKES, JONATHAN.

On the Author of the "Connubia Florum," 1196.

STRONG, CHARLES, 1785-1864, poet. Allibone; Blunden, Keats's Publisher.

Sonnet, 1055, 1078, 1098.

Specimens of Sonnets, 1138, 1149, 1180, 1233, 1266, 1296.

Forest Legends, 1292, 1423.

Hymn to the Monad, 1381.

The Revelation of Beauty, 1404.

See also Nos. 206, 280, 673, 849.

TALFOURD, THOMAS NOON, 1795-1854, barrister and dramatist. DNB.

On Pulpit Oratory, 327, 356.

Mr. Charles Lloyd's Poems, 380.

The Drama, 385.

Paris in 1815 by Croly, 410.

Hazlitt's Table Talk, 411.

Sardanapalus, 587.

On the Profession of the Bar, 1488

See also Nos. 308, 384, 415.

TAYLOR, HENRY, 1800-86, dramatist. DNB.

Recent Poetical Plagiarisms, 1124, 1198.

TAYLOR, JOHN, 1781-1864, editor and publisher of The London Magazine. DNB; Blunden, Keats's Publisher; Chilcott.

Sonnet on the Death of the Poet, J. Keats, 404.

The Lion's Head, 1073, 1213, 1237, 1261, 1283, 1309, 1337, 1362, 1386, 1413.

Necrological Table, 442, 709.

Monthly Register, from No. 444 (June 1821) monthly to No. 1435 (Dec. 1824); see note at No. 878.

On Spenser's supposed acquaintance with Shakespeare, 496.

The Poet, 521.

A Visit to John Clare, 548.

Sonnet, 568, 640.

On a Free Paper Currency, 615.

The Inconstant Lady, 714.

The Phrenological System, 760.

Original Letter from Sir Philip Francis, 943.

The Quarterly Review on Tithes, 1172.

Reply to Blackwood, 1363.

The London Tithe Question, 1459, 1495.

The First Edition of Hamlet, 1517.

Proceedings in Parliament Relative to the Currency, 1726.

See also Nos. 419, 431, 445, 636, 669, 702, 704, 849, 1044, 1084, 1177, 1208, 1297, 1371, 1401.

THORNTON, THOMAS, 1786-1866, journalist. DNB.

H. Crabb Robinson's Diary for 14 December 1824 mentions "Mr. Thornton" who Southern was to employ to do the monthly review of commerce. Thomas Thornton was H. Crabb Robinson's nephew and was a Parliamentary reporter for The Times. Possibly he was responsible for the commerce report, included in this Index under Monthly Intelligence, from No. 1464 (Jan. 1825) monthly to No. 2082 (March 1828). See also No. 1825.

UNDERWOOD, THOMAS RICHARD, 1772-1835, artist and naturalist. Allibone.

The Journal of a Detenu, 1618, 1641, 1652, 1665.

VANCOUVER, CHARLES, fl. 1785-1813, American writer on agriculture. DNB.

Rural Economics, 27, 49, 78, 106.

VAN DYK, HARRY STOE, d. 1828, poet. Allibone; Tibble; Clare, Letters.

The Roses, 966.

Stanzas to --, 1017, 1321.

Poem...Jacob Westerbaen, 1020.

The Flower Spirit, 1035.

Poems...Gerbrand Brederode, 1037.

Birth-Day Verses, 1064.

Serenade, 1123.

The Nightingale, 1168.

Sonnet, 1202, 1223.

Letter from Van Dyk, 1213.

On the Death of an Infant, 1247.

Old Letters, 1267.

John A'Schaffelaar, 1291.

Tropical Recollections, 1315.

Elements of Vocal Science, 1317.

Ballad, 1323.

Song, 1339.

Hearts' Ease, 1354.

Contrasted Scenes, 1355.

On Dying for Love, 1368.

My Harp, 1388.

Stanzas, 1397.

Karl and his Horse Nicolaus, 1398.

See also Nos. 1059, 1128.

WAINEWRIGHT, THOMAS GRIFFITHS, 1794-1847, artist and art critic. DNB; Curling.

Modest Offer of Service from Mr. Bonmot, 6.

Sentimentalities on the Fine Arts, 36, 67, 92.

Notices of the Fine Arts, 46, 75, 103, 153.

Mr. Bonmot's Visit to the Editor, 55.

Janus's Jumble, 142.

Much Ado About Nothing, 149.

Mr. Weathercock's Private Correspondence, 212.

Letter from a Roué, 382, 439.

The British Institution, 386.

Exhibition of the Royal Academy, 460.

C. Van Vinkbooms, his Dogmas for Dilettanti, 502, 522, 566.

Letter from Janus Weathercock, 682.

Janus Weathercock's Reasons Against writing an account of "The Exhibition," 700.

The Delicate Intricacies, 727.

The Academy of Taste, 819.

Janus Weatherbound; or the Weathercock Steadfast for Lack of Oil, 864.

See also Nos. 430, 547.

WASHINGTON, GEORGE, 1732-99, President of U.S.A. DAB.

Original Letter of General Washington, 900.

WATKINS.

Letter of John Locke, 150.

See also No. 275.

WEBB, CORNELIUS, 1790?-1850?, poet. Allibone; Marsh, PQ.

Sonnets, 98, 122, 168, 245, 278.

Etchings of Different Kinds of Men, 399.

Song, 423.

WILKS, RICHARD, d. 1824, Rector of Enville, friend of H. F. Cary. King.

See No. 1117.

WILLIAMS, HELEN MARIA, 1762-1827, poet. DNB.

The Leper of the City of Aosta, 97.

WILLIAMS, JANE, d.c. 1884, friend of Shelley and T. J. Hogg.

The Brooke-Taylor MSS mention her writing on 31 January 1823 to ask if her tales will appear in the magazine. Nothing has been traced.

WILLIAMS, THOMAS, convict.

The Narrative of a Convict, 2200.

WILLIAMSON, J. W. Rollins.

Letter signed J. W. W., 879.

A Day of a Persian Jew, 880.

The King of Persia's Female Guards, 908.

A Road to Preferment in Persia, 932, 959.

WILLMOTT, ROBERT ELDRIDGE ARIS, 1809-63, divine and essayist. DNB; Venn.

A Thought of Harrow, 2177.

Gale of the Waters, 2188.

The Dramas of Euripides: The Hecuba, 2279.

To a Friend on his Birthday, 2294.

WOLFE and EDMONDS, stockbrokers.

Account of Canal, Dock, Bridge, Water Works Prices (included under Monthly Register), from No. 31 (Jan. 1820) monthly to No. 853 (Dec. 1822).

WOODHOUSE, RICHARD, 1788-1834, barrister. Rollins.

The Garden of Florence, 458.

"Beauty is Truth, Truth Beauty," 469.

See also No. 476.

WORDSWORTH, WILLIAM, 1770-1850, poet.   DNB; Harper.

Dion, 157.

PART THREE:

INDEX OF SIGNATURES

A.--Richard Ayton (973), Peter G. Patmore (167), 1505.

A.B.--O. Gilchrist (185).

A.B.C.--John Neal (1469).

A.B.M.--A. B. Jameson (809).

A.H.--Solomon Atkinson (1660), 1379.

A.S.--? A. Skottowe (730).

A.Y.--2040.

Abraham Twaddler.--H. Southern (1475).

AEvah.--2153.

Alexis.--1482.

Amante.--1501.

Amen.--? T. Hood or J. H. Reynolds (1520).

Ancient Amateur, An.--1546.

Anthony Rushtowne.--T. Hood (596).

Ardelius.--George Darley (1454).

Author of the Essays on English Versification, The.--W. Crowe (934).

Author of The River Derwent, The.--W. B. Clarke (928).

B.--Bernard Barton (428), John Bowring (935), B. W. Procter (190).

/B./--B. W. Procter (845).

B.B.--Bernard Barton (207).

B.C.--(for Barry Cornwall) B. W. Procter (41).

B.F.--Barron Field (624).

Barrister, A.--2204.

Billy O'Rourke.--George Darley (1366).

Bob Trimmings.--1897.

Bridget Oozeley.--1816.

C.--William Crowe (860), Allan Cunningham (668), B. W. Procter (1087), James Smith (754), 14.

C.D.--Stendhal (1619).

C.F.G.--2141, 2159.

C.S.--Charles Strong (1055).

C.W.--Cornelius Webb (245).

Chatterton, Richard.--1155, 1203.

Chevalier.--? P. G. Patmore or T. G. Wainewright (430).

Cistus.--100.

Coelebs, Agt.--H. Southern (1840).

Cogin.--T. Hood (583).

Constant Reader, \.--H. Southern (1685).

Cornelius Van Vinkbooms.--T. G. Wainewright (460).

Counselor O'D----.--John O'Driscoll (1713).

Crito-Galen.--B. W. Procter (989).

Cyril.--1079, 1146.

D.--? John Taylor (1401), ? T. De Quincey or John Taylor (1084).

Dicatus.--B. W. Procter (873).

Dissenter, A.--? John Taylor (431).

D.L.R.----n.--D. L. Richardson (1283).

Drue Digby.--Leigh Hunt (115).

E.--Hartley Coleridge (716), 1478.

E.A.--? T. Hood or J. H. Reynolds (1473).

E.B.--(for Egomet Bonmot) T. G. Wainewright (149).

E.D.--? George Darling (1305).

E.H.--(for Edward Herbert) John Hamilton Reynolds (612).

E.R.--? Eugenius Roche (403).

E.W.--(for Edward Ward) J. H. Reynolds (962).

Edgeworth Benson.--John Scott (292).

Edward Herbert (also Ed. Herbert).--J. H. Reynolds (485).

Edward Ward, Jun.--J. H. Reynolds (1151).

Egomet Bonmot.--T. G. Wainewright (6).

Eheu!--1892.

Elia.--Charles Lamb (178).

Elia's Ghost.--Charles Lamb (855).

Ellen.--1019.

English Opium-Eater.--Thomas De Quincey (503).

Ex-Theorist.--1813.

F.A.B.B.--830.

F.K.--1864.

F.R.--? Cyrus Redding (719).

F.V.--1647.

Father, A.--Horace Smith (338).

Foreign Contributor, A.--? C. L. Eastlake or John Scott (38).

Friend of Education, A.--? M. D. Hill (2266).

g.--Octavius Gilchrist (146).

G.--Octavius Gilchrist (849).

G.D.--George Darley (1601).

G.F.--1868.

G.H.P.--319.

G.O.B.--(for George Olaus Borrow) George Henry Borrow (1416).

G.S.--George Soane (736).

Gent. One &c.--J. H. Reynolds (747).

Granby.--1789.

Grasmeriensis Teutonizans.--T. De Quincey (557).

Grimm's Grandson.--Stendhal (1447).

Guilliame.--George Darley (341).

Gust. Vostermann.--B. W. Procter (873).

Gymnast.--1827.

H.--T. Hood (873), Thomas Poole (1066), Horace Smith (15), H. Southern (1804).

H.B.M.--596.

H.H.--873.

H.L.--596.

H.M.--2225.

H.O.--1754.

H.T.S.--T. J. Hogg (1636).

Handel.--? R. M. Bacon (See No. 211).
Hannibal.--? T. Hood (1040).
Harrovian, The.--R. E. A. Willmott (2177).
Henry Francis Vere Harrington Delamore.--Charles Lamb (373).
Horrida Bella.--T. Hood (1239).
Humphrey Nixon.--? J. H. Reynolds (426).

Idler, An.--C. A. Elton (497).
Incog.--T. Hood (538).
Index.--1802.

J.--John Taylor (1517).
J.A.G.--J. A. Galiffe (432).
J.B.--John Bowring (1118).
J.C.--John Clare (973).
J.C.F.--1833.
J.C.H.--J. C. Hare (1254).
J.D.--Charles Lamb (1542).
J.M.--James Montgomery (605).
J.N.--John Neal (1783).
J.P.C.--John Payne Collier (1221).
J.W.--(for Janus Weathercock) T. G. Wainewright (700).
J,W.--2200.
J.W.W.--J. W. Williamson (879).
Jack Daw.--1922.
Jacob Goosequill.--George Darley (1253).
Janus Weathercock.--T. G. Wainewright (36).

Jehu.--1606.

Jerry Sneak.--? T. Hood (1309).

John Bull.--? C. A. Elton (1015), 1320, 1356.

John Huggins.--Horace Smith (371).

John Lacy.--George Darley (1036).

John O'D----.--John O'Driscoll (1713).

Joseph Munden.--Charles Lamb (1474).

Julius.--George Darley (1327).

K.--H. S. Van Dyk (1321), ? C. A. Elton or H. S. Van Dyk (1128).

K.N.--H. Southern (1821).

K.Q.A.E.--John Payne Collier (234).

K.Q.X.--John Payne Collier (121).

L.--W. Hazlitt (131), Charles Lamb (1054), B. W. Procter (63), John Taylor (714).

---- L.--? John Bull (1320).

L.C.D.--Stendhal (1678).

L.I.--1662.

L.I.T.--H. Southern (1699).

L.L.--1891, 1901.

LL.D.--? J. Bowring or O. Gilchrist (777).

L.M.--W. Hazlitt (21).

L.S.C.--L. S. Costello (160).

L'Anonyme Litteraire.--1715.

Lacento.--C. A. Elton (1171).

Laelius.--John Payne Collier (1134).

Lauchlin Galloway.--Thomas M. Cunningham (457).

Lunatic, A.--1492.

M.--Charles Macfarlane (259), James Montgomery (567),
B. W. Procter (89), ? J. H. Reynolds (239).

M.M.--? M. M. Busk or M. R. Mitford (232).

Master Slender.--? T. Hood or B. W. Procter or J. H.
Reynolds (1581).

Mazeppa.--P. G. Patmore (294).

Minimum.--1870.

Modern Dilworth, The.--1540.

N.--James Broughton (1331), James Harley (302), John
Neal (1731), Stendhal (1536), 1882.

N.B.--1874.

N.N.--Solomon Atkinson (1553).

N.O.H.I.--John Payne Collier (1144).

N.O.H.J.--John Payne Collier (1133).

N.T.H.B.--39.

Nalla.--Allan Cunningham (790).

Navita.--1655.

Ned Ward, Jun.--J. H. Reynolds (960).

Nepos.--482.

Nimrod.--T. Hood (809).

Noemon.--H. F. Cary (447).

Old Mortality.--? Allan Cunningham (531).

Olen.--C. A. Elton (474).

One &c.--J. H. Reynolds (427).

One of the Fancy.--Octavius Gilchrist (183).

Opium-Eater.--Thomas De Quincey (503).

Ovid.--T. Hood (789).

Oxoniensis.--1791.

P.--P. G. Patmore (94).

P*.--John Poole (629).

P.A.Z.--T. Hood (1477).

P.C.--(for Peregrine Courtenay) Winthrop Mackworth Praed (2235).

P.N.D.G.--Stendhal (1447).

P.P.--(for Peter Pickleherring) George Darley (480).

P.Q.--2118.

Papinian.--1480.

Percy Green.--John Clare (1021).

Person of Sentiment, A.--J. H. Reynolds (1590).

Peter Pith.--H. Southern (1457).

P. Pickle.--George Darley (1441).

Philanthropist, A.--1446.

Philarchaeus.--John Taylor (1459).

Phil-Elia.--Charles Lamb (858).

Philopatris Londiniensis.--Charles Lamb (1097).

Pomarius.--B. W. Procter (228).

Poor Italian, A.--Antonio Panizzi (1721).

Pupil, A (of Mr. Broster).--George Darley (1601).

Quaestor.--1831.

R.--James Rice (609), and for some questionable possibilities, see Nos. 493, 571, 621.

R----.--? W. Read or J. Rice or E. Roche (634).

R.A.--Richard Ayton (741).

R.E.S.--1894, 1900, 1902.

R.H.--Reginald Heber (19).

R.N.--H. Southern (1364).

R.P.--Stendhal (1577).

R.R.--1427.

R.S.--830.

R.S.W.--? W. S. Rose (1328).

Rev. Tom Foggy Dribble.--T. De Quincey (1451).

R---d***.--1888.

Richard Chatterton.--1155, 1203.

Roué, A.--T. G. Wainewright (382).

Rustica.--402.

S.--Horace Smith (798), Charles Strong (1138), John Taylor (521), 1642, 1854.

S.D.S.--1365.

St. Alcohol.--1884.

Senex.--J. H. Reynolds (547).

Senior Wrangler.--Solomon Atkinson (1511).

Sombrerus.--1836.

Strephon.--? T. Hood or J. H. Reynolds (1467).

Surrey.--1294.

Suspensurus.--Charles Lamb (1523).

T.--W. Hazlitt (75), T. Hood (832), B. W. Procter (249).

T.C.--1788.

T.H.--? T. Hood (1651).

T.N.--1664.

T.R.--129, 272.

T.Y.--(for Tom Young), 437, 462.

Terentius Secundus.--B. W. Procter (1197).

Theodosius.--T. Hood (759).

Thersites.--Hartley Coleridge (534).

Theta.--B. W. Procter (391).

Thomas Pam.--? Charles Lamb (1689).

Thurma.--C. W. Dilke (494).

Thyrsis.--? J. H. Reynolds (359).

Timothy Walkinshaw.--Robert Hay (1324).

T. L. Dustington.--1718.

Tom Thumb the Great.--Hartley Coleridge (655).

Tom Young.--406.

U.--Cyrus Redding (764).

U.B.D.!--? T. Hood or J. H. Reynolds (1458).

Umbra.--1218.

Umbroso.--B. W. Procter (1438).

Unworthy Rector, An.--? Thomas Price or Richard Wilks (1117).

V.--W. Quin (492), John Taylor (568), 1785.

V.D.--H. S. Van Dyk (1017).

Veritas.--1799.

Veteranus.--124.

Vida.--C. A. Elton (795).

Vitruvius.--88.

W.--B. W. Procter (8), Cyrus Redding (745), H. Southern (1710).

W.H.--W. Hazlitt (285).

W.H.S.S.--1760.

W.M.I.--? J. Gordon Smith (35).

W.R.--? William Read (393).

W.S.--1539.

W. Cornelius.--Cornelius Webb (98).

Winifred Lloyd.--T. Hood (672).

X.--B. W. Procter (152), 1883.

Xx.--Charles Phillips (544).

X.Y.Z.--T. De Quincey (553).

Y.--? W. Y. Ottley (1426), 527, 2285.

Young Gentleman of the Fancy, A.--B. W. Procter (119).

Z.--T. De Quincey (946).

Zara.--596.

ΑΙΛΟΥΡΟΦΙΛΟΣ.   --Hartley Coleridge (638).

Δ.   --(delta) George Darley (849).

Ερημος.--1898.

ΘΨ.   --(theta, psi) George Croly (400).

ΜΑΙΩΝ.   --George Croly (291).

Ξ.   --(xi) W. M. Praed (2224).

[1]   --(probably an error for Ξ) W. M. Praed (2249).

ξ.   --(xi) E. M. Fitzgerald (2230).

Ουτις.   --1450.

Σ.   --(sigma) George Darley (1325).

Σς.   --(sigma, sigma) M. W. Shelley (1192).

Φορμιο.   --George Croly (425).

Ω.   --(omega) B. W. Procter (861), T. N. Talfourd (327).

Ωτος. --George Croly (523).

**
*.--? T. Hood (563).

***.--T. Hood (631), Charles Lamb (584), John Taylor (548).

****.--Charles Lamb (213).

*****.--John Clare (723).

*******.--? B. W. Procter (61).

** ************.--T. G. Wainewright (864).

✠ .--1271.

PART FOUR:

BOOK REVIEW INDEX

AUTHOR LIST

Abernethy, John. Reflections on Gall and Spurzheim's System of Physiognomy and Phrenology. 760.

Adams, Samuel and Sarah. The Complete Servant. 1627.

Addison, William. On the Nature and Properties of the Malvern Water. 2163.

Alcock, Thomas. An Essay on...Powerful Disinfecting Agents. 1893.

Alexander, James Edward. Travels from India to England. 1954.

Alighieri, Dante. L'Enfer de Dante Alighieri, trans. John C. Tarver into French. 1405.

Anciro. See Frediano, Enegildo.

Andrews, Joseph. Journey from Buenos Ayres...to Potosi. 2004.

Angeloni, Luigi. Della Forza nelle Cose Politiche. 1774.

Antommarchi, Francesco A. The Last Days of the Emperor Napoleon. 1503.

Appleyard, Ernest S. Letters from Cambridge. 2163.

Arago, Jacques E. V. Narrative of a Voyage round the World by Captain Freycinet. 917.

Ariosto, Ludovico. The Orlando Furioso, trans. William S. Rose. 1270.

Arlincourt, Charles V. P., vicomte d'. L'Etrangere. 1500.

Arrowsmith, Aaron. Eton Comparative Atlas. 2259.

Ashbach, Dr. I. (?Joseph Aschbach). History of the Western Goths. 2128.

Atherstone, Edwin. The Last Days of Herculaneum. 372.

Author of the Lives of Haydn and Mozart, The. See Beyle, Marie Henri.

Author of the Peerage and Baronetage Charts, The. See Kingdom, William.

Bacon, Richard Mackenzie. Elements of Vocal Science. 1317.

Banim, John. Tales by the O'Hara Family. 1630; second series, 1872.

Barbaroux, Charles O. (Robert Guillemard, pseud.). Adventures of a French Serjeant. 1803.

Barker, Edmund Henry. Parriana: or Notices of the Rev. Samuel Parr. 2190.

Barker, Henry. The Panorama of Matlock. 2163.

Barrington, Sir Jonah. Personal Sketches of His Own Times. 1956.

Barthélemy, Auguste M., Joseph Méry, and Jérome L. Vidal. Biographie des Quarante de l'Academie Française. 1793.

Barton, Bernard. Poems. 192.

Beamish, North Ludlow. Peace Campaigns of a Cornet. 2297.

Beaufoy, Mark. Mexican Illustrations...of Society, Manners, Religion, and Morals. 2116.

Beaumont, J. A. B. Travels in Buenos Ayres and the Adjacent Provinces. 2052.

Beazley, Samuel. The Roué. 2088.

Beddoes, Thomas Lovell. The Brides' Tragedy. 887.

Bedemar, Vargas. Travels through Sweden, Norway and Lapland. 151.

Beltrami, Giacomo C. A Pilgrimage in Europe and America. 2099.

Belzoni, Giovanni B. Travels in Egypt and Nubia. 309, 443.

Bennet, Grey. A Letter to Earl Bathurst...on New South Wales and Van Dieman's Land. 192.

Bentzel-Sternau, Christian E. K., graf von. Royal Theatre of Barataria. 2128.

Bérard, Auguste Simon Louis, Marquis de Châteaugiron, and Jean Duchesne. Isographie des Hommes Célèbres. 2139.

Bernays, Adolphus. German Poetical Anthology. 2259.

Best, Henry (afterwards Henry Digby Beste). Four Years in France. 1820.

_____. Italy as it is. 2116.

Bevan, Edward. The Honey-Bee; its Natural History, Physiology and Management. 1936.

Beyle, Marie Henri (Stendhal, the Author of the Lives of Haydn and Mozart, pseuds.). Memoirs of Rossini. 1176.

Blakiston, John. Twelve Years' Military Adventure. 2297.

Blanchard, Samuel L. Lyric Offerings. 2195.

Blanqui, Jérome A. Voyage d'un jeune Francaise en Angleterre et en Écosse. 1518.

Blunt, Joseph, ed. The American Annual Register. 1989.

Bohn, Henry George, ed. Bibliotheca Parriana. 1993.

Bowles, William Lisle. The Parochial History of Bremhill. 2105.

Bowring, John. Servian Popular Poetry. 1928.

_____. Specimens of the Polish Poets. 2012.

_____. Specimens of the Russian Poets. 358.

_____ and Harry Stoe Van Dyk. Batavian Anthology, or Specimens of the Dutch Poets. 1204.

Brady, John. Varieties of Literature, ed. John Henry Brady. 1692.

Brasbridge, Joseph. The Fruits of Experience; or Memoir of Joseph Brasbridge. 1229.

Brooke, Arthur de Capell. A Winter in Lapland and Sweden. 1940.

Brougham, Lord. A Discourse on the Objects, Advantages, and Pleasures of Science. 2099.

Brown, Capt. Biographical Sketches of Dogs. 2297.

Brown, John, of Great Yarmouth (Mandanis, pseud.). Patronage; a poem in imitation of the seventh Satire of Juvenal. 274.

Browne, John Murray. An Historical View of the Revolutions in Portugal since the close of the Peninsular War. 2116.

Browne, Mary Ann. Ada, and Other Poems. 2130.

Brydges, Sir Egerton. Res Literariae. 331, 357.

Buckingham, James S. Travels in Mesopotamia. 1926.

Bullock, William. Six Months' Residence and Travels in Mexico. 1403.

Bulwer, Sir Henry, Baron Dalling and Bulwer. An Autumn in Greece. 1677.

Bulwer-Lytton, Edward G., Baron Lytton. The Disowned. 2221, 2226.

_____. Pelham; or the Adventures of a Gentleman. 2192.

Burchell, William J. Travels in the Interior of Southern Africa. 1350.

Burnet, Gilbert. History of His Own Times. 914.

Burney, F. H., ed. The Musical Bijou. 2245.

Burton, Thomas. Diary of Thomas Burton, Esq., Member in the Parliament of Oliver Cromwell, ed. John T. Rutt. 2099.

Butler, Charles. The Life of Erasmus. 1692.

Byron, George Gordon Noel, Lord. Beauties of Don Juan. 2163.

_____. Corsair. 416.

_____. The Deformed Transformed. 1208.

_____. Don Juan. 1454.

_____. Extract from Lord Byron's Journal. 71.

_____. The Giaour. 362.

_____. Letter to **** ****** on the Rev. W. L. Bowles's Strictures on the Life and Writings of Pope. 420.

_____. Manfred. 120.

_____. Marino Faliero, Doge of Venice. 305, 412, 440.

_____. Mazeppa. 362.

_____. Sardanapalus; the Two Foscari; Cain. 587.

Campan, Jeanne L. H. Journal Anecdotique de Madame Campan, ed. M. Maigne. 1452, 1481.

Carnarvon, Henry John, Lord Porchester. Don Pedro; A Tragedy. 2099.

Caro, Annibale, trans. See Virgil.

Casanova de Seingalt, Giacomo Girolamo. Memoirs of Casanova. 1837.

Castelneau, Gabriel de, marquis. History of Russia. 488.

Catullus, Caius Valerius. The Poems of Caius Valerius Catullus, trans. George Lamb. 465.

Channing, William Ellery. Analysis of the Character of Napoleon Buonaparte. 2058, 2148.

Charles Bernard, Duke of Saxe-Weimer-Eisenach. Travels through North America. 2128.

Châteaugiron, Marquis de. See Bérard, Auguste Simon Louis et al.

255

Choiseul-Gouffier, Count. Voyage Pittoresque de la Grèce, ed. Barbié du Bocage. 196.

Cicero, Marcus Tullius. De Re Publica, ed. Angelo Maio. 57, 941.

Clapperton, Hugh. See Denham, Dixon.

Clare, John. Poems descriptive of Rural Life and Scenery. 80.

_____. The Village Minstrel and other Poems. 548.

Clarke, Edward Daniel. The Life and Remains of the Rev. Edward Daniel Clarke. 1371.

_____. Travels in...Europe, Asia, and Africa. 151.

Clarke, William. The Boy's Own Book. 2130.

Clavier, Étienne. On the Oracles of the Ancients. 40.

Cochrane, John Dundas. Narrative of a Pedestrian Journey through Russia and Siberian Tartary. 1290.

Coleridge, Henry Nelson. Six Months in the West Indies. 1749; second edition, 1883.

Collingwood, Cuthbert. A Selection from the Public and Private Correspondence of Vice-Admiral Lord Collingwood, ed. G. L. Newnham Collingwood. 2051.

Conder, Josiah. The Modern Traveller: India. 2116.

Constant, Benjamin. De la Religion. 1394.

Cooper, James Fenimore. The Last of the Mohicans. 1750.

_____. The Red Rover, a Tale. 2048.

Cornwall, Barry. See Procter, Bryan Waller.

Costello, Louisa Stuart. Redwald; a Tale of Mona and other Poems. 274.

Country Curate, A. See Neale, Erskine.

Cradock, Joseph. Literary and Miscellaneous Memoirs. 1745.

Crayon, Geoffrey. See Irving, Washington.

Croker, Thomas Crofton, ed. The Christmas Box; an
Annual Present for Children. For 1828, 2043. For
1829, 2221.

_____. Legends of the Lakes. 2231.

Croly, George. The Angel of the World. 260.

_____. Catiline. 331.

_____. May Fair. In Four Cantos. 1953.

_____. Paris in 1815, Second Part. 384, 410.

_____. Salathiel. 2107.

_____. Tales of the Great St. Bernard. 2221.

Crow, Eyre Evans. To-Day in Ireland. 1586.

Cunningham, Allan, ed. The Anniversary. 2209.

_____. Sir Marmaduke Maxwell. 823.

_____. Sir Michael Scott, a Romance. 2047.

Cunningham, Peter M. Two Years in New South Wales.
1983.

Cuvier, Georges, Baron. The Animal Kingdom, trans.
Edward Griffith. 1984, 1998.

_____. Eloges. 196.

Dalling and Bulwer, Lord. See Bulwer, Sir Henry.

Dance, Henry. Remarks on the Practical Effect of Imprisonment for Debt. 2234.

Dante. See Alighieri, Dante.

Darley, George. The Errors of Ecstasie. 1415.

Davy, Sir Humphry. Salmonia, or Days of Fly Fishing.
2158.

Deale, _____. Crockford's: or, Life in the West. 2062.

de Chaboulon, Fleury. Memoires...Napoleon in 1815. 51.

Delamotte, William Alfred. Illustrations of Virginia Water. 2176.

de la Motte-Fouqué, Frederic, Baron. Sintram and his Companions. 170.

de la Motte-Fouqué, Madame. Lodoiska and her daughter. 233.

Delanglard, C. F. P. Observations on Geographical Projections. 2135.

de la Roche-Arnaud, L'Abbé Martial-Marcet. Memoires d'un Jeune Jésuite. 2139.

d'Emden, Monsr., ed. Le Petit Bijou, for 1829. 2221.

Denham, Dixon and Hugh Clapperton. Narrative of Travels and Discoveries in Northern and Central Africa. 1773.

Denman, Thomas. Inaugural Discourse, on the Opening of the Theatre ... 2148.

De Quincey, Thomas, trans. Walladmor. 1367.

De Roos, Frederic Fitzgerald (also John F. F. De Ros). Personal Narrative of Travels in the United States and Canada. 1975.

Dibdin, Thomas J. The Reminiscences of Thomas Dibdin. 1955.

Diez de Gamez, Guttiere. The Chronicle of Don Pierre Nino, Count of Buelna. 114.

Dirom, Alexander. Remarks on Free Trade and on the State of the British Empire. 2163.

Disraeli, Benjamin. Vivian Grey. 1772; second part, 1920.

Donaldson, Joseph. Recollections of an Eventful Life. 1650.

Drake, Nathan. Memorials of Shakespeare. 2116.

du Bocage, Barbié, ed. See Choiseul-Gouffier, Count.

Duchesne, Jean. See Bérard, Auguste Simon Louis et al.

Dufief, Nicholas G. Nature Displayed, in Her System of
    Teaching Language to Man. 2245.

Du Hausset, Madame. Memoires de Madame du Hausset,
    Femme de Chambre de Madame de Pompadour. 1504.

Ebers, John. Seven Years of the King's Theatre. 2163.

Ebert, Frederich Adolf. Allgemeines Bibliographisches
    Lexikon. 164.

_____. Mr. Ebert and Mr. Dibdin. 183.

Edgcumbe, Richard, Second Earl of Mount-Edgcumbe.
    Musical Reminiscences of an Old Amateur. 1947.

Edgeworth, Maria. Harry and Lucy. 1683.

_____. Memoirs of the late R. L. Edgeworth. 130.

Egerton, Francis, First Earl of Ellesmere. Boyle Farm.
    A Poem. 2044.

Ellesmere, Earl of. See Egerton, Francis.

Ellis, George Agar. Historical Inquiries Respecting the
    Character of Edward Hyde, Earl of Clarendon. 1991.

Elton, Charles A. The Brothers. 216.

Emerson, James, Count Pecchio, and W. H. Humphreys.
    A Picture of Greece in 1825. 1677.

Faulkner, Arthur Brooke. Rambling Notes and Reflections
    Suggested during a Visit to Paris. 2007.

Field, Barron, ed. See Vaux, James Hardy.

Field, William. Memoirs of the Life, Writing and
    Opinions of the Rev. Samuel Parr. 2190.

Finlayson, George. The Mission to Siam and Huè. 1692.

Forsyth, J. S. The Natural and Medical Dieteticon.
    1562.

Forteguerri, Nicolo. The First Canto of Ricciardetto,
    trans. Lord Glenbervie. 673.

Foscolo, Ugo. Essays on Petrarch. 972.

Frank, Elizabeth. See Murray, Lindley.

Franklin, John. Narrative of a Journey to the Shores of the Polar Sea. 974.

Fraser, James Baillie. The Kuzzilbash, a Tale of Khorasan. 2116.

⎯⎯⎯⎯. Narrative of a Journey into Khorasan. 1725.

⎯⎯⎯⎯. Travels and Adventures in the Persian Provinces. 1776.

Frediano, Enegildo (Anciro, pseud.). Some Account of the Travels of the Count Enegildo Frediano in Egypt...under the assumed name of Anciro. 265.

Galt, John. The Earthquake. 310.

Gaspey, Thomas. History of George Godfrey. 2116.

Gazul, Clara. See Mérimée, Prosper.

Gent, Thomas. Poems. 384.

Gilbart, James W. A Practical Treatise on Banking. 1964.

Gioja, Melchiorre. Filosofia della Statistica. 2254.

Glascock, William Nugent. The Naval Sketch-Book. 1698.

Gleig, George R. A Narrative of the Campaigns of the British Army...in the years 1814 and 1815 /in America/. 1859.

Glenbervie, Lord, trans. See Forteguerri, Nicolo.

Godwin, William. History of the Commonwealth. 1297.

⎯⎯⎯⎯. On Population...answer to Mr. Malthus. 281.

Goethe, Johann W. von. Faust, trans. Francis Leveson Gower. 177; second edition, 1828.

⎯⎯⎯⎯. Sketches from my Life. 868.

⎯⎯⎯⎯. Ueber Kunst und Alterthum. 120, 383.

Goethe, Johann W. von. Werter /Werther/. 12.

_____. Wilhelm Meister's Apprenticeship. 1329, 1353.

_____. See Maempel, Johann C.

Goodhugh, William. The English Gentleman's Library Manual. 1978.

Gore, Catherine G. F. Hungarian Tales. 2229.

Gorton, John. A General Biographical Dictionary. 2099.

Gower, Francis Leveson, trans. See Goethe.

Graham, Maria. Three Months passed in the Mountains East of Rome. 216.

Graham, Thomas J. Sure Methods of Improving Health and Prolonging Life. 2009.

Grattan, Thomas Colley (A Walking Gentleman). High-Ways and By-Ways; or Tales of the Roadside. 1468; third series, 1977.

Green, Philip James. Sketches of the War in Greece, ed. R. L. Green. 2036.

Gregory, Olinthus G. Mathematics for Practical Men. 1692.

Grey, Elizabeth C. The Trials of Life. 2231.

Griffin, Gerald. The Collegians. 2285.

_____. Holland Tide; or Munster Popular Tales. 1908.

_____. Tales of the Munster Festivals. 2031.

Griffith, Edward, trans. See Cuvier, Georges, Baron.

Grimm, Jakob and Wilhelm. German Popular Stories. 872.

Guillemard, Robert. See Barbaroux, Charles O.

Hall, Anna Maria (Mrs. Samuel C.). The Juvenile Forget-me-not, for 1829. 2221.

Hall, Basil. Extracts from a Journal, written on the
Coasts of Chili, Peru and Mexico. 1340.

Hall, Samuel Carter, ed. The Amulet, or Christian
and Literary Remembrancer. For 1824, 2024. For
1829, 2209.

Hare, Julius Charles, trans. See Niebuhr, Barthold
Georg.

Harwood, William. On the Curative Influence of the
Southern Coast of England. 2163.

Hazlitt, William. Lectures on the Literature of the Age
of Elizabeth. 51.

_____. The Spirit of the Age. 1554.

_____. Table Talk. 384, 411, 1001.

Head, Francis Bond. Rough Notes. 1835.

Hervey, Thomas Kibble, ed. Friendship's Offering; a
Literary Album and Christmas and New Year's Gift.
For 1826, 1673. For 1827, 1856. For 1828, 2043.
For 1829, 2209.

_____. The Poetical Sketch-Book. 2297.

Hill, Isabel. The Poet's Child. 357.

Hockley, William Browne. Pandurang Hàri; or Memoirs of a
Hindoo. 1692.

Hofland, Barbara Wreaks Hoole. Africa Described. 2099.

Hogg, James. Winter Evening Tales. 151.

Hogg, Thomas Jefferson. Two Hundred and Nine Days.
1952.

Holberg, Ludwig. Journey to the World Under-ground.
2148.

Holmes, Edward. A Ramble Among the Musicians in Germany.
2130.

Hood, Thomas. National Tales. 1917.

_____. The Progress of Cant, an Etching. 1681.

Hood, Thomas. Whims and Oddities, in Prose and Verse. 1858; second series, 2034.

———— and John Hamilton Reynolds. Odes and Addresses to Great People. 1490.

Hook, Theodore E. Sayings and Doings, or Sketches from Life. Second series, 1496; third series, 2076.

Hope, Thomas. Anastasius: or Memoirs of a Greek. 24.

Horace. The Lyrics of Horace, trans. Francis Wrangham. 636.

Hughes, Thomas Smart. Travels in Sicily, Greece and Albania. 262.

Hugo, Victor Marie. Les Orientales. 2252.

Humphreys, W. H. See Emerson, James et al.

Hunt, Henry. The Memoirs of Henry Hunt. 274.

Hunt, J. H. Leigh. Hero and Leander and Bacchus and Ariadne. 167.

————. The Literary Pocket-Book. 304.

————. Lord Byron and some of his Contemporaries. 2057.

Hurwitz, Hyman. Hebrew Tales. 1707.

Irving, Edward. For the Oracles of God. 1044.

Irving, Washington (Geoffrey Crayon, pseud.). Bracebridge-Hall. 817.

————. A Chronicle of the Conquest of Granada. 2286.

————. A History of the Life and Voyages of Christopher Columbus. 2065.

————. Tales of a Traveller. 1373.

Jacob, William. A View of the Agriculture, Manufactures, Statistics and State of Germany. 352.

James, Edwin. Account of an Expedition from Pittsburgh to the Rocky Mountains. 938.

James, William. The Naval History of Great Britain. 1877, 1905.

Jennings, James. The Pleasures of Ornithology. A Poem. 2172.

Johnson, Samuel. Johnson's Dictionary of the English Language. 2099.

Johnstone, Christian Isobel. Diversions of Hollycot. 2245.

Johnstone, John, ed. See Parr, Samuel.

Judson, Ann H. An Account of the American Baptist Mission to the Burman Empire. 1961.

Keating, William H. Narrative of an Expedition /to Canada/. 1519.

Keats, John. Endymion. 87.

_____. Lamia, Isabella, the Eve of Saint Agnes. 216.

Keightley, Thomas. The Fairy Mythology. 2099.

Kennedy, William. Fitful Fancies. 2016.

_____. My Early Days. 2195.

Kent, Elizabeth. Flora Domestica. 1038.

King, Philip Parker. Narrative of a Survey of the Intertropical and Western Coasts of Australia. 1906.

Kingdom, William (The Author of the Peerage and Baronetage Charts). A Dictionary of Quotations from the British Poets. 1786.

Kitchiner, William (also Kitchener in London). The Cook's Oracle. 526, 2285.

_____. The Housekeeper's Oracle. 2297.

_____. The Traveller's Oracle. 2005.

Knapp, John Leonard. The Journal of a Naturalist. 2282.

Körner, Christian Gottfried. The Life of Carl Theodore Korner, trans., G. F. Richardson. 1985.

Lamartine, Alphonse de. Méditations Poétiques. 500.

Lamb, George, trans. See Catullus, Caius Valerius.

Lameth, Alexandre. Histoire de l'Assemblée Constituante. 2139.

Landor, Walter Savage. Imaginary Conversations. 1254.

Lawrence, James. The Etonian Out of Bounds. 2163.

Leclercq, Michael Théodore. Proverbes Dramatiques. 1536.

Liddiard, William. The Legend of Einsidlin. 2297.

Lingard, John. A Vindication of certain Passages in... the History of England. 1911.

Lister, Thomas Henry. Granby, a Novel. 1692.

_____. Herbert Lacy. 2059.

Llanos, Valentin. Don Esteban; or Memoirs of a Spaniard. 1561.

Lloyd, Charles. Desultory Thoughts in London. 380.

Lockhart, John Gibson. The Life of Robert Burns. 2100.

_____. Some Passages in the Life of Mr. Adam Blair. 686.

Longchamps, Marcelin. See Rengger, Johann R.

Lyall, Alfred. Rambles in Madeira and in Portugal. 1976.

Lyttleton, George, Baron. Lord Lyttleton's Letters. 2221.

Lytton, Lord. See Bulwer-Lytton, Edward G.

Maccormac, Henry. A Treatise on the Cause and Cure of Hesitation of Speech or Stammering. 2195.

McCrie, Thomas. History of the Progress and Suppression of the Reformation in Italy. 2042.

Macculloch, John. The Highlands and Western Isles of Scotland. 1582.

Macdonnel, D. E. A Dictionary of Quotations. 1786.

Macgregor, Duncan. A Narrative of the Loss of the Kent East Indiaman. 1666.

Maempel, Johann C. Der Junge Feldjäger, preface by Johann W. von Goethe. 1706.

Magalotti, Lorenzo. Travels of Cosmo the Third, Grand Duke of Tuscany. 478.

Maginn, William (An Officer of the Line). The Military Sketch-Book. 1941.

Mahon, Lord. See Stanhope, Philip H.

Maigne, M., ed. See Campan, Madame Jeanne L. H.

Maio, Angelo, ed. See Cicero, Marcus Tullius.

Maitland, Frederick Lewis. Narrative of the Surrender of Buonaparte and of his Residence on Board H. M. S. Bellerophon. 1777.

Major, John, ed. See Walton, Izaak.

Malcolm, Sir John. Sketches of Persia. 2022.

_____. Tales of Field and Flood. 2297.

Malet, Alexander. Some Account of the System of Fagging at Winchester School. 2216.

Malone, Edmund, ed. See Spence, Joseph.

Mandanis. See Brown, John, of Great Yarmouth.

Manzoni, Alexander. Il Conte di Carmagnola. 209, 252, 383.

?Marvell, Andrew. Flagellum Parliamentarium. 1942.

Mathias, Thomas J., trans. See Spenser, Edmund.

Matthews, Henry. The Diary of an Invalid. 170.

Matthews, William. An Historical Sketch of the Origin, Progress and Present State of Gas-Lighting. 2032.

Maturin, Charles R. Melmoth the Wanderer. 311, 401.

_____. See Wills, James.

Maugham, Robert. A Treatise on the Laws of Literary Property. 2217.

Medwin, Thomas. Journal of the Conversations of Lord Byron. 1387.

Meissner, Edward. Observations...in a Journey From Odessa, through a part of Germany, Holland, England and Scotland. 108.

Meli, Giovanni. Don Chisciotte e Sancio Panza nella Scizia. 381.

Mérimée, Prosper (Clara Gazul, pseud.). Théatre de Clara Gazul, Comédienne Espagnole. 1588, 1692.

Méry, Joseph. See Barthélemy, Auguste M. et al.

Miers, John. Travels in Chile and La Plata. 1822.

Miller, John. Memoirs of General Miller. 2194.

Milman, Henry Hart. The Fall of Jerusalem. 151.

Mitford, Mary Russell. Our Village. 2119.

Mitford, William. History of Greece. 1556.

Monkland, Mrs. Life in India. 2209.

Montgomery, James. The Pelican Island and Other Poems. 1996.

_____. Polyhymnia. 702.

_____. Prose by a Poet. 1179.

_____. Songs of Zion. 849.

Moore, Thomas. Irish Melodies. 438.

_____. The Loves of the Angels. 899.

_____. Memoirs of Captain Rock. 1262.

Morgan, Sydney (Owenson), Lady. The O'Briens and the O'Flahertys, a National Tale. 2041.

Morgann, Maurice. An Essay on the Dramatic Character of Sir John Falstaff. 51.

Morier, James J. Adventures of Hajji Baba of Ispahan. 1177, 2130.

Mount-Edgcumbe, Second Earl of. See Edgcumbe, Richard.

Moxon, Edward. Christmas; a Poem. 2231.

Mudie, Robert. Babylon the Great...the British Capital. 2163.

————. A Second Judgment of Babylon the Great. 2259.

Murray, Lindley. Memoirs of the Life and Writings of Lindley Murray, with a continuation by Elizabeth Frank. 1848.

Neale, Erskine (A Country Curate). The Living and the Dead. 1919.

Neele, Henry. The Romance of History. England. 2030.

Nicolas, Nicholas Harris, ed. An Account of the Expenses of the Privy Purse of King Henry VIII. 1995.

————. The History of the Battle of Agincourt. 2017.

Niebuhr, Barthold Georg. Carsten Niebuhr's Leben. 2270.

————. The History of Rome. Trans. F. A. Walter, 1968. Trans. Julius Charles Hare and Connop Thirlwall, 2094.

Niemeyer, August Hermann. Travels. 752.

Nodier, Charles. Jean Sbogar. 204.

Norgate, E. Mr. John Hunter defended. 1783.

Normanby, Lord. See Phipps, Constantine Henry.

Oehlenschläger, Adam Gottlob (Ochlenschäger in London). Correggio. 231.

Officer of the Line, An. See Maginn, William.

O'Meara, Barry E. A Voice from St. Helena. 705, 724.

Opie, Amelia (Alderson). Illustrations of Lying, in all its Branches. 1547.

Paris, John Ayrton. Philosophy in Sport made Science in Earnest. 1969.

_____. A Treatise on Diet. 1801.

Parkes, Joseph. A History of the Court of Chancery. 2060.

Parr, Samuel. Aphorisms, Opinions and Reflections of the Late Dr. Parr. 2190.

_____. The Works of Samuel Parr, ed. John Johnstone. 2190.

Parry, William E. Journal of a Second Voyage for the Discovery of a North-West Passage. 1242.

_____. Journal of a Voyage for the Discovery of a North-West Passage. 434.

Pecchio, Count. See Emerson, James et al.

Pennie, John F. The Tale of a Modern Genius, or the Miseries of Parnassus. 2028.

Pepys, Samuel. Diary of Samuel Pepys. 1669.

Philidor, François A. D. Studies of Chess. 1608.

Phillips, Sir Richard. Personal Tour Through the United Kingdom. 2221.

Phipps, Constantine H., Lord Normanby. Historiettes, or Tales of Continental Life. 1951.

_____. Matilda. 1682.

Pichot, Amedee. Voyage Historique et Littéraire en Angleterre et en Écosse. 1607.

Planche, James R. Descent of the Danube. 2163.

Plumptre, James (Plumtre in London). Original Dramas. 59.

Poole, Richard. An Essay on Education. 1692.

Porchester, Lord. See Carnarvon, Henry John.

Prévôt, C. V. See Arlincourt, vicomte d'.

Pringle, Thomas. Ephemerides, or Occasional Poems. 2099.

Procter, Bryan Waller (Barry Cornwall, pseud.). The Flood of Thessaly. 946, 996.

_____. Marcian Colonna. 170.

_____. Mirandola. 305, 332.

_____. A Sicilian Story. 24.

Radcliffe, Anne. Gaston de Blondeville. 1814.

Reade, Edmund. Sybil Leaves. 1934.

Rengger, Johann R. and Marcelin Longchamps. The Reign of Doctor Joseph Gaspard Roderick De Francia in Paraguay, trans. J. R. Rengger. 1990.

Rennie, Elizabeth. Poems. 2130.

Reynolds, Frederick. The Life and Times of Frederick Reynolds. 1794.

Reynolds, Frederic Mansel, ed. The Keepsake, for 1829. 2221.

Reynolds, John Hamilton. The Fancy. 170.

_____. The Garden of Florence. 357, 458.

_____ and Thomas Hood. Odes and Addresses to Great People. 1490.

Rhodes, Edward. Peak Scenery, or Excursions in Derbyshire. 1130.

Richardson, Charlotte C. Poems. 2163.

Richardson, G. F., trans. See Körner, Christian G.

Ritchie, Leitch. Tales and Confessions. 2231.

Robarts, Anne. Memoirs of the Rival Houses of York and Lancaster. 1971.

Roberts, Orlando W. Narrative of Voyages and Excursions ...in...Central America. 2039.

Roche, Regina M. Contrast. A Novel. 2116.

Roederer, Pierre L. Memoirs of Louis XII and Francis I. 2003.

Room, Charles. Herculaneum and Other Poems. 2099.

Rose, William S., trans. See Ariosto, Ludovico.

Rovigo, duc de. See Savary, Anne J. M. R.

Rutt, John T., ed. See Burton, Thomas.

Saint-Elme, Ida. See Versfelt, Maria E. J.

Savary, Anne Jean Marie René, duc de Rovigo. Memoirs of the Duke of Rovigo. 2139, 2148, 2163.

Saxe-Weimar-Eisenach, Duke of. See Charles Bernard.

Scargill, William Pitt. Elizabeth Evanshaw, a Novel. 2046.

_____. Truckleborough Hall, A Novel. 1907.

Schiller, Johann C. F. von. Wallenstein, a dramatic poem. 1918.

?Schlegel, August W. von. Berichtigung einiger Missductungen. 2128.

Scott, Sir Walter. The Abbot. 237.

_____. The Chronicles of the Canongate. 2025.

_____. Halidon Hill. 754.

_____. Ivanhoe. 24.

_____. Kenilworth. 305, 328.

Scott, Sir Walter. The Monastery. 130.

———. Peveril of the Peak. 897.

———. The Pirate. 590.

———. Redgauntlet. 1300.

———. Tales of the Crusaders. 1612.

———. The Waverley Novels, a new edition. 2295.

———. Woodstock, or the Cavalier. 1768.

Sebastani, D. Leopoldo. A New System of Moral Philosophy. 57.

Ségur, Philippe Paul, comte de. Histoire de Napoleon et de la Grande Armee. 1471.

———. A History of Russia. 2297.

Senior, Nassau W. An Introductory Lecture on Political Economy. 1962.

———. Two Lectures on Population. 2289.

Shelley, Percy Bysshe. The Cenci. 130.

———. Charles the First. 305.

Sheridan, Richard B. Sheridaniana. 1759.

Shipp, John. Scenes and Sketches of a Soldier's Life in Ireland. 1886.

Shoberl, Frederic, ed. Forget Me Not, A Christmas and New Year's Present. For 1826, 1673. For 1827, 1856. For 1828, 2024. For 1829, 2209.

Siddons, Sarah. The Story of our First Parents, selected from Milton's Paradise Lost. 900.

Singer, S. W., ed. See Spence, Joseph.

Smart, Christopher. Song to David. 80.

Smith, Horace. Brambletye House. 1712.

———. Gaieties and Gravities. 1545.

Smyth, William H. Memoir descriptive of...Sicily.
    1190, 1224.

_____. Sketch of the Present State...of Sardinia.
    2099.

Snodgrass, John J. Narrative of the Burmese War. 1890.

Southey, Robert. The Life of Wesley. 192, 431.

_____. A Tale of Paraguay. 1640.

_____. A Vision of Judgment. 384.

Southey, Thomas. Chronological History of the West
    Indies. 2011.

Spence, Joseph. Anecdotes, Observations and Characters
    of Books and Men, editions by S. W. Singer and by
    Edmund Malone. 51.

Spenser, Edmund. Il Cavaliero della Croce Rossa, trans.
    Thomas J. Mathias into Italian. 1784.

Spiker, Samuel H. Tour Through England, Wales and Scot-
    land. 117.

Staël, Madame de. Ten Years' Exile. 516.

Stanhope, Marianne S. Almack's, A Novel. 1875.

Stanhope, Philip H., Lord Mahon. Life of Belisarius.
    2297.

Stendhal. See Beyle, Marie Henri.

Sternau, Ernst Benzel. See Bentzel-Sternau,
    Christian E. K., graf von.

Stewart, Alexander. Stories from the History of Scot-
    land. 2297.

Sydney, pseud. Sydney's Letters...on the reported ex-
    clusion of Lord Byron's monument from Westminster
    Abbey. 2195.

Taaffe, John. A Comment on the Divine Comedy. 918, 933.

Tarver, John C. A Complete System of French Pronunciation. 2163.

_____, trans. See Alighieri, Dante.

Taylor, Arthur. The Glory of Regality. 170.

Taylor, William. Historic Survey of German Poetry. 2168.

Telesforo de Trueba y Cossio. See Trueba y Cossio, Telesforo de.

Teonge, Henry. The Diary of Henry Teonge. 1566.

Thackeray, Francis. A History of the Right Honorable William Pitt. 1972.

Thirlwall, Connop, trans. See Niebuhr, Barthold Georg.

Thompson, George. Travels and Adventures in Southern Africa. 1981.

Timbs, John, ed. The Arcana of Science and Art. 2099.

_____. Cameleon Sketches. 2116.

Todd, Henry J. Some Account of the Life and Writings of John Milton. 1845.

Tone, Theobald Wolfe. Memoirs. 1946.

Tooke, Thomas. A Letter to Lord Grenville on...the Currency. 2246.

Townsend, Chauncy H. The Reigning Vice, a satirical essay. 2130.

Trant, Thomas A. Two Years in Ava. 1999.

Trueba y Cossio, Telesford de. The Castillian. 2259.

Turner, Sharon. The History of the Reign of Henry VIII. 1889.

Ude, Louis Eustace. The French Cook. 1449, 2285.

Van Dyk, Harry Stoe. The Gondola. 1904.

Van Dyk, Harry Stoe and John Bowring. Batavian Anthology. 1204.

Varley, John. A Treatise on Zodiacal Physiognomy. 2231.

Vaux, James Hardy. Memoirs, ed. Barron Field. 7; second edition, 1992.

Vernon, Henry. See Wightwick, George.

Versfelt, Maria E. J. (Ida Saint-Elme, pseud.). Memoires d'une Contemporaine. 2081.

Vidal, Jérome L. See Barthélemy, Auguste M. et al.

Virgil. The Eneid of Virgil, trans. Annibale Caro into Italian. 154.

Voss, Johann H. Life of Hölty. 544.

Wadd, William. Comments on Corpulency. 2231.

_____. Mems, Maxims and Memoirs. 2002.

Wade, John. Appendix to the Black Book. 1852.

Walking Gentleman, A. See Grattan, Thomas Colley.

Walter, F. A., trans. See Niebuhr, Barthold Georg.

Walton, Izaak. The Complete Angler, ed. John Major. 986.

Ward, Robert Plumer. De Vere; or the Man of Independence. 1935.

_____. Tremaine; or the Man of Refinement. 1515, 1549.

Warner, Richard. Church of England Theology. 543.

Waterton, Charles. Wanderings in South America, etc. 1716.

Watts, Alaric A., ed. The Literary Souvenir, for 1829. 2209.

Watts, Zillah, ed. The New Year's Gift, for 1829. 2221.

White, Charles. Herbert Milton. 2059.

Wightwick, George (Henry Vernon, pseud.). The Life and
   Remains of Wilmot Warwick. 2195.

Williams, Cynric R. A Tour in the Island of Jamaica.
   1742.

Wills, James. The Universe. Although the poem bears
   Charles R. Maturin's name, it is by Wills. 415.

Wilmot, Edward. Ugolino, or the Towers of Famine.
   2148.

Wilson, Thomas. The Yule Log. 2231.

Wrangham, Francis, trans. See Horace.

Wright, T. Some Account of the Life of Richard Wilson.
   1559.

TITLE LIST

Abbott, The. Sir Walter Scott. 237.

Account of a New Process in Painting, An. 955.

Account of an Expedition from Pittsburgh to the Rocky Mountains. Edwin James. 938.

Account of the American Baptist Mission to the Burman Empire, An. Ann H. Judson. 1961.

Account of the Expenses of the Privy Purse of King Henry VIII, An. Nicholas Harris Nicolas, ed. 1995.

Ada and Other Poems. Mary Ann Browne. 2130.

Adventures of a French Serjeant. Charles O. Barbaroux (Robert Guillemard, pseud.). 1803.

Adventures of Hajji Baba of Ispahan. James J. Morier. 1177, 2130.

Africa Described. Barbara Wreaks Hoole Hofland. 2099.

Allgemeines Bibliographisches Lexikon. Frederich Adolf Ebert. 164.

Almack's, A Novel. Marianne S. Stanhope. 1875.

Alma Mater, or Seven Years at the University of Cambridge. 1916.

America, An Epistle in Verse. 274.

American Annual Register, The. Joseph Blunt, ed. 1989.

Amulet, or Christian and Literary Remembrancer, The. Samuel Carter Hall, ed. For 1828, 2024; for 1829, 2209.

Analysis of the Character of Napoleon Buonaparte. William Ellery Channing. 2148.

Anastasius: or Memoirs of a Greek. Thomas Hope. 24.

Anecdotes, Observations and Characters of Books and Men, editions by S. W. Singer and Edmund Malone. Joseph Spence. 51.

Angel of the World, The. George Croly. 260.

Animal Kingdom, The, trans. Edward Griffith. Baron Georges Cuvier. 1984, 1998.

Anniversary, The. Allan Cunningham, ed. 2209.

Aphorisms, Opinions and Reflections of the Late Dr. Parr. Samuel Parr. 2190.

Appendix to the Black Book. John Wade. 1852.

Arcana of Science and Art, The. John Timbs, ed. 2099.

Atlantic Souvenir: A Christmas and New Year Offering for 1829. 2221.

Attempt to Remove the Differences Caused by Count Munster, An. 2128.

Autumn in Greece, An. Sir Henry Bulwer, Lord Dalling and Bulwer. 1677.

Babylon the Great. Robert Mudie. 2163.

Batavian Anthology, or Specimens of the Dutch Poets. John Bowring and Harry Stoe Van Dyk. 1204.

Beauties of Don Juan. Lord Byron. 2163.

Beauties of Mozart, Handel, Pleyel, Haydn, Beethoven... adapted to the words of popular psalms and hymns, The. 508.

Berichtigung einiger Missductungen. ?August W. von Schlegel. 2128.

Bibliotheca Parriana. Henry George Bohn, ed. 1993.

Bijou, or Annual of Literature and Arts, The. 2024.

Biographical Sketches of Dogs. Capt. Brown. 2297.

Biographie des Quarante de l'Academie Française. Auguste M. Barthélemy, Joseph Méry and Jérome L. Vidal. 1793.

Boyle Farm. A Poem. Francis Egerton, First Earl of
    Ellesmere. 2044.

Boy's Own Book, The. William Clarke. 2130.

Bracebridge-Hall. Washington Irving. 817.

Brambletye House. Horace Smith. 1712.

Brides' Tragedy, The. Thomas Lovell Beddoes. 887.

British Code of Duel, The. 1470.

Brothers, The. Charles A. Elton. 216.

Cameleon Sketches. John Timbs. 2116.

Carsten Niebuhr's Leben. Barthold Georg Niebuhr. 2270.

Castilian, The. Telesforo de Trueba y Cossio. 2259.

Catiline. George Croly. 331.

Cavaliero della Croce Rossa...di Edmundo Spenser, Il.
    Thomas J. Mathias, trans. 1784.

Cenci, The. Percy Bysshe Shelley. 130.

Charles the First. Percy Bysshe Shelley. 305.

Christmas: A Poem. Edward Moxon. 2231.

Christmas Box; an Annual Present for Children, The.
    Thomas Crofton Croker, ed. For 1828, 2043; for
    1829, 2221.

Chronological History of the West Indies. Thomas
    Southey. 2011.

Chronicle of Don Pierre Nino, Count of Buelna, The.
    Guttiere Diez de Gamez. 114.

Chronicle of the Conquest of Granada, A. Washington
    Irving. 2286.

Chronicles of the Canongate, The. Sir Walter Scott.
    2025.

Church of England Theology. Richard Warner. 543.

Collegians, The. Gerald Griffin. 2285.

Comment on the Divine Comedy, A. John Taaffe. 918, 933.

Comments on Corpulency. William Wadd. 2231.

Companion to the Almanac. 2099.

Complete Angler, The, ed. John Major. Izaak Walton. 986.

Complete Servant, The. Sarah and Samuel Adams. 1627.

Complete System of French Pronunciation, A. John C. Tarver. 2163.

Conte di Carmagnola, Il. Alexander Manzoni. 209, 252, 383.

Contrast. A Novel. Regina M. Roche. 2116.

Cook's Oracle, The. William Kitchiner. 526, 2285.

Correggio. Adam Gottlob Oehlenschlager. 231.

Corsair. Lord Byron. 416.

Crockford's: or Life in the West. _____ Deale. 2062.

Deformed Transformed, The. Lord Byron. 1208.

De la Religion. Benjamin Constant. 1394.

Della Forza nelle Cose Poliliche. Luigi Angeloni. 1774.

De Re Publica, ed. Angelo Maio. Cicero. 57, 941.

Der Junge Feldjäger, preface by J. W. von Goethe. Johann C. Maempel. 1706.

Descent of the Danube. James R. Planché. 2163.

Desultory Thoughts in London. Charles Lloyd. 380.

De Vere; or the Man of Independence. Robert Plumer Ward. 1935.

Diary of an Invalid, The. Henry Matthews. 170.

Diary of Henry Teonge, The. Henry Teonge. 1566.

Diary of Samuel Pepys. Samuel Pepys. 1669.

Diary of Thomas Burton, Esq., Member in the Parliament of Oliver Cromwell, ed. John T. Rutt. Thomas Burton. 2099.

Dictionary of Quotations, A. D. E. Macdonnel. 1786.

Dictionary of Quotations from the British Poets, A. William Kingdom. 1786.

Discourse on the Objects, Advantages and Pleasures of Science, A. Lord Brougham. 2099.

Disowned, The. Edward G. Bulwer-Lytton, Baron Lytton, 2221, 2226.

Diversions of Hollycot. Mrs. Christian Isobel Johnstone. 2245.

Don Chisciotte e Sancio Panza nella Scizia. Giovanni Meli. 381.

Don Esteban; or, Memoirs of a Spaniard. Valentin Llanos. 1561.

Don Juan. Lord Byron. 1454.

Don Pedro; a Tragedy. Henry John Carnarvon, Lord Porchester. 2099.

Doveri dei Sudditi verso il loro Monarca. 1770.

Duties of a Lady's Maid. 1699.

Earthquake, The. John Galt. 310.

Elements of Vocal Science. Richard Mackenzie Bacon. 1317.

Elizabeth Evanshaw, a Novel. William Pitt Scargill. 2046.

Eloges. Baron Georges Cuvier. 196.

Endymion. John Keats. 87.

Eneid of Virgil, The, trans. Annibale Caro into Italian. Virgil. 154.

L'Enfer de Dante Alighieri, trans. John C. Tarver into
French. Dante Alighieri. 1405.

English Gentleman's Library Manual, The. William
Goodhugh. 1978.

Ephemerides, or Occasional Poems. Thomas Pringle.
2099.

Errors of Ecstasie, The. George Darley. 1415.

Essay on Education, An. Richard Poole. 1692.

Essay on the Dramatic Character of Sir John Falstaff, An.
Maurice Morgann. 51.

Essay on...Powerful Disinfecting Agents, An. Thomas
Alcock. 1893.

Essays on Petrarch. Ugo Foscolo. 972.

Eton Comparative Atlas. Aaron Arrowsmith. 2259.

Etonian Out of Bounds, The. James Lawrence. 2163.

Etrangère, L',Charles V. P., vicomte d'Arlincourt. 1500.

Extract from Lord Byron's Journal. Lord Byron. 71.

Extracts from a Journal, written on the Coasts of Chili,
Peru and Mexico. Basil Hall. 1340.

Fairy Mythology, The. Thomas Keightley. 2099.

Fall of Jerusalem, The. Henry Hart Milman. 151.

Fancy, The. John Hamilton Reynolds. 170.

Faust, trans. Francis Leveson Gower. J. W. von Goethe.
177; second edition, 1828.

Filosofia della Statistica. Melchiorre Gioja. 2254.

First Canto of Ricciardetto, The, trans. Lord Glenbervie. Nicolo Forteguerri. 673.

Fitful Fancies. William Kennedy. 2016.

Flagellum Parliamentarium. ?Andrew Marvell. 1942.

Flood of Thessaly, The. Bryan Waller Procter (Barry Cornwall, pseud.). 946, 996.

Flora Domestica. Elizabeth Kent. 1038.

Forget Me Not, a Christmas and New Year's Present. Frederic Shoberl, ed. For 1826, 1673; for 1827, 1856; for 1828, 2024; for 1829, 2209.

For the Oracles of God. Edward Irving. 1044.

Four Years in France. Henry Best. 1820.

French Cook, The. Louis Eustace Ude. 1449, 2285.

Friendship's Offering; a Literary Album and Christmas and New Year's Gift. Thomas Kibble Hervey, ed. For 1826, 1673; for 1827, 1856; for 1828, 2043; for 1829, 2209.

Fruits of Experience; or Memoir of Joseph Brasbridge, The. Joseph Brasbridge. 1229.

Gaieties and Gravities. Horace Smith. 1545.

Garden of Florence, The. John Hamilton Reynolds. 357, 458.

Gaston de Blondeville. Anne Radcliffe. 1814.

General Biographical Dictionary, A. John Gorton. 2099.

German Poetical Anthology. Adolphus Bernays. 2259.

German Popular Stories. Jakob and Wilhelm Grimm. 872.

Gift of an Uncle, The. 2245.

Giour, The. Lord Byron. 362.

Glory of Regality, The. Arthur Taylor. 170.

Gondola, The. Harry Stoe Van Dyk. 1904.

Granby, a Novel. Thomas Henry Lister. 1692.

Halidon Hill. Sir Walter Scott. 754.

Hamel, the Obeah Man. 1950.

Harrovian, The. 2116.

Harry and Lucy. Maria Edgeworth. 1683.

Hebrew Tales. Hyman Hurwitz. 1707.

Herbert Lacy. Thomas Henry Lister. 2059.

Herbert Milton. Charles White. 2059.

Herculaneum and Other Poems. Charles Room. 2099.

Hero and Leander and Bacchus and Ariadne. J. H. Leigh Hunt. 167.

Highlands and Western Isles of Scotland, The. John Macculloch. 1582.

High-Ways and By-Ways; or, Tales of the Road-Side. Thomas Colley Grattan. 1468; third series, 1977.

Histoire de l'Assemblée Constituante. Alexandre Lameth. 2139.

Histoire de Napoleon et de la Grande Armée. Philippe Paul, comte de Ségur. 1471.

Historic Survey of German Poetry. William Taylor. 2168.

Historical Inquiries respecting the Character of Edward Hyde, Earl of Clarendon. George Agar Ellis. 1991.

Historical Sketch of the Origin, Progress and Present State of Gas-Lighting, An. William Matthews. 2032.

Historical View of the Revolutions in Portugal since the Close of the Peninsular War, An. John Murray Browne. 2116.

Historiettes, or Tales of Continental Life. Constantine H. Phipps, Lord Normanby. 1951.

History of George Godfrey. Thomas Gaspey. 2116.

History of Greece. William Mitford. 1556.

History of His Own Times. Gilbert Burnet. 914.

History of Rome, The. Barthold Georg Niebuhr. Trans.
F. A. Walter, 1968; trans. J. C. Hare and Connop
Thirlwall, 2094.

History of Russia. Gabriel, marquis de Castelneau. 488.

History of Russia, A. Philippe Paul, comte de Ségur.
2297.

History of the Battle of Agincourt, The. Nicholas
Harris Nicolas. 2017.

History of the Commonwealth. William Godwin. 1297.

History of the Court of Chancery, A. Joseph Parkes.
2060.

History of the Life and Voyages of Christopher
Columbus, A. Washington Irving. 2065.

History of the Progress and Suppression of the Reformation in Italy. Thomas McCrie. 2042.

History of the Reign of Henry VIII, The. Sharon
Turner. 1889.

History of the Right Honourable William Pitt, A.
Francis Thackeray. 1972.

History of the Western Goths. Dr. I. Ashbach. 2128.

Holland Tide; or Munster Popular Tales. Gerald Griffin.
1908.

Honey-bee; its Natural History, Physiology and Management, The. Edward Bevan. 1936.

Housekeeper's Oracle, The. William Kitchiner. 2297.

Hungarian Tales. Catherine G. F. Gore. 2229.

Illustrations of Lying, in all its Branches. Amelia
(Alderson) Opie. 1547.

Illustrations of Virginia Water. William Alfred Delamotte. 2176.

Imaginary Conversations. Walter Savage Landor. 1254.

Inaugural Discourse on the Opening of the Theatre.
    Thomas Denman. 2148.

Introductory Lecture on Political Economy, An. Nassau
    W. Senior. 1962.

Irish Melodies. Thomas Moore. 438.

Isographie des Hommes Célèbres. Auguste Simon Louis
    Bérard, Marquis de Châteaugiron and Jean Duchesne.
    2139.

Italy as it is. Henry Best. 2116.

Ivanhoe. Sir Walter Scott. 24.

Jean Sbogar. Charles Nodier. 204.

Johnson's Dictionary of the English Language. Samuel
    Johnson. 2099.

Journal Anecdotique de Madame Campan, ed. M. Maigne.
    Jeanne L. H. Campan. 1452, 1481.

Journal of a Naturalist, The. John Leonard Knapp. 2282.

Journal of a Second Voyage for the Discovery of a North-
    West Passage. William E. Parry. 1242.

Journal of a Voyage for the Discovery of a North-West
    Passage. William E. Parry. 434.

Journal of the Conversations of Lord Byron. Thomas
    Medwin. 1387.

Journey from Buenos Ayres...to Potosi. Joseph Andrews.
    2004.

Journey to the World Under-ground. Ludwig Holberg.
    2148.

Juvenile Forget-Me-Not, The. Anna Maria Hall, ed. 2221.

Keepsake, The. Frederic Mansel Reynolds, ed. 2221.

Kenilworth. Sir Walter Scott. 305, 328.

Kuzzilbash, a Tale of Khorasan, The. James Baillie
    Fraser. 2116.

Lamia, Isabella, the Eve of Saint Agnes. John Keats. 216.

Last Days of Herculaneum, The. Edwin Atherstone. 372.

Last Days of the Emperor Napoleon, The. Francesco A. Antommarchi. 1503.

Last of the Mohicans, The. James Fenimore Cooper. 1750.

Lectures on the Literature of the Age of Elizabeth. William Hazlitt. 51.

Legend of Einsidlin, The. William Liddiard. 2297.

Legends of the Lakes. Thomas Crofton Croker. 2231.

Les Orientales. Victor Marie Hugo. 2252.

Letter to Earl Bathurst...on New South Wales and Van Dieman's Land, A. Grey Bennet. 192.

Letter to Lord Grenville on...the Currency. Thomas Tooke. 2246.

Letter to **** ****** on the Rev. W. L. Bowles's Strictures on the Life and Writings of Pope. Lord Byron. 420.

Letters from Cambridge. Ernest S. Appleyard. 2163.

Life and Remains of the Rev. Edward Daniel Clarke, The. Edward Daniel Clarke. 1371.

Life and Remains of Wilmot Warwick, The. George Wightwick. 2195.

Life and Times of Frederick Reynolds, The. Frederick Reynolds. 1794.

Life in India. Mrs. Monkland. 2209.

Life of Belisarius. Philip H. Stanhope, Lord Mahon. 2297.

Life of Carl Theodore Körner, The, trans. G. F. Richardson. Christian Gottfried Körner. 1985.

Life of Erasmus, The. Charles Butler. 1692.

Life of Hölty. Johann H. Voss. 544.

Life of Robert Burns, The. John Gibson Lockhart. 2100.

Life of Wesley, The. Robert Southey. 192, 431.

Life, Political and Official, of John, Earl of Eldon,
    late Lord High Chancellor, The. 1980.

Literary and Miscellaneous Memoirs. Joseph Cradock.
    1745.

Literary Pocket-Book, The. J. H. Leigh Hunt. 304.

Literary Souvenir, The. Alaric A. Watts, ed. For 1829,
    2209.

Living and the Dead, The. Erskine Neale. 1919.

Lodoiska and her daughter. Madame de la Motte-Fouqué.
    233.

London in 1819. By the Author of a Year in London. 108.

London Lithograph Album for 1828. 2092.

Lord Byron and Some of his Contemporaries. J. H. Leigh
    Hunt. 2057.

Lord Lyttleton's Letters. George, Baron Lyttleton.
    2221.

Loves of the Angels, The. Thomas Moore. 899.

Lyric Offerings. Samuel L. Blanchard. 2195.

Lyrics of Horace, The, trans. Francis Wrangham. Horace,
    636.

Manfred. Lord Byron. 120.

Marcian Colonna. Bryan Waller Procter. 170.

Marino Faliero, Doge of Venice. Lord Byron. 305, 412,
    440.

Marly; or a Planter's Life in Jamaica. 2099.

Mary Harland, or a Journey to London, a Tale of Humble
    Life. 2099.

Mathematics for Practical Men. Olinthus G. Gregory.
    1692.

Matilda. Constantine H. Phipps, Lord Normanby. 1682.

May Fair. In Four Cantos. George Croly. 1953.

Mazeppa. Lord Byron. 362.

Méditations Poétiques. Alphonse de Lamartine. 500.

Melmoth the Wanderer. Charles R. Maturin. 311, 401.

Memoir descriptive of...Sicily. William H. Smyth. 1190, 1224.

Memoires de Madame du Hausset, Femme de Chambre de Madame de Pompadour. Madame du Hausset. 1504.

Memoires d'une Contemporaine. Maria E. J. Versfelt. 2081.

Memoires d'un Jeune Jésuite. L'Abbé Martial-Marcet de la Roche-Arnaud. 2139.

Memoires...Napoleon in 1815. Fleury de Chaboulon. 51.

Memoirs. Theobald Wolfe Tone. 1946.

Memoirs, ed. Barron Field. James Hardy Vaux. 7, 1992.

Memoirs of Captain Rock. Thomas Moore. 1262.

Memoirs of Casanova. Giacomo Girolamo Casanova de Seingalt. 1837.

Memoirs of General Miller. John Miller. 2194.

Memoirs of Henry Hunt, The. Henry Hunt. 274.

Memoirs of Louix XII and Francis I. Pierre L. Roederer. 2003.

Memoirs of Rossini. Marie Henri Beyle (Stendhal, pseud.). 1176.

Memoirs of the Duke of Rovigo. Anne J. M. R. Savary, duc de Rovigo. 2139, 2148, 2163.

Memoirs of the late R. L. Edgeworth. Maria Edgeworth. 130.

Memoirs of the Life and Writings of Lindley Murray, continued by Elizabeth Frank. Lindley Murray. 1848.

Memoirs of the Life, Writing and Opinions of the Rev. Samuel Parr. William Field. 2190.

Memoirs of the Margravine of Anspach. By herself. 1705.

Memoirs of the Rival Houses of York and Lancaster. Anne Robarts. 1971.

Memorials of Shakespeare. Nathan Drake. 2116.

Mems, Maxims and Memoirs. William Wadd. 2002.

Mengelingen van waderlanschen Inhond. 2139.

Mexican Illustrations...of Society, Manners, Religion and Morals. Mark Beaufoy. 2116.

Military Sketch-Book, The. William Maginn. 1941.

Mirandola. Bryan Waller Procter (Barry Cornwall, pseud.). 305, 332.

Mission to Siam and Huè, The. George Finlayson. 1692.

Mr. Ebert and Mr. Dibdin. Frederich Adolf Ebert. 183.

Mr. John Hunter defended. E. Norgate. 1783.

Modern Traveller: India, The. Josiah Conder. 2116.

Monastery, The. Sir Walter Scott. 130.

Musical Bijou, The. F. H. Burney, ed. 2245.

Musical Reminiscences of an Old Amateur. Richard Edgcumbe, Second Earl of Mount-Edgcumbe. 1947.

My Early Days. William Kennedy. 2195.

Narrative of a Journey into Khorasan. James Baillie Fraser. 1725.

Narrative of a Journey to the Shores of the Polar Sea. John Franklin. 974.

Narrative of an Expedition /̄to Canada_/. William H. Keating. 1519.

Narrative of a Pedestrian Journey through Russia and
    Siberian Tartary. John Dundas Cochrane. 1290.

Narrative of a Survey of the Intertropical and Western
    Coasts of Australia. Philip Parker King. 1906.

Narrative of a Voyage round the World by Captain Frey-
    cinet. Jacques E. V. Arago. 917.

Narrative of the Burmese War. John J. Snodgrass. 1890.

Narrative of the Campaigns of the British Army...in the
    years 1814 and 1815, A. George R. Gleig. 1859.

Narrative of the Loss of the Kent East Indiaman, A.
    Duncan Macgregor. 1666.

Narrative of the Surrender of Buonaparte and of his
    Residence on Board H. M. S. Bellerophon. Frederick
    Lewis Maitland. 1777.

Narrative of Travels and Discoveries in Northern and
    Central Africa. Dixon Denham and Hugh Clapperton.
    1773.

Narrative of Voyages and Excursions...in...Central
    America. Orlando W. Roberts. 2039.

National Tales. Thomas Hood. 1917.

Natural and Medical Dieteticon, The. J. S. Forsyth.
    1562.

Nature Displayed in Her System of Teaching Language to
    Man. Nicolas G. Dufief. 2245.

Naval History of Great Britain from...1793 to...1820,
    The. William James. 1877, 1905.

Naval Sketch-Book, The. William Nugent Glascock. 1698.

New System of Moral Philosophy, A. D. Leopoldo
    Sebastani. 57.

New Year's Gift, for 1829. Zillah Watts, ed. 2221.

Night Watch, or Tales of the Sea, The. 2116.

Notes on the Various Sciences. 1634.

O'Briens and the O'Flahertys, a National Tale, The. Sydney (Owenson), Lady Morgan. 2041.

Observations...in a Journey from Odessa, through a part of Germany, Holland, England and Scotland. Edward Meissner. 108.

Observations on Geographical Projections. C. F. P. Delanglard. 2135.

Observations on Phrenology. 761.

Odes and Addresses to Great People. Thomas Hood and John Hamilton Reynolds. 1490.

On Population...answer to Mr. Malthus. William Godwin. 281.

On the Curative Influence of the Southern Coast of England. William Harwood. 2163.

On the Nature and Properties of the Malvern Water. William Addison. 2163.

On the Oracles of the Ancients. Étienne Clavier. 40.

Original Dramas. James Plumptre. 59.

Orlando Furioso, The, trans. William S. Rose. Ludovico Ariosto. 1270.

Our Village. Mary Russell Mitford. 2119.

Pandurang Hàri; or, Memoirs of a Hindoo. William Browne Hockley. 1692.

Panorama of Matlock, The. Henry Barker. 2163.

Paris in 1815, Second Part. George Croly. 384, 410.

Parochial History of Bremhill, The. William Lisle Bowles. 2105.

Parriana; or Notices of the Rev. Samuel Parr. Edmund Henry Barker. 2190.

Patronage; a poem in imitation of the seventh Satire of Juvenal. John Brown, of Great Yarmouth (Mandanis, pseud.). 274.

Peace Campaigns of a Cornet. North Ludlow Beamish. 2297.

Peak Scenery, or Excursions in Derbyshire. Edward
    Rhodes. 1130.

Pelham; or the Adventures of a Gentleman. Edward G.
    Bulwer-Lytton, Lord Lytton. 2192.

Pelican Island and other Poems, The. James Montgomery.
    1996.

Personal Narrative of Travels in the United States and
    Canada. Frederic Fitzgerald De Roos. 1975.

Personal Sketches of his own Times. Sir Jonah Barring-
    ton. 1956.

Personal Tour Through the United Kingdom. Sir Richard
    Phillips. 2221.

Petit Bijou, Le, for 1829. Monsr. d'Emden, ed. 2221.

Peveril of the Peak. Sir Walter Scott. 897.

Philosophy in Sport made Science in Earnest. John
    Ayrton Paris. 1969.

Picture of Greece in 1825, A. James Emerson, Count
    Pecchio, and W. H. Humphreys. 1677.

Pilgrimage in Europe and America, A. Giacomo C.
    Beltrami, 2099.

Pirate, The. Sir Walter Scott. 590.

Pleasures of Ornithology, a Poem, The. James Jennings.
    2172.

Pledge of Friendship; a Christmas Present and New Year's
    Gift, The. 2043.

Plutarque des Pays-Bas, ou Vie des hommes illustres de ce
    Royaume. 2139.

Poems. Bernard Barton. 192.

Poems. Thomas Gent. 384.

Poems. Elizabeth Rennie. 2130.

Poems. Charlotte C. Richardson. 2163.

Poems descriptive of Rural Life and Scenery. John Clare.
    80.

Poems of Caius Valerius Catullus, The, trans. George
    Lamb. Caius Valerius Catullus. 465.

Poetical Sketch-Book, The. Thomas Kibble Hervey. 2297.

Poetry and Prose by a Member of Parliament and Free
    Mason. 33.

Poet's Child, The. Isabel Hill. 357.

Polyhymnia. James Montgomery. 702.

Practical Treatise on Banking, A. James W. Gilbart.
    1964.

Progress of Cant, an Etching, The. Thomas Hood. 1681.

Prose by a Poet. James Montgomery. 1179.

Proverbes Dramatiques. Théodore Michel Leclercq. 1536.

Provincial Antiquities of Scotland. 75.

Ramble Among the Musicians in Germany, A. Edward Holmes.
    2130.

Rambles in Madeira and in Portugal. Alfred Lyall. 1976.

Rambling Notes and Reflections Suggested during a Visit
    to Paris. Arthur Brooke Faulkner. 2007.

Recollections of an Eventful Life. Joseph Donaldson.
    1650.

Redgauntlet. Sir Walter Scott. 1300.

Red Rover, a Tale, The. James Fenimore Cooper. 2048.

Redwald; a Tale of Mona and other poems. Louisa Stuart
    Costello. 274.

Reflections on Gall and Spurzheim's System of Physiog-
    nomy and Phrenology. John Abernethy. 760.

Reigning Vice, a satirical essay, The. Chauncy H.
    Townsend. 2130.

Reign of Doctor Joseph Gaspard Roderick De Francia in
    Paraguay, The. Johann R. Rengger and Marcelin
    Longchamps. 1990.

Remarks on Free Trade and on the State of the British
Empire. Alexander Dirom. 2163.

Remarks on the Practical Effect of Imprisonment for
Debt. Henry Dance. 2234.

Reminiscences of Thomas Dibdin, The. Thomas J. Dibdin.
1955.

Res Literariae. Sir Egerton Brydges. 331, 357.

Romance of History: England, The. Henry Neele. 2030.

Roué, The. Samuel Beazley. 2088.

Rough Notes. Francis Bond Head. 1835.

Royal Theatre of Barataria. Christian E. K., graf von
Bentzel-Sternau. 2128.

Sabbath among the Mountains, a Poem, A. 1200.

Salathiel. George Croly. 2107.

Salmonia, or Days of Fly Fishing. Sir Humphry Davy.
2158.

Sardanapalus; the Two Foscari; Cain. Lord Byron. 587.

Sayings and Doings, or Sketches from Life. Theodore E.
Hook. Second Series, 1496; third series, 2076.

Scenes and Sketches of a Soldier's Life in Ireland.
John Shipp. 1886.

Second Judgment of Babylon the Great, A. Robert Mudie.
2259.

Selection from the Public and Private Correspondence of
Vice-Admiral Lord Collingwood, A., ed. G. L.
Newnham Collingwood. Lord Cuthbert Collingwood.
2051.

Servian Popular Poetry. John Bowring, trans. 1928.

Seven Years of the King's Theatre. John Ebers. 2163.

Sheridaniana. Richard B. Sheridan. . 1759.

Shreds and Patches of History, in the Form of Riddles. 2297.

Sicilian Story, A. Bryan Waller Procter (Barry Cornwall, pseud.). 24.

Sintram and his Companions. Frederic, Baron de la Motte-Fouqué. 170.

Sir Marmaduke Maxwell. Allan Cunningham. 823.

Sir Michael Scott, a Romance. Allan Cunningham. 2047.

Six Months in the West Indies. Henry Nelson Coleridge. 1749; second edition, 1883.

Six Months' Residence and Travels in Mexico. William Bullock. 1403.

Sketches from my Life. J. W. von Goethe. 868.

Sketches of Persia. Sir John Malcolm. 2022.

Sketches of the War in Greece, ed. R. L. Green. Philip James Green. 2036.

Sketch of the Present State of...Sardinia. William H. Smyth. 2099.

Some Account of the Life and Writings of John Milton. Henry J. Todd. 1845.

Some Account of the Life of Richard Wilson. T. Wright. 1559.

Some Account of the System of Fagging at Winchester School. Alexander Malet. 2216.

Some Account of the Travels of the Count Enegildo Frediano in Egypt...under the assumed name of Anciro. Enegildo Frediano. 265.

Some Passages in the Life of Mr. Adam Blair. John Gibson Lockhart. 686.

Songs of Zion. James Montgomery. 849.

Song to David. Christopher Smart. 80.

Souverains de l'Europe en 1828, Les. 2139.

Specimens of the Lyrical, Descriptive and Narrative
Poets of Great Britain. 2148.

Specimens of the Polish Poets. John Bowring. 2012.

Specimens of the Russian Poets. John Bowring. 358.

Spirit of the Age, The. William Hazlitt. 1554.

Stories from the History of Scotland. Alexander Stewart.
2297.

Story of our First Parents, Selected from Milton's
Paradise Lost, The. Sarah Siddons. 900.

Studies of Chess. François A. D. Philidor. 1608.

Sunday Book, A. 2245.

Sure Methods of Improving Health and Prolonging Life.
Thomas J. Graham. 2009.

Sybil Leaves. Edmund Reade. 1934.

Sydney's Letters...on the reported exclusion of Lord
Byron's monument from Westminister Abbey. Sydney,
pseud. 2195.

Table Talk. William Hazlitt. 384, 411, 1001.

Tale of a Modern Genius, or the Miseries of Parnassus,
The. John F. Pennie. 2028.

Tale of Paraguay, A. Robert Southey. 1640.

Tales and Confessions. Leitch Ritchie. 2231.

Tales by the O'Hara Family. John Banim. 1630; second
series, 1872.

Tales of a Traveller. Washington Irving. 1373.

Tales of Field and Flood. John Malcolm. 2297.

Tales of the Crusaders. Sir Walter Scott. 1612.

Tales of the Great St. Bernard. George Croly. 2221.

Tales of the Munster Festivals. Gerald Griffin. 2031.

Ten Years' Exile. Madame de Staël. 516.

Théatre de Clara Gazul, Comédienne Espagnole. Prosper
    Mérimée (Clara Gazul, pseud.). 1588, 1692.

Three Months Passed in the Mountains East of Rome.
    Maria Graham. 216.

Time's Telescope, or a Complete Guide to the Almanac for
    1821. 331.

To-Day in Ireland. Eyre Evans Crow. 1586.

Tour in the Island of Jamaica, A. Cynric R. Williams.
    1742.

Tour Through England, Wales and Scotland. Samuel H.
    Spiker. 117.

Transactions of the Phrenological Society. 1111.

Traveller's Oracle, The. William Kitchiner. 2005.

Travels. August Hermann Niemeyer. 752.

Travels and Adventures in Southern Africa. George
    Thompson. 1981.

Travels and Adventures in the Persian Provinces. James
    Baillie Fraser. 1776.

Travels from India to England. James Edward Alexander.
    1954.

Travels in Buenos Ayres and the Adjacent Provinces. J.
    A. B. Beaumont. 2052.

Travels in Chile and La Plata. John Miers. 1822.

Travels in Egypt and Nubia. Giovanni B. Belzoni. 309,
    443.

Travels in...Europe, Asia and Africa. Edward Daniel
    Clarke. 151.

Travels in Mesopotamia. James S. Buckingham. 1926.

Travels in Sicily, Greece and Albania. Thomas Smart
    Hughes. 262.

Travels in the Interior of Southern Africa. William J.
    Burchell. 1350.

Travels of Cosmo the Third, Grand Duke of Tuscany.
    Lorenzo Magalotti. 478.

Travels through North America. Charles Bernard, Duke of
    Saxe-Weimar-Eisenach. 2128.

Travels through Sweden, Norway and Lapland. Vargas
    Bedemar. 151.

Treatise on Diet, A. John Ayrton Paris. 1801.

Treatise on the Cause and Cure of Hesitation of Speech,
    or Stammering, A. Henry Maccormac. 2195.

Treatise on the Laws of Literary Property, A. Robert
    Maugham. 2217.

Treatise on Zodiacal Physiognomy, A. John Varley. 2231.

Tremaine, or the Man of Refinement. Robert Plumer Ward.
    1515, 1549.

Trials of Life, The. Elizabeth C. Grey. 2231.

Truckleborough Hall, A Novel. William Pitt Scargill.
    1907.

Twelve Years' Military Adventure. John Blakiston.
    2297.

Two Hundred and Nine Days. Thomas Jefferson Hogg. 1952.

Two Lectures on Population. Nassau W. Senior. 2289.

Two Years in Ava. Thomas A. Trant. 1999.

Two Years in New South Wales. Peter M. Cunningham.
    1983.

Ueber Kunst and Alterthum. J. W. von Goethe. 120, 383.

Ugolino, or the Towers of Famine. Edward Wilmot. 2148.

Universe, The. James Wills (incorrectly ascribed to
    Charles R. Maturin). 415.

Varieties of Literature, ed. John Henry Brady. John
    Brady. 1692.

Viaggio di un Livornese al Canada. 2142.

View of the Agriculture, Manufactures, Statistics and State of Germany, A. William Jacob. 352.

Village Minstrel and other Poems, The. John Clare. 548.

Vindication of Certain Passages in...the History of England, A. John Lingard. 1911.

Vision of Judgment, A. Robert Southey. 384.

Vivian Grey. Benjamin Disraeli. 1772; second part, 1920.

Voice from St. Helena, A. Barry E. O'Meara. 705, 724.

Voyage d'un jeune Francaise en Angleterre et en Écosse. Jérôme A. Blanqui. 1518.

Voyage Historique et Littéraire en Angleterre et en Écosse. Amédée Pichot. 1607.

Voyage Pittoresque de la Grèce, ed. Barbié du Bocage. Count Choiseul-Gouffier. 196.

Walladmor. Thomas De Quincey, trans. 1367.

Wallenstein, A Dramatic Poem. Johann C. F. von Schiller. 1918.

Wanderings in South America, etc. Charles Waterton. 1716.

Waverley Novels, The (a new edition). Sir Walter Scott. 2295.

Week at Margate, A. 2163.

Werter /Werther7. J. W. von Goethe. 12.

Whims and Oddities, in Prose and Verse. Thomas Hood. 1858; second series, 2034.

Wilhelm Meister's Apprenticeship. J. W. von Goethe. 1329, 1353.

Wine and Spirit Adulterators Unmasked. 2029.

Winter Evening Tales. James Hogg. 151.

Winter in Lapland and Sweden, A. Arthur de Capell
    Brooke. 1940.

Winter's Wreath, The. For 1828, 2043; for 1829, 2209
    and 2221.

Woodstock, or the Cavalier. Sir Walter Scott. 1768.

Works of Samuel Parr, The, ed. John Johnstone. Samuel
    Parr. 2190.

Young Man of Honor's Vade-Mecum, being a Salutary
    Treatise on Duelling, The. 1470.

Yule Log, The. Thomas Wilson. 2231.

BIBLIOGRAPHY

Abbott, Claude Colleer. *The Life and Letters of George Darley: Poet and Critic*. London: Humphrey Milford, 1928.

Ainsworth, William Harrison. *December Tales*. London: Whittaker, 1823.

Allibone, S. Austin. *A Critical Dictionary of English Literature and British and American Authors*. 3 vols. Philadelphia: Lippincott, 1858-71; 2 vol. sup., 1891.

Armour, Richard Willard. *Barry Cornwall: A Biography of B. W. Procter*. Boston, Mass.: Meandor, 1935.

_____. *Literary Recollections of Barry Cornwall*. Boston, Mass.: Meandor, 1936.

Axon, W. E. A. "De Quincey and T. F. Dibdin," *The Library*, n. s. VIII (1907), 267-74.

Ayton, Richard. *Essays and Sketches of Character by the late Richard Ayton*. London: Taylor and Hessey, 1825.

BMCat. *British Museum General Catalogue of Printed Books*. London, 1959-66.

B. M. Egerton MSS. The Egerton MSS 2245-47 in the British Museum contain letters to John Clare from Taylor, Hessey and others.

Baker, Herschel. *William Hazlitt*. Cambridge, Mass.: Harvard Un. Pr., 1962.

Bakewell MSS. These manuscripts contain hundreds of letters from John Taylor to his mother, father and brother James, dated from 1801 to 1864, and are now in the possession of Mr. R. W. P. Cockerton of Bakewell, Derbyshire.

Barnett, George L. *Charles Lamb: The Evolution of Elia*. Bloomington, Ind.: Indiana Un. Pr., 1964.

_____. *Charles Lamb*. Boston, Mass.: Twayne, 1976.

Barton, Bernard. Poems. London: Baldwin, Cradock and Joy, 1821.

_____. Poetic Vigils. London: Baldwin, Cradock and Joy, 1824.

_____. Minor Poems. London: Boys, 1824.

Barwick, G. F. "The Magazines of the 19th Century," Transactions of the Bibliographical Society, XI (Oct. 1909-March 1911), 237-49.

Bauer, Josephine. The London Magazine 1820-29. Copenhagen: Rosenkilde and Bagger, 1953.

Beavan, Arthur H. James and Horace Smith. London: Hurst and Blackett, 1899.

Beddoes, Thomas Lovell. Letters, ed. E. Gosse. London; Elkin Mathews and John Lane, 1894.

Blunden, Edmund. Leigh Hunt. London: Cobden-Sanderson, 1930.

_____. Keats's Publisher: A Memoir of John Taylor 1781-1864. London: Jonathan Cape, 1936; repr. 1940.

_____. Shelley: A Life Story. London: Collins, 1946.

_____. "The obscure Webb(e)," Times Literary Supplement (18 December 1959), p. 748.

Boase, George C. and William P. Courtney. Bibliotheca Cornubiensis. 3 vols. London: Longman, 1874.

Borrow, George. Romantic Ballads. Norwich: Wilkin, 1826.

Bowring, Sir John. Ancient Poetry and Romances of Spain. London: Taylor and Hessey, 1824.

_____. Autobiographical Recollections. London: King, 1877.

Broderip, F. F. and Thomas Hood, Jr. Memorials of Thomas Hood. 2 vols. London: Moxon, 1860.

Brooke-Taylor MSS. These manuscripts contain some documents and many letters to and from Taylor and Hessey concerning the London and are now in the possession of Michael Brooke-Taylor of Bakewell, but deposited in the Derbyshire County Hall, Matlock, England.

Brooks, Elmer L. "Coleridge's Second Packet for Blackwood's Magazine," Philological Quarterly, XXX (October 1951), 426-30.

_____. "The Poet--A Possible Error in the Keats Canon," Modern Language Notes, LXVII (November 1952), 450-52.

_____. "Was Hazlitt a News Reporter?" Notes and Queries, n. s. I (August 1954), 355-56.

_____. "Studies in The London Magazine," Harvard University, Ph.D. Dissertation, 1954.

_____. Review of Josephine Bauer, The London Magazine, Keats-Shelley Journal, IV (Winter 1955), 106-08.

Brydges, Sir Samuel Egerton. The Autobiography, Times, Opinions and Contemporaries. 2 vols. London: Cochrane and McCrone, 1834.

Butterworth, Samuel. "The old London Magazine and some of its contributors," The Bookman, LXIII (October 1922), 12-17.

Byrne, Julia. Gossip of the Century. London: Ward and Downey, 1892.

Carlyle, Thomas. The Life of Frederich Schiller. London: Taylor and Hessey, 1825.

Cary, Henry Francis. Pindar in English Verse. London: Moxon, 1833.

_____. The Early French Poets. London: Bohn, 1846.

_____. The Lives of the English Poets. London: Bohn, 1846.

Cary, Henry. Memoir of the Rev. Henry Francis Cary, Translator of Dante, with his Literary Journals and Letters. 2 vols. London: Moxon, 1847.

Cassell's Encyclopaedia of Literature, ed. S. H. Steinberg. 2 vols. London: Cassell, 1953.

Champneys, Basil. Coventry Patmore: Memoirs and Correspondence. London: Bell, 1900.

Chilcott, Tim. A Publisher and his Circle. London: Routledge and Kegan Paul, 1972.

Clare, John. The Village Minstrel. London: Taylor and Hessey, 1821.

──────────. The Shepherd's Calendar. London: Taylor, 1827.

──────────. The Rural Muse. London: Whittaker, 1835.

──────────. The Poems of John Clare, ed. J. W. Tibble. 2 vols. London: Dent, 1935.

──────────. The Letters of John Clare, ed. J. W. and A. Tibble. London: Routledge and Kegan Paul, 1951.

Clowes, Alice A. Charles Knight: A Sketch. London: Bentley, 1892.

Coleridge, Hartley. Poems. Leeds: Bingley, 1833.

──────────. Essays and Marginalia, ed. Derwent Coleridge. 2 vols. London: Moxon, 1851.

Coles, William A. "Magazine and other contributions by Mary Russell Mitford and Thomas Noon Talfourd," Studies in Bibliography, XII (1959), 218-26.

Collier, John Payne. An Old Man's Diary. London: privately printed, 1871.

Conder, Josiah. The Star in the East. London: Taylor and Hessey, 1824.

Croly, George. Cataline...with other pieces. London: Hurst, Robinson, 1822.

Crowe, William. A Treatise on English Versification. London: Murray, 1827.

Cunningham, Allan. Sir Marmaduke Maxwell. London: Taylor and Hessey, 1822.

Cunningham, Allan. Traditional Tales of the English and
Scotch Peasantry. London: Taylor and Hessey, 1822.

_____. Songs of Scotland. 4 vols. London: Taylor,
1825.

_____. Poems and Songs. London: Murray, 1847.

Curling, Jonathan. Janus Weathercock: The Life of
Thomas Griffiths Wainewright 1794-1847. London:
Nelson, 1938.

DAB. Dictionary of American Biography, ed. Dumas
Malone. 20 vols. and index. New York: Scribners,
1928-37.

DBF. Dictionnaire de Biographie Français. Paris, 1933-.

DEI. Dizionario Enciclopediea Italiano. 12 vols.
Rome, 1955-61.

DNB. Dictionary of National Biography, ed. Leslie
Stephen and Sidney Lee. 21 vols. repr. London;
Oxford Un. Pr., 1885-1900.

Darley, George. The Complete Poetical Works of George
Darley, ed. Ramsay Colles. London: Routledge, 1908.

De Quincey, Thomas. Confessions of an English Opium-
Eater. London: Taylor and Hessey, 1822.

_____. The Collected Writings of Thomas De Quincey,
ed. David Masson. 14 vols. London: Black, 1896.

Dilke, Charles Wentworth. The Papers of a Critic. 2
vols. London: Murray, 1875.

Dobell, Bertram. Sidelights on Charles Lamb. London:
Dobell, 1903.

_____. "Lamb's Trouvailles," The Athenaeum,
No. 3965 (24 Oct. 1903), 548-49.

EI. Enciclopedia Italiana di Scienze, Lettere ed Arti.
Rome: Treccani, 1934.

Eastlake, Sir Charles. Contributions to the Literature
of the Fine Arts by Sir Charles Eastlake, ed. Lady
Eastlake. 2nd. Series. London: Murray, 1870.

Eaton, Horace Ainsworth. Thomas De Quincey: A Biography.
London: Oxford Un. Pr., 1936.

Ellis, Stewart M. William Harrison Ainsworth and his
Friends. 2 vols. London: Lane, 1911.

Elton, Sir Charles Abraham. Boyhood: With Other Poems
and Translations. London: Longman, 1835.

Encyclopaedia Britannica. 11th ed. 29 vols. New York:
Encyclopaedia Britannica, 1910-11.

Felton, Felix. Thomas Love Peacock. London: Allen and
Unwin, 1973.

Field, Barron. Geographical Memoir of New South Wales.
London: Murray, 1825.

Fitzgerald, Percy. Charles Lamb: His Friends, His Haunts
and His Books. London: Bentley, 1866.

Fortin, Andre. Frederic Degeorge. Lille, 1964.

Galignani. The Poetical Works of Milman, Bowles, Wilson
and Barry Cornwall. Paris: Galignani, 1829.

George, Eric. The Life and Death of Benjamin Robert
Haydon. Oxford: Clarendon Press, 1948: 2nd. edition,
1976.

Gibson, Strickland and C. J. Hindle. "Philip Bliss
(1787-1857), Editor and Bibliographer," Oxford
Bibliographical Society Proceedings and Papers, III,
pt. 2 (1932), 177-260.

Gilchrist, Anne. Mary Lamb. London: Allen, 1883.

Graham, Walter. English Literary Periodicals. New
York: Thomas Nelson and Sons, 1930.

Greever, Garland. A Wiltshire Parson and his friends.
London: Constable, 1926.

Grierson, Herbert J. C. Sir Walter Scott, Bart.
London: Constable, 1938.

Gunnell, Doris. Stendhal et l'Angleterre. Paris: C.
Bosse, 1909.

Harley, James. Nonsense Verse. London: Cadell, 1822.

Harper, George McLean. William Wordsworth: His Life,
Works and Influence. London: Murray, 1916; revised
and abridged, 1929.

Hartman, Herbert. Hartley Coleridge: Poet's Son and
Poet. Oxford: Oxford Un. Pr., 1931.

Haydon, Frederic W. Benjamin Robert Haydon: Correspondence and Table Talk. 2 vols. London: Chatto and
Windus, 1876.

Hazlitt, William. Criticisms on Art: and Sketches of
the Picture Galleries of England, edited by his son.
London: Templeman, 1843.

_____. New Writings: Second Series, ed. P. P. Howe.
London: Martin Secker, 1927.

_____. Works of William Hazlitt, ed. P. P. Howe.
21 vols. London: Dent, 1930-34.

Hazlitt, William Carew. Memoirs of William Hazlitt.
London: Bentley, 1867.

Hewlett, Dorothy. A Life of John Keats. London:
Hutchinson, 1970; orig. 1937.

Hogg, David. The Life of Allan Cunningham. London:
Hodder and Stoughton, 1875.

Hogg, Thomas Jefferson. Two hundred and nine days or
The Journal of a Traveller on the Continent.
London: Hunt and Clarke, 1827.

Hood, Thomas. Whims and Oddities. London: 1st. series
Lupton Relfe, 1826; 2nd. series Tilt, 1827.

_____. The Plea of the Midsummer Fairies. London:
Longman, Rees, Orme, Brown and Green, 1827.

Hood, Thomas. Hood's Own. London: Baily, 1839.

_____. The Works of Thomas Hood. 7 vols. London: Moxon, 1862.

_____. Poetical Works, ed. W. Jerrold. London: Humphrey Milford, 1920.

_____ and J. Hamilton Reynolds. Odes and Addresses to Great People. London: Baldwin, Cradock, and Joy, 1825.

Howe, P. P. The Life of William Hazlitt. London: Martin Secker, 1922; Hamilton, 1947.

Hughes, T. Rowland. "The London Magazine," Jesus College, Oxford University, Doctoral Dissertation, 1931.

Jameson, Anna Brownell. Diary of an Ennuyée. London: Colburn, 1826.

Jerrold, Walter. Thomas Hood: His Life and His Times. London: Alston Rivers, 1907.

_____. Thomas Hood and Charles Lamb. London: Benn, 1930.

Jones, Leonidas M., ed. Selected Prose of John Hamilton Reynolds. Cambridge, Mass.: Harvard Un. Pr., 1966. Includes "The Writings of Reynolds," the most complete published list of Reynolds's work.

Keynes, Geoffrey. Bibliography of William Hazlitt. London: Nonesuch Press, 1931.

King, R. W. The Translator of Dante: The Life, Work and Friendships of Henry Francis Cary (1772-1844). London: Martin Secker, 1925.

Knight, Charles. Once Upon a Time. 2 vols. London: Murray, 1854.

_____. Passages of a Working Life during Half a Century. 3 vols. London: Bradbury and Evans, 1864-65.

LCCat. A Catalog of Books Represented by Library of
Congress Printed Cards. Ann Arbor, 1942-46; with
all supplements and continuations, including The
National Union Catalog: Pre-1956 Imprints.

Lamb, Charles. The Essays of Elia. London: Taylor and
Hessey, 1823.

_____. The Last Essays of Elia. London: Moxon,
1833.

_____. The Works of Charles and Mary Lamb, ed. E.
V. Lucas. 7 vols. London: Methuen, 1903-05.

_____. The Letters of Charles and Mary Lamb, ed. E.
V. Lucas. 3 vols. London: Dent, 1935.

Landor, Walter Savage. Imaginary Conversations. 2 vols.
London: Taylor and Hessey, 1824.

Landrè, Louis. Leigh Hunt: Contribution à l'Histoire
du Romantisme Anglais. 2 vols. Paris: Société d'
edition "Les Belles-Lettres," 1935-36.

Leeds/Turner Letters. The letters of W. H. Leeds to
Dawson Turner, dated from Aug. 1820 to July 1825, MS
Nos. 13.20-13.30, held by Trinity College, Cambridge.

Lowndes, William T. The Bibliographer's Manual of English Literature. 4 vols. London: Bell, 1858-64.

Lucas, E. V. Bernard Barton and his friends. London:
Hicks, 1893.

_____. The Life of Charles Lamb. 2 vols. London:
Methuen, 1905.

Macfarlane, Charles. Reminiscences of a Literary Life.
London: Murray, 1917.

Maclean, Catherine Macdonald. Born Under Saturn: A
Biography of William Hazlitt. London: Collins,
1943.

Marsh, George L. John Hamilton Reynolds: Poetry and
Prose. London: Humphrey Milford, 1928.

_____. "A Forgotten Cockney Poet--Cornelius Webb,"
Philological Quarterly, XXI (1942), 323-33.

Martineau, Henri, ed. Stendhal, Courrier Anglais. 2
vols. Paris: Le Divan, 1935-36.

Mathews, Anne. Memoirs of Charles Mathews, Comedian.
4 vols. London: Bentley, 1839.

Miller, Edward. Prince of Librarians: The Life and
Times of Antonio Panizzi. London: Andre Deutsch,
1967.

Mitford, Mary Russell. The Dramatic Works of M. R.
Mitford. 2 vols. London: Hurst and Blackett, 1854.

Montgomery, James. Songs of Zion. London: Longman,
Hurst, Rees, Orme and Brown, 1822.

_____. Poetical Works. 4 vols. London: Longman,
Orme, Brown, Green, and Longmans, 1841.

Morgan, P. F. "John Hamilton Reynolds and Thomas Hood,"
Keats-Shelley Journal, XI (Winter 1962), 83-95.

_____. The Letters of Thomas Hood. Edinburgh:
Oliver and Boyd, 1973.

Morley, Edith J. The Life and Times of Henry Crabb
Robinson. London: Dent, 1935.

_____, ed. Henry Crabb Robinson on Books
and their Writers. 3 vols. London: Dent, 1938.

N.L. of S. MSS. This collection, MSS 1706, in the
National Library of Scotland, Edinburgh, contains
a number of letters concerning the London during the
editorships of Scott and Taylor.

Neal, John. Wandering Recollections of a Somewhat Busy
Life. Boston, Mass.: Roberts Brothers, 1869.

Nitchie, Elizabeth. Mary Shelley. New Brunswick, N. J.:
Rutgers Un. Pr., 1953.

OCAL. Oxford Companion to American Literature, ed. James
D. Hart. 4th ed. New York: Oxford Un. Pr., 1965.

OCFL. Oxford Companion to French Literature, ed. Sir
Paul Harvey and J. E. Heseltine. Oxford: Clarendon
Press, 1959.

Ottolini, Angelo. Bibliografia Foscoliano. Florence:
L. Battistelli, 1921.

Patmore, Derek. The Life and Times of Coventry Patmore.
London: Constable, 1949.

Patmore, Peter George. Rejected Articles. London:
Colburn, 1826.

"Periodical Literature," The Athenaeum, No. 13 (7 March 1828), 203-04.

Poole, John. Christmas Festivities, Tales, Sketches and Characters. London: Smith, Elder, 1845-48.

Praed, Winthrop M. Praed's Essays, ed. George Young.
London: Routledge, 1890.

Prance, Claude A. "A Forgotten Skit by Charles Lamb,"
Times Literary Supplement (9 February 1951), p. 92.

_____. Peppercorn Papers. Cambridge, England:
Golden Head Press, 1964.

Procter, Bryan Waller. Poetical Works. 3 vols. London:
Colburn, 1822.

_____. The Flood of Thessaly. London: Colburn, 1823.

_____. Charles Lamb: A Memoir by Barry Cornwall.
London: Moxon, 1866.

_____. An Autobiographical Fragment and Biographical Notes, ed. Coventry Patmore. London: Bell, 1877.

_____. English Songs. London: Bell, 1880.

Procter/Taylor Letters. Thirty-one manuscript letters
from B. W. Procter to Taylor and Hessey, mainly concerning the London, located in the Houghton Library,
Harvard University. Though undated they relate to
the period 1822-24.

Read, William. Sketches from Dover Castle. London: Smith, Elder, 1859.

Reid, J. C. Thomas Hood. London: Routledge and Kegan Paul, 1963.

Reiman, Donald H. Shelley and his Circle 1773-1822. Vol. VI. Cambridge, Mass.: Harvard Un. Pr., 1973.

Reynolds. Volumes of The London Magazine owned and marked by John Hamilton Reynolds, now in the Keats Museum, Hampstead, England.

Richardson, Joanna. "Richard Woodhouse and his family," Keats-Shelley Memorial Bulletin, V (1953), 39-44.

Robinson, Charles E. "Mary Shelley and the Roger Dodsworth Hoax," Keats-Shelley Journal, XXIV (1975), 20-28.

Robinson, H. C. Diary, Reminiscences and Correspondence of Henry Crabb Robinson. Selected and edited by Thomas Sadler. 2 vols. London: Macmillan, 1872.

_____. Manuscript diary of Henry Crabb Robinson deposited in Dr. Williams's Library, 14 Gordon Square, London.

Rollins, Hyder E., ed. The Keats Circle: Letters and Papers. 2 vols. Cambridge, Mass.: Harvard Un. Pr., 2nd. ed., 1965.

Ross, Ernest C. The Ordeal of Bridget Elia. Norman: Un. of Oklahoma Pr., 1940.

Ross, Janet A. Three Generations of English Women. 2 vols. London: Murray, 1888.

Sackville-West, Edward. A Flame in Sunlight: The Life and Work of Thomas De Quincey. London: Cassell, 1936.

Scott/Baldwin Letters. Eight letters, in typescript copies, from John Scott to Robert Baldwin, dated from March 1818 to Jan. 1820, in the Houghton Library, Harvard University.

Scott, John. The House of Mourning. London: Taylor and Hessey, 1817.

Scott, John. Sketches of Manners, Scenery &c., in the French Provinces, Switzerland and Italy. With an Essay on French Literature. London: Longman, Hurst, Rees, Orme and Brown, 1821.

Scott, Winifred. Jefferson Hogg. London: Cape, 1951.

Sestini, Bartolomeo. Poesie di B. Sestini. Florence, 1855.

Sikes, H. M. "Hazlitt, the London Magazine and the 'Anonymous Reviewer,'" New York Public Library Bulletin, LXV (March 1961), 159-74.

Smith, Horace. Gaieties and Gravities. 3 vols. London: Colburn, 1825.

_____. Poetical Works. London: Colburn, 1846.

Southern Letters. Several MS letters from Henry Southern to Henry Crabb Robinson in Dr. Williams's Library, London, which deal with Southern's direction of the London.

Steele, Mabel A. E. "The Authorship of 'The Poet' and other studies," Keats-Shelley Journal, V (Winter 1956), 69-80.

Strong, Charles. Specimens of Sonnets from the most celebrated Italian Poets with translations. London, 1827.

Talfourd, Thomas Noon. Final Memorials of Charles Lamb. 2 vols. London: Moxon, 1848.

_____. Critical and Miscellaneous Writings. Philadelphia: Hart, late Carey and Hart, 1850; 2nd. American ed., 1853.

Tatchell, Molly. "Elizabeth Kent and Flora Domestica," Keats-Shelley Memorial Association Bulletin, XXVII (1976), 15-18.

Taylor, Sir Henry. Autobiography of Henry Taylor 1800-75. 2 vols. London: Longmans, Green, 1885.

Taylor, John. The Identity of Junius. London: Taylor and Hessey, 1818.

Taylor, London. Volumes of The London Magazine owned and marked by John Taylor, now in the possession of Mr. R. W. P. Cockerton of Bakewell, Derbyshire.

Taylor Commonplace Book. The first of nine numbered commonplace books in John Taylor's handwriting, located in the Henry W. and Albert A. Berg Collection, New York Public Library.

Taylor, Olive M. "John Taylor, Author and Publisher, 1781-1864," London Mercury, XII (June and July, 1925), 158-66, 258-67.

Thomas, Clara. Love and Work Enough. Toronto: Toronto Un. Pr., 1967.

Tibble, J. W. and A. John Clare: A Life. London: Cobden-Sanderson, 1932.

Turnbull. Volumes of The London Magazine owned and marked by John M. Turnbull, now in the Charles Lamb Society's Library, London.

Underwood, Thomas Richard. A Narrative of Memorable Events in Paris...extracts from the journal of a detenu. London: printed for John Britton, 1828.

Van Dyk, Harry Stoe. The Gondola. London: Lupton Relfe, 1827.

_____ and John Bowring. Batavian Anthology. London: Taylor and Hessey, 1824.

Venn, J. A., ed. Alumni Cantabrigienses. Part II, from 1752 to 1900. 6 vols. Cambridge: Cambridge Un. Pr., 1940-54.

Vincent, E. R. Ugo Foscolo. Cambridge: Cambridge Un. Pr., 1953.

Wainewright, T. G. Essays and Criticism by Thomas Griffiths Wainewright, ed. W. Carew Hazlitt. London: Reeves and Turner, 1880.

Wasserman, Earl L. "Keats's Sonnet 'The Poet,'" Modern Language Notes, LXVII (Nov. 1952), 454-56.

Watson, Vera. *Mary Russell Mitford*. London: Evans, 1949.

_____. "Thomas Noon Talfourd and his friends," *Times Literary Supplement* (20 and 27 April 1956), p. 244 and p. 260.

Watts, Alaric A. *Poetical Album*. London: Hurst, Chance and Co., 1828.

Watts, Alaric A. Watts's correspondence with William Blackwood, located in the National Library of Scotland, Edinburgh.

Webb (also Webbe), Cornelius. *Sonnets, amatory, incidental and descriptive with other poems*. London: privately printed, 1820.

_____. *Summer: an Invocation to Sleep*. London, 1821.

_____. *Posthumous Papers...of a Person lately about Town*. London, 1828.

_____. *Lyric Leaves*. London, 1832.

Young, Sir George, ed. *Political and Occasional Writings of W. M. Praed*. London: Routledge, 1888.

Zeitlin, Jacob. "The Editor of The London Magazine," *Journal of English and Germanic Philology*, XX (July 1921), 328-54.

APPENDIX:

LIST OF ILLUSTRATIONS

IN THE LONDON

Note. The plates are inserted at various places in the London, somewhat at the whim of the binder, and may vary from copy to copy. The page number given in the first line of the entry is that given on the contents page. We have noted the variations we have seen. The index number follows the title of the item illustrated.

Volume II, Number XII (December 1820), p. 615.
Illustration in the text. A facsimile of an illustration from Sir Thomas Parkyns's book, Art of Wrestling, here illustrating John Hamilton Reynolds's essay, "Exmouth Wrestling," No. 270.

Volume III, Number XIII (January 1821), p. 81.
Apotheosis of Homer, from a Bas Relief in the British Museum. A Plate. Illustrates John Conrath's essay, "The Apotheosis of Homer," No. 307. In some volumes this is bound in as frontispiece.

Volume III, Number XIV (February 1821), p. 125.
Memnon's Head, from a Bust in the British Museum. A Plate. Illustrates Horace Smith's essay, "Memnon's Head," No. 317. In some volumes this is bound in facing the contents page, p. 121.

Volume III, Number XV (March 1821), p. 245.
Theseus, from the Statue in the British Museum. A Plate. Illustrates Horace Smith's essay, "The Statue of Theseus and the Sculpture Room of Phidias," No. 337. In some volumes this is bound in facing the contents page, p. 241.

Volume III, Number XVII (May 1821), p. 537.
Christ's Agony in the Garden, a Sketch from Mr. Haydon's picture. A Plate. Illustrates William Hazlitt's essay, "Mr. Haydon's picture of Christ's Agony in the Garden exhibiting in Pall Mall," No. 409. In some volumes this is bound in facing the contents page, p. 473.

Volume IV, Number XX (August 1821), p. 117.
Nature Blowing Bubbles for her Children, a Sketch from Mr. Hilton's picture. A Plate, etched by Mr. George Cook. Illustrates the note to Richard Woodhouse's verses, "Beauty is Truth, Truth Beauty," contained in The Lion's Head, No. 469.

Volume V, Number XXVI (February 1822), frontispiece. The Ilissus, from the Elgin Marbles. A Plate, etched by J. Shury. Illustrates William Hazlitt's essay, "On the Elgin Marbles," No. 606.

Volume VI, Number XXXIII (September 1822), p. 197. Plate of Craniology. Illustrates John Taylor's essay, "The Phrenological System of Dr. Gall and Spurzheim," No. 760.

New Series, Volume I, Number I (January 1825), p. 1. Plan of Part of the Thames. A Plate, in color (probably hand colored). Illustrates Henry Southern's essay, "The Thames Quay," No. 1436.

New Series, Volume V, Number XVII (May 1826), p. 65. Cleopatra with an asp, ΕΓΚΑΥΣΤΟΝ. A Plate, etched by J. Shury. Illustrates Ugo Foscolo's essay, "Ancient Encaustic Painting of Cleopatra," No. 1755. In some volumes this is bound in as frontispiece.

For Product Safety Concerns and Information please contact our EU
representative GPSR@taylorandfrancis.com
Taylor & Francis Verlag GmbH, Kaufingerstraße 24, 80331 München, Germany

www.ingramcontent.com/pod-product-compliance
Lightning Source LLC
Chambersburg PA
CBHW071757300426
44116CB00009B/1111